The People Shall Rule

The People Shall Rule

ACORN, Community Organizing,

and the Struggle for Economic Justice

Robert Fisher, Editor

Vanderbilt University Press

Nashville

© 2009 by Vanderbilt University Press
Nashville, Tennessee 37235
All rights reserved

13 12 11 10 09   1 2 3 4 5

This book is printed on acid-free paper
made from 50% post-consumer recycled content.
Manufactured in the United States of America
Cover design: Gary Gore
Text design: Dariel Mayer

Library of Congress Cataloging-in-Publication Data

The people shall rule : ACORN, community organizing, and
the struggle for economic justice / Robert Fisher, editor.
p. cm.
Includes bibliographical references and index.
ISBN 978-0-8265-1656-5 (cloth : alk. paper)
ISBN 978-0-8265-1657-2 (pbk. : alk. paper)
1. ACORN (Organization)   2. Community organization—
United States.   3. Community development, Urban—United
States. I. Fisher, Robert, 1947–
HN65.P395 2009
361.80973—dc22
2008039357

Contents

Acknowledgments

As with any volume, there are many people to thank. Most of all, the editor would like to thank the authors for their timely submissions, commitment to the book project, and patience. Staff at the Urban and Community Studies program at the University of Connecticut—Maria Winnick and Lola Elliott-Hugh—provided invaluable assistance, especially with the "Researching ACORN" conference we assembled in December 2005. Much thanks also goes to Edna McBreen, then Associate Vice Provost of the Tri-Campus, and Kay Davidson, then Dean of the School of Social Work, for their support with that event. Students in my graduate course on community organizing, especially Suzanne Accashian, Erin Bryne, Rebecca DeSimone, Lynn Mercieri, and Christine Sullivan, took on the task of focusing on ACORN and putting on a conference with good cheer and intellectual interest. Allison Fisher, a graduate student in the School of Social Work, was an incredible asset in overseeing transportation of participants, no small organizing feat. I'd also like to thank some friends and fellow academics who attended the conference and provided helpful comments, including James DeFilippis, Lee Staples, and Heidi Swarts. Tara Smollen and Nora Bishop were critical in completing this manuscript, and Nora provided additional research on ACORN and community organizing. Sally Tamarkin also helped with the last stages of the book. Jeff Ordower, Midwest Field Director for ACORN, first planted the idea for this book. Wade Rathke got the project moving much quicker than normal, encouraging an organizer's rather than an academic's schedule. Unfortunately, since then we've been on academic time. Lastly, in the final throes of putting together the manuscript, Michael Ames, editor at Vanderbilt University Press, helped shape it into a more cogent book. I want to thank all those mentioned here and those unintentionally skipped for this rich experience and for making this book possible.

I'd also like to add that this book has deep roots. It grows out of work I've done on the field of community organizing since the late 1970s, which includes five books and dozens of articles. It grows out of my current research with Eric Shragge and James DeFilippis on developing a critical perspective of community initiatives. But it also grows out of work I've done with ACORN, starting with interviews in Houston with new ACORN organizers in the early 1980s, to participating in a rainbow-coalition style campaign in Houston around a living wage referendum that was resoundingly defeated, to studying ACORN's effort to build a comprehensive community initiative in the south Bronx in the 1990s, to more recently evaluating their campaign against predatory refund anticipation loans. Like those of a lot of other authors in this volume, my political history, as well as academic career, runs parallel with the growth of the field of community organizing as well as that of ACORN. I've been a sympathetic but critical observer of both for decades. In December 2005, in order to better understand ACORN and where it fits with contemporary community organization, we held a conference at the University of Connecticut, where I teach. Many of the contributors to this volume presented their initial ideas there and received feedback not only from fellow authors but also from ACORN staff and leaders, as well as from independent scholars interested in and critical of ACORN's work.

Preface
Why Study Community Organizing and ACORN?

The time is right for this book. Community-based initiatives are a popular form of social change. The "turn to community" is a hallmark of our era, especially in the United States but increasingly worldwide. At the same time that community-based organizations have proliferated, however, there has been since at least 1980 an ascendancy of conservative and re-actionary politics and policies throughout most of the world. This trend has produced a paradoxical context of growing efforts at the local level occurring simultaneously with harsher conditions and greater obstacles to change at the community level. When compared with the dramatic shift to the Right in society, the outcomes of all this community-based work hardly seem to equal its sum total. We need to better understand the lim-its and potential of community organizing.

Moreover, it is an excellent time for a study of contemporary com-munity organizing to focus on ACORN. Founded in 1970, ACORN has caught a "second wind" since 2002, more than doubling in size. As the organization has become more visible, so have its chroniclers and crit-ics, both Left and Right. Up until recently, however, arms-length re-search on the organization has been rare. The only two published books on ACORN—Gary Delgado's *Organizing the Movement: The Roots and Growth of ACORN*, a seminal account of the organization's first ten to fifteen years, and Daniel Russell's *Political Organizing in Grassroots Poli-tics*—were written in 1986 and 1990, respectively. Both were revised PhD dissertations by authors very close to ACORN. Interestingly enough, the absence of a literature is not the case for the overall field of community-based organizations. There is, for example, a growing scholarship on the work of the Industrial Areas Foundation (IAF), the direct descendant to Saul Alinsky's work. In the last decade alone, new books on the IAF have included at least four studies by academics and two by IAF insiders.

Our title, *The People Shall Rule*, reflects well the populist ideals behind the community organizing phenomenon that took off in the 1960s and early 1970s, and ACORN continues to use that phrase as its credo. While the words ring of political naiveté, many ACORN staff and members (and certainly the contributors to this book) understand the limits of local-based activism and the need for critical inquiry as well as populist fervor. For example, community-level interventions may be the natural site of grassroots activism, but the problems people face in their communities are almost always caused by decisions and structures set in motion far beyond their local borders.

To address such issues and advance understanding of the potential and limits of contemporary community organizing, *The People Shall Rule* offers a dozen descriptions and analyses, by both "insiders" and "outsiders," of ACORN organizing and its place in the struggle for economic justice. ACORN's organizing model addresses boundaries and dualisms that constrain other efforts—tensions such as local or national scale, organizing or mobilizing, community building and service delivery or social activism, issue focus on culture or political economy, moderate or conflict tactics, community or labor organizing, electoral politics or social movement activism. This book highlights how this model distinguishes ACORN from other large community organizing networks (such as the IAF, PICO, DART, the Gamaliel Foundation, and others) with which its model overlaps and separates ACORN even further from community organizations that focus on social capital or asset-building. On the heels of the 2008 presidential election and in the midst of the greatest economic disaster since the Great Depression, we offer the following chapters as evidence of the continuing value of community organizing to American democracy and as an example of an alternative model of organizing for economic justice worthy of greater consideration.

PART I

Contextualizing Community Organizing and ACORN
History, Theory, and Comparative Perspectives

1

Community Organizing, ACORN, and Progressive Politics in America

Peter Dreier

During the 2008 presidential campaign, for the first time in memory, America had a national conversation about community organizing. That's because, at its September national convention in St. Paul, the Republican Party attacked the community organizing experience of Barack Obama, the Democratic candidate, who spent three years in the early 1980s working for a church-based group in Chicago. Former New York governor George Pataki sneered, "[Obama] was a community organizer. What in God's name is a community organizer? I don't even know if that's a job." Then former New York City mayor Rudy Giuliani snickered, "He worked as a community organizer. What? Maybe this is the first problem on the résumé." A few minutes later, in her acceptance speech for the GOP vice-presidential nomination, Gov. Sarah Palin declared, "I guess a small-town mayor is sort of like a community organizer, except that you have actual responsibilities." Within hours, Obama released a statement challenging the Republicans who "mocked, dismissed, and actually laughed out loud at Americans who engage in community service and organizing." His campaign manager David Plouffe sent an e-mail saying, "Let's clarify something for them right now. Community organizing is how ordinary people respond to out-of-touch politicians and their failed policies."

These comments triggered a blizzard of newspaper articles and editorials, radio talk show discussions, e-mails, and blogosphere commentary. Stories about and columns by community organizers multiplied—describing, explaining, defending, and criticizing what organizers do and the role of community organizing in American life. (See, for example, Barone 2008; Bhargava 2008; Boyte 2008; Dickens 2008; Dreier 2008b; Dreier and Atlas 2008; Finfer 2008; Garnick 2008; Geoghegan 2008; Hubbke 2008; Kellman 2008; Kelly and Lee 2008; Kwon 2008; Lawrence 2008;

McKitrick 2008; Sege 2008; and Simpson 2008.) In addition to attacking Obama's own organizing experience, the increasingly desperate Republicans mounted an attack on ACORN. John McCain's campaign ran a one-and-a-half-minute video that claimed that Obama once worked for ACORN, alleged that ACORN was responsible for widespread voter registration fraud, and accused ACORN of "bullying banks, intimidation tactics, and disruption of business." The ad claimed that ACORN "forced banks to issue risky home loans—the same types of loans that caused the financial crisis we're in today." The McCain campaign was simply echoing what right-wing bloggers, columnists, editorial writers, and TV and radio talk-show hosts, led by the *Wall Street Journal, National Review*, and Fox News, had been saying about ACORN for months (Atlas and Dreier 2008; Kurtz 2008; Malkin 2008; Moran 2008).

The Republicans had expected that their attack on Obama's organizing efforts as well as on ACORN would, in Americans' minds, link the Democratic candidate with inner cities, the poor, racial minorities, troublemakers, radicals, and "socialism." But, unwittingly, the Republicans' attacks helped introduce Americans to the relatively invisible work of the organizers who get paid to help millions of people improve their families and communities through grassroots activism.

Some of the comments linked the work of community organizers to the American tradition of collective self-help that goes back to the Boston Tea Party. After visiting the United States in the 1830s, Alexis de Tocqueville observed in *Democracy in America* how impressed he was by the outpouring of local voluntary organizations that brought Americans together to solve problems, provide a sense of community and public purpose, and tame the hyperindividualism that Tocqueville considered a threat to democracy. The Republicans' nasty attacks on grassroots organizing reflect another longstanding tradition in American politics—the conservative elite's fear of "the people." Some of the founding fathers worried that ordinary people—people without property, indentured servants, slaves, women, and others—might challenge the economic and political status quo. In *The Federalist Papers* and other documents, they debated how to restrain the masses from gaining too much influence. To maintain their privilege, the elite has denied them the vote, limited their ability to protest, censored their publications, thrown them in jail, and ridiculed their ideas about how to expand democracy. Both the self-help and the elite traditions were on display during the 2008 campaign, catalyzed by the possibility that America might elect its first president who had once been a community organizer.

This chapter takes a broad look at the nation's largest community organizing group, ACORN, not only in terms of its role within the community organizing world but also in terms of America's progressive movement, the contemporary political landscape, and, as the Obama campaign observed, the capacity of ordinary people, if organized, to gain political power. ACORN's longevity is quite remarkable. Founded in the 1970s, it has grown almost steadily, especially since the early 1980s. Many community groups, despite the best intentions, are unable to sustain their work amid victories and defeats. They can't juggle the myriad aspects of effective community organizing. ACORN has been successful not only as a community organizing group but also as a political vehicle; its approach has been similar to those taken by the Populist movement in the late 1800s and by the labor movement since at least the 1930s. ACORN's impact should be evaluated in this broader context, given its strategic innovations and the "ripple effects" of its work beyond its own organizational activities.

Grassroots Organizing and Progressive Politics

Every crusade for reform draws on America's self-help tradition—the abolitionists who helped end slavery; the progressive housing and health reformers who fought slums, sweatshops, and epidemic diseases in the early 1900s; the suffragists who battled to give women the vote; the labor unionists who fought for the eight-hour workday, better working conditions, and living wages; the civil rights pioneers who helped dismantle Jim Crow; and the activists who since the 1960s have won hard-fought victories for environmental protection, women's equality, decent conditions for farmworkers, and gay rights. The purpose of progressive politics and movements is to reduce the level of class, racial, and gender inequality in the nation, shrink the number of people living in poverty, promote sustainable growth, and promote peace and human rights at home and overseas. Despite America's vast wealth, no other major industrial nation has allowed the level of sheer destitution that exists in the United States. Americans accept as "normal" levels of poverty, hunger, crime, and homelessness that would cause national alarm in Canada, Western Europe, or Australia.

All movements for social justice face enormous challenges to success. Disparities in financial resources give big business and its allies disproportionate influence in getting their voices heard and gaining access to political decision makers. This influence does not guarantee that they will get everything they seek, but it does mean that they have an advantage. To be effective, progressive forces must be well organized, strategic, clever, and willing to do battle for the long haul. Too often, however, the Left has suffered from self-inflicted wounds of fragmentation. Since the 1960s, the Left has been a mosaic of organizations that focus on separate issues and separate constituencies, which has undermined its effectiveness. The thousands of local community organizing groups, and the major community organizing networks, comprise a small part of the progressive Left. The largest component of the Left is the labor movement (the AFL-CIO, the new Change to Win union coalition, and the national unions) in terms of the number of members and staff and the size of the budget. It also includes environmental groups like the Sierra Club, the National Wildlife Federation, and Greenpeace; national women's groups like NOW and NARAL; civil rights and immigrants rights organizations; gay rights groups; the network of "public interest" groups like Common Cause, Public Campaign, the Center for Responsive Politics, OMB Watch, and Congress Watch; and civil liberties groups like People for the American Way and the American Civil Liberties Union (ACLU).

The progressive movement also includes national policy groups and think tanks like the Economic Policy Institute, the Center for American Progress, the Center on Budget and Policy Priorities, Citizens for Tax Justice, the Campaign for America's Future, the Institute for Women's Policy Research, Policy Link, Demos, Good Jobs First, Families USA, the Fiscal Policy Institute, Fairness and Accuracy in Reporting (FAIR), and many others, as well as some local counterparts like the Center on Wisconsin Strategy and the Los Angeles Alliance for a New Economy. Throw into the mix the various progressive media outlets—*Mother Jones*, the *Nation*, the *Progressive*, *American Prospect*, *Sojourners*, *Ms.*, *Dollars and Sense*, the handful of liberal radio talk shows, websites like AlterNet, TomPaine. com, and Common Dreams, and many others. Include the various progressive nonprofit public interest legal groups like the Mexican American Legal Defense and Education Fund (MALDEF), the National Association for the Advancement of Colored People (NAACP) Legal Defense Fund, Natural Resources Defense Fund, Lambda Legal Defense Fund, Southern Poverty Law Center, the National Women's Law Center, and others. Add the various national and regional organizer-training programs. Consider also the various political action committees (PACs) (the union PACs, Emily's List, and others), the liberal churches and Jewish groups, the AARP,

MoveOn.org, and the many peace, human rights, and international "solidarity" groups.

All of these organizations do good work, but there is little coordination or strategizing among them and no mechanism for a discussion of how to best utilize their substantial resources in the most effective way. If they were to pool their resources and sit around a large table, they might discuss the following issues: How many organizers, researchers, lawyers, public relations and communications staffers should there be? What kind of organizations—single issue and multi-issue, online groups, and training centers for organizers, volunteers, and candidates? How much should be allocated to unions, community organizing, environmental groups, women's rights groups, civil rights organizations, and gay rights groups? In what parts of the country—which cities, states, congressional districts—should they focus organizing work? How many staff would be based in Washington, DC? How many in "the field"? What issues should they focus on? What policy agenda?

But, of course, the Left has no coordinating committee to assemble all these resources and make a rational allocation of money based on agreed-upon criteria. It is not really a coherent "movement" but rather a mosaic of organizations and interests that share a broad notion of social justice and a general belief in the positive potential of activist government, and that occasionally collaborate on election and issue campaigns.

Although these groups share a broad consensus about policy issues (for example, progressive taxation, reducing the arms race, and supporting reproductive rights, stronger environmental laws, and expanded anti-poverty programs), they rarely join forces to mount sustained organizing campaigns to get policies adopted at the local, state, or federal levels. The one time these groups break out of their separate "issue silos" and work together is at election time, typically by supporting liberal Democrats through endorsements, voter drives, campaign contributions, policy work, publicity, and other means. (Occasionally, they get their own leaders to run for office, but more typically they work for candidates who have no preexisting organic connection to their organizations.) These fragile electoral coalitions are typically forged by the candidates, or the Democratic Party, or some loose and temporary alliance, and are soon dismantled after each election is over, such as the Americans Coming Together collaboration in 2004 (Bai 2004, 2007).

In some ways, the Obama campaign learned from the mistakes of the past. It hired hundreds of organizers from labor unions, community and environmental organizations, and religious groups. They, in turn, recruited tens of thousands of volunteers and trained them in the skills of community organizing. They used door knocking, small house meetings, cell phones, and the Internet to motivate and energize supporters. They used the Internet and social networks to raise funds, in small and large amounts, from the largest-ever donor base. They opened more local offices than any other presidential campaign, including outposts in small towns and suburbs in traditionally Republican areas.

Many organizations and constituencies, outside the official campaign, had a hand in Obama's win. Groups as diverse as MoveOn.org, labor unions, community groups like ACORN, environmental and consumer organizations like the Sierra Club and U.S. Action, civil rights and women's groups, student activist groups, and many others who educated and mobilized voters legitimately claimed a part not only in Obama's triumph but also the dramatic increase in Democratic victories in the House and Senate. These organizing efforts account for the unprecedented increase in voter registration and voter turnout, especially among first-time voters, young people, African Americans, Hispanics, and union members, in the 2008 elections.

But can Obama's supporters—inside and outside the official campaign—transform that electoral energy into a grassroots movement for change? Political campaigns frequently promise to sustain the momentum after election day, but they rarely do. E-mail addresses, donor lists, and other key ingredients get lost or put on the shelf until the next election, when the campaign almost starts from scratch. In a handful of cities and states, the various segments of the progressive movement have built ongoing coalitions to work together around a common policy agenda during and in between election cycles, but these are still rare and remain fragile (Clarkson 2003; Dreier et al. 2006; Fine 1996; Reynolds 2004; Simmons 1994, 2000; Weir and Ganz 1997). The 2008 election created new opportunities and new challenges. Can the progressive Left build the organizational infrastructure needed to build, sustain, and expand a broad movement and to maintain a presence in between elections to mobilize people around issues?

The Fragmented Mosaic of Community Organizing

The world of community organizing reflects the progressive Left's strengths and weaknesses. Historians trace modern community organizing to Jane Addams, who founded Hull House in Chicago in the late 1800s and inspired the settlement house movement. These activists—upper-class philanthropists, middle-class reformers, and working-class radicals—organized immigrants to clean up sweatshops and tenement slums, improve sanitation and public health, and battle against child labor and crime. In the 1930s, another Chicagoan, Saul Alinsky, took community organizing to the next level. He sought to create community-based "people's organizations" to organize residents the way unions organized workers. He drew on existing groups—particularly churches, block clubs, sports leagues, and unions—to form the Back of the Yards Neighborhood Council in an effort to get the city to improve services to a working-class neighborhood adjacent to meatpacking factories.

The past several decades have seen an explosion of community organizing in every American city. With funding from private foundations, some unions, the federal government, and members' dues, thousands of community groups have emerged that work on a variety of issues, using a variety of organizing strategies, with uneven effectiveness. Almost every U.S. city (and a few suburbs) now has at least one—and in many cases dozens of—community organizing groups.

For years, critics viewed community organizing as too fragmented and isolated, unable to translate local victories into a wider movement for social justice. During the past decade, however, community organizing groups have forged links with labor unions, environmental organizations, immigrant rights groups, women's groups, and others to build a stronger multi-issue progressive movement. For example, the Los Angeles Alliance for a New Economy (LAANE) has created a powerful coalition of unions, environmental groups, community organizers, clergy, and immigrant rights groups to change business and development practices in the nation's second-largest city. At the national level, the Apollo Alliance—a coalition of unions, community groups, and environmental groups like the Sierra Club—is pushing for a major federal investment in "green" jobs and energy-efficient technologies.

Although most community organizing groups are rooted in local neighborhoods, often drawing on religious congregations and block clubs, there are now several national organizing networks with local affiliates, enabling groups to address problems at the local, state, and national levels, sometimes even simultaneously. These groups include ACORN, the Industrial Areas Foundation (IAF), People in Communities Organized (PICO), the Center for Community Change, National People's Action, Direct Action Research and Training (DART), and the Gamaliel Foundation (the network affiliated with the Developing Communities Project that hired Obama). These networks, as well as a growing number of training centers for community organizers—such as the Midwest Academy in Chicago, the Highlander Center in Tennessee, and a few dozen universities that offer courses in community and labor organizing—have helped recruit and train thousands of people into the organizing world and strengthened the community organizing movement's political power.

Even so, fragmentation within the community organizing world undermines its total impact. This is due, in part, to "turf" competition between groups for funding, membership, and media attention. With some notable exceptions, the various community organizing networks and groups rarely work together, they don't forge a sense of common purpose, and they don't engage in collaborative campaigns. For example, ACORN and IAF have chapters in some of the same cities and often work on similar issues (schools, housing, and public services), but they never work together. Foundations contribute to this turf competition in the way they evaluate organizing groups, requiring each group to distinguish its accomplishments from those of other groups within a broader movement. To please funders, community organizing groups have to be able to claim credit for specific accomplishments, effectively thwarting cooperation among groups.

This fragmentation is not inevitable. There were many divisions within the civil rights movement, but there was also some coordination and a sense of common history and purpose. The labor movement is split into dozens of separate unions and two separate umbrella groups (the AFL-CIO and the Change to Win coalition), but it has some capacity to work politically as a unified movement. The environmental movement is composed of dozens of national organizations, but they coordinate their political work through an umbrella group. There is no similar coordination among community organizing groups.

Without being part of a broader movement, there is no way for organizing groups to decide how to allocate progressive resources, to prioritize where and how to organize, or to figure out which campaigns would be most effective in recruiting and mobilizing people. Moreover, as a strategy for broad political and policy change—especially at the state and federal levels—simply organizing the poor is inadequate. The poor alone don't constitute a majority in any city, state, or congressional district, or nationwide.

When people read about or see large-scale protest demonstrations in the media, they rarely think about the organizational resources required to make it happen. Mobilizing protests is only one aspect of effective organizing. Few people recognize how hard it is to build membership-based community organizations among the poor. It is extremely labor intensive, requiring constant attention to identifying and developing leaders, fundraising, engaging in traditional lobbying and occasional direct action, conducting research and policy analysis, as well as media savvy and other skills.

The discussion about community organizing triggered by the Republicans' comments during the 2008 presidential campaign was unusual because the news media rarely pay attention to the small miracles that happen when ordinary people join together to channel their frustration and anger into solid organizations that win improvements in workplaces, neighborhoods, and schools. The media are generally more interested in political theater and confrontation—when workers strike, when community activists protest, or when hopeless people resort to rioting. As a result, with some exceptions, much of the best organizing work during the past decade has been unheralded in the mainstream press (Eckholm 2006).

Many (perhaps most) of the community organizing groups that have emerged in the past four decades eventually fell apart or remained small and marginal, unable to sustain themselves financially, economically, and politically. A few grew and gained in strength, in part by becoming part of broader networks at the city, regional, or national levels. Most local community groups are not linked to any regional or national organizing or training networks. Local groups that are tied to such networks have been helped to improve their capacity to develop leaders, mobilize campaigns, and win local victories as well as participate in citywide, state, and national campaigns beyond their local bases.

No one really knows how many community organizations exist, the total size of their budgets, the number of staff people who work for them, how long they've been in business, how many are linked to larger networks, or how effective they are. What seems clear, however, is that most community organizations engage in relatively modest efforts. These include, for example, pressuring the police to close down a local crack house, getting city hall to fix potholes, or getting the parks department to clean up a local playground. Some groups are more ambitious. Their community organizing has included enacting living wage laws, forming tenant unions, building community development corporations, combating redlining, challenging police abuses, fighting against environmental and health problems, mobilizing against plant closings and layoffs, reforming public education, setting up housing trust funds, encouraging inclusionary zoning laws, expanding funding for health services and public schools, and even setting up charter schools.

Despite the thousands of grassroots community organizations that have emerged in America's urban neighborhoods, and the existence of citywide coalitions, state-level activism, and national networks of community organizing groups, however, the whole is smaller than the sum of its parts. Karen Paget (1990) described this reality almost two decade ago, and it remains true today. With some important exceptions, community groups that do win important local victories are not always capable of building on their success and moving on to other issues and larger problems. For the most part, community organizing has been unable to affect the national agenda—or, in most cases, even state agendas. As a result, they often only marginally improve conditions in urban neighborhoods.

ACORN's Balancing Act: A Federated Structure

Observers and practitioners of community organizing sometimes examine the differences between various "schools" of organizing. There are certainly differences between various organizing networks and training centers in terms of the class and racial/ethnic base of their constituencies, how or whether they deal with religious congregations, how they train leaders, how they raise money, and other matters. But those engaged in the organizing itself typically exaggerate the distinctions—what Freud called the "the narcissism of small differences." On a larger level, though, because many community groups don't ask their "members" to pay dues, it is difficult to know with any certainty the overall magnitude of community organizing efforts. What's clear is that compared with groups like organized labor (with 13 million members) or even AARP (with 35 million members), the world of community organizing is not very large or powerful at the national level.

Within the world of community organizing, no other group or network has been able to achieve what ACORN has accomplished: a national organization with local chapters and the ability to simultaneously wage organizing campaigns at the neighborhood, city, state, and federal levels. ACORN—which claims to have 220,000 dues-paying families organized into 850 neighborhoods spread across more than one hundred American cities—is the largest of the community organizing networks. The ACORN family of organizations includes two public-employee unions, two southern-based radio stations (KNON and KABF), several publications (including the magazine *Social Policy*), a housing development corporation (ACORN Housing), a law office, and a variety of other vehicles that support its direct organizing and issue campaigns, such as Project Vote and the Living Wage Resource Center.

A major obstacle for community organizing groups is the reality that the sources of urban decline and its symptoms—poverty, unemployment, homelessness, violent crime, racial segregation, high infant mortality rates—have their roots in large-scale economic forces and federal government policy outside the boundaries of local neighborhoods. What influence, then, can neighborhood organizing groups be expected to have on policies made in city halls, state capitals, Washington, and corporate board rooms? Perhaps ACORN's most impressive attribute is its ability to work *simultaneously* at the neighborhood, local, state, and federal levels, so that its chapter members are always "in motion" on a variety of issues, and so that its local chapters can link up with their counterparts around the country to change national policy on key issues that can't be solved at the neighborhood, municipal, regional, or state levels.

In *Diminished Democracy: From Membership to Management in American Civil Life*, Theda Skocpol (2003) laments that since the early 1900s mass membership grassroots and mixed-income organizations have declined and been replaced by advocacy/lobbying groups run by professional staff with little capacity to mobilize large numbers of people. One of ACORN's most important attributes is that it is a *federated* organization with local bases but with a national infrastructure and the capacity to wage campaigns simultaneously at the local, state, and national levels. Its staff works to build strong local organizations and leaders that can influence municipal and county governments as well as major corporations (such as banks) to address the needs of the poor and their neighborhoods. Local organizing defines ACORN's core issues, but when national leaders and staff recognize problems that are energizing members in several cities, they can consider whether changes in state or federal policy would more effectively address the issue. ACORN employs a staff of researchers and lobbyists in its national offices in Brooklyn, New York, and Washington, DC, to serve the needs of local chapters. Issues such as welfare reform, redlining, predatory lending, school reform, and low wages provide ACORN with organizing "handles" at the local, state, and national levels. Recent work in mobilizing the residents of New Orleans forced to evacuate by Hurricane Katrina benefited from ACORN's capacity to work simultaneously to put pressure on politicians and policymakers in several cities, in at least two states, and at the national level (Dreier and Atlas 2007).

ACORN's federated structure is perhaps its most important difference from the Industrial Areas Foundation (IAF), the oldest organizing network (founded by Saul Alinsky in the late 1940s) and, in terms of chapters and members, the second largest. Many of the key strategic concepts of community organizing come from Alinsky's writings. The IAF now has fifty-four affiliated chapters in twenty-one states, organized into regional clusters, and it has evolved significantly since Alinsky died in 1972. The national office, however, has a limited role. It is primarily responsible for training staff members and leaders, but it does not seek to coordinate organizing campaigns, raise money, or conduct research for its affiliates, nor does it encourage chapter leaders to strongly identify with the IAF as a national organization. The IAF has built strong local multi-issue organizations among the poor and the nearly poor in many cities, but it has not sought to build the kind of federated organization that can wage policy campaigns at the national level.

The IAF is, instead, a network of local and regional organizations that have little contact with each other, except at occasional meetings among the lead organizers in each region. Each local or regional group is essentially on its own in terms of designing campaigns, hiring staff, and raising money. As a result, it lacks the capacity to coordinate the organizing work of its chapters in different cities to build a national campaign. That is why, ironically, the IAF—whose Baltimore affiliate (Baltimoreans United in Leadership Development, or BUILD) mobilized the first successful "living wage" campaign in 1994—was not able to translate that pioneering local victory into a broader movement. ACORN, meanwhile, has used its federated structure to help sustain a national "living wage" movement, with victories in dozens of cities.

ACORN tends to recruit its members through door knocking in poor neighborhoods. This work is extremely labor intensive. In contrast, the IAF, PICO, and Gamaliel networks organize through already-established organizations, mostly churches. In these three networks, organizations, not individuals, pay dues. As a result, the IAF's local chapters typically have more members than ACORN's because the IAF counts all the members of its affiliated congregations and unions, whereas ACORN counts only individual dues payers as members. The IAF tends to recruit its leaders primarily from among people who have already demonstrated some leadership potential in religious congregations and other affiliated organizations. ACORN, in contrast, recruits its leaders from neighborhoods, and its members are generally poorer, and less involved in organizational and civic life, than their IAF counterparts. As a result, ACORN is probably more staff driven than it claims to be, although many of its local grass-roots leaders are very effective.

ACORN's organizing model of intensive door knocking to recruit members, collect dues, and identify potential leaders is difficult for many novice organizers. As a result, there is considerable turnover and burnout among novice staff. This situation is not unique to ACORN, but because it has grown so quickly and required additional organizers to staff its new and growing chapters, ACORN has often hired young activists who were not ready for the stresses of grassroots organizing. The shortage of experienced organizers also means that ACORN puts some young staff in positions of responsibility—including managing local offices and even supervising young staff—before they may be ready. Those who remain with ACORN for more than about five years fare considerably better, financially, emotionally, and politically. Because ACORN is a large federated organization, with chapters around the country and many different kinds of jobs, it is able to provide upward mobility and new challenges. So, despite the revolving door of young organizers, ACORN has been reasonably successful in holding onto its most promising and effective staff. ACORN can also take credit for training hundreds of organizers over the years who have gone on to start or work for other groups. Like the United Farm Workers in the past, ACORN has become (perhaps unwittingly) a school for organizers for the wider progressive movement.

Community Reinvestment and Living Wage Movements

ACORN's involvement in the community reinvestment and living wage movements illustrates the strengths of its federated approach to organizing. The community reinvestment movement is primarily a place-based movement that has linked together local groups to change federal policy and negotiate with national and local lenders. ACORN was involved in early efforts to address the reality of declining urban neighborhoods and persistent racial discrimination in housing and lending. In the 1970s some neighborhood groups, including ACORN's St. Louis chapter, achieved small victories, including getting banks to provide loans or maintain branches in their neighborhoods. Eventually, activists across the country working on similar issues discovered one another and recognized their common agendas. From such localized efforts grew a national "community reinvestment" movement to address the problem of bank redlining.

Local community groups came together to focus attention on the role lenders played in exacerbating urban neighborhood decline and racial segregation. Its first major victory, the Home Mortgage Disclosure Act (HMDA), was passed by Congress in 1975, followed by the Community Reinvestment Act (CRA) in 1977 (Sidney 2003). These laws had minimal impact at first but gained momentum in the 1980s as a result of grassroots organizing (despite resistance from the Reagan and Bush administrations and their appointed federal bank regulators). By the mid-1980s, local groups coalesced into a significant national presence, thanks to the work of several national community organizing networks. The national effort around community reinvestment issues was carried out by loose networks of local groups coordinated by national organizations that primarily provided technical assistance. These included National Peoples Action (NPA), the Center for Community Change (CCC) and the National Community Reinvestment Coalition (NCRC), the Woodstock Institute, and the Inner City Press.

ACORN, in contrast, viewed the community reinvestment issue as a tool for building its national organization and its local chapters. It waged anti-redlining campaigns in many different cities in the 1980s and 1990s, drawing on its national staff to conduct research, issue reports on lending disparities, provide legal assistance for mounting CRA challenges against lenders, and offer strategic lessons. ACORN organizers who led successful community reinvestment campaigns helped train their counterparts in other cities. ACORN used these local campaigns to develop national campaigns around federal banking and housing legislation. At any given time, chapters would be engaged in local and national campaigns. These efforts paid off in helping enact federal legislation during the early 1990s savings and loan bailout scandal and in subsequent battles to reform CRA and HMDA, for which ACORN deserves considerable credit. In the following decade, ACORN took a leading role in injecting the issue of predatory lending into local and national political agendas.

ACORN has used its community reinvestment campaigns to build its organization. It targeted several major national banks and mortgage companies, waged campaigns against them, brought them to the bargaining table, and got them to change their lending practices. Equally important, ACORN got major national lenders to provide philanthropic support to pay for ACORN's homeownership counseling and homebuilding programs and to work with ACORN to provide its members with mortgage loans. Other groups working on community reinvestment issues have accomplished some of these same goals, but only ACORN has used its federal structure to bundle these accomplishments to build its political clout, organizational funding, and constituency base. ACORN has received considerable media attention for its community reinvestment work representing the voice of consumers in stories about redlining and predatory lending. In addition, ACORN has used its local and national campaigns around banking issues to strengthen its relationships with elected officials at the local, state, and national levels—forming political ties that ACORN could draw on for help with other issues and for help in obtaining funding from the Democratic Party and some of its key funders to wage voter education and get-out-the-vote drives.

The living wage movement, in which ACORN has played a major role, has helped change the public's view of the poor and the social contract. Two decades ago, the concept of a living wage was a radical idea. Today, it is part of the mainstream public debate. The movement was spurred by Congress's failure to raise the national minimum wage for almost ten years (after raising it to $5.15 an hour in 1997). The momentum for change was also catalyzed by the proliferation of low-wage jobs, and by city governments' efforts to contract public services to private firms paying lower wages and benefits than prevail in the public sector. Most Americans now agree that people working full-time should not be trapped in poverty. There is now widespread popular support, among most Democrats and many Republicans, for the Earned Income Tax Credit, which provides income assistance to the working poor. The popularity of Barbara Ehrenreich's best-selling book, *Nickel and Dimed*, about America's working poor, and the growing protests against Wal-Mart's low pay, indicate that concerns about inequality and poverty are moving from the margin to the mainstream of American politics.

Baltimore passed the first living wage law in 1994, following a grassroots campaign organized by BUILD (an affiliate of the Industrial Areas Foundation) and the American Federation of State, County, and Municipal Employees (whose members work for local governments). By 2008, community, labor, and religious coalitions had won living wage ordinances in over 150 cities and counties as well as the state of Maryland. The movement's effectiveness is due in large measure to the existence of two national networks and federated structures—the labor movement and ACORN—that have separately and together spearheaded local living wage campaigns and spread their strategic and tactical experience to new cities (Martin 2006). In some cities, unions or union-sponsored organizations (such as the Los Angeles Alliance for a New Economy) initiated the living wage campaigns, and then brought community, religious, and other groups into the coalition. Elsewhere, ACORN took the lead and (in most cities) recruited labor unions, religious groups, and other community groups into the organizing effort. The national unions and ACORN's national office provided training, research, fundraising, strategizing, and coordination. ACORN sponsors a Living Wage Resource Center that provides model ordinances, arguments to rebut opponents, and tactical and strategic advice.

ACORN's federated structure made it possible to juggle several local living wage campaigns at the same time. Moreover, the group's close ties to the labor movement—particularly SEIU, the nation's largest union, which it has been working with for two decades—provide resources for national and local living wage efforts that a locally based organization would not have. ACORN has used local living wage battles to build its local chapters and national organization, and to test organizing strategies that can be utilized in broader campaigns with more significant consequences. In 2002, for example, ACORN mounted a successful grassroots campaign in New Orleans to enact a citywide minimum wage pegged at a dollar above the federal wage level. After the surprise victory, the city's business leaders sued, and the state's right-wing Supreme Court overturned the wage law. But ACORN had made a name for itself as a grassroots David willing to take on powerful Goliaths.

ACORN has also brought the minimum wage issue into state ballot measures. In 2004, ACORN and its union and faith-based allies organized a statewide ballot initiative in Florida to raise the state minimum wage, registered thousands of residents (mostly in low-income, minority urban neighborhoods) to increase turnout on election day, and won a decisive victory in November. In November 2006, ACORN led ballot measures to raise the minimum wage in four other states (Missouri, Ohio, Colorado, and Arizona), while unions led similar successful campaigns in Montana and Nevada. In each state, they forged broad coalitions between community groups, clergy and churches, unions, and other constituencies. They mobilized effective voter registration and get-out-the-vote campaigns. All six measures prevailed, most by wide margins, and included provisions for annual increases based on the cost of living. Importantly, these grassroots minimum-wage campaigns increased voter turnout enough to help Democrats Claire McCaskill in Missouri, John Tester in Montana, and Sherrod Brown in Ohio defeat incumbent Republicans and cement the

Democrats' majority in the U.S. Senate (Atlas and Dreier 2006). This state-by-state strategy also laid the groundwork for raising the federal minimum wage. After the Democrats regained their majority in Congress in November 2006, both the House (by a 280 to 142 margin) and Senate (eighty to fourteen) voted to increase the minimum wage to $7.25 an hour over three years. President Bush reluctantly signed the bill in May 2007, giving almost 6 million minimum wage workers a pay raise.

ACORN and the Organizing Tradition

Alinsky viewed community organizing as part of the broader movement for redistributing economic and political power. However, for pragmatic reasons—especially to cement ties to the Catholic Church and most labor unions—he warned community groups to avoid becoming too "ideological," which in the context of the 1930s meant resisting being identified with or influenced by the Communist Party. That legacy continues today. Most community organizing groups, despite their efforts to gain political influence for poor and working class people, identify their campaigns in terms of promoting "democracy" or "fairness" rather than a broader ideology.

ACORN has always explicitly identified itself with America's Populist and Progressive traditions in its publications, its training for organizers and leaders, and its public rhetoric. It incorporates into its training curriculum a history of the Populist and Progressive movements, the labor movement, and the civil rights movement. It is willing to challenge specific businesses (such as banks and insurance companies) as well as to attack corporations for being socially irresponsible, for preying on consumers, workers, and ordinary people, and for having too much political influence.

One of ACORN's strengths is its combination of "inside" and "outside" tactics and strategies. Like most community organizing groups, ACORN is not shy about using confrontational protest tactics. Indeed, regular public protest is a key part of ACORN's organizational culture. ACORN is unapologetic about its tactics, in part because they not only help draw public attention to neglected issues but also help build membership. Equally important, these tactics typically get results. Public officials and private businesses that decry ACORN's tactics often wind up agreeing with its agenda—or at least negotiating with its leaders to forge compromises.

At the same time, ACORN acknowledges the limits of protest as a tactic as well as the limits of community organizing as a strategy for influencing public policy. It recognizes the fundamental paradox that even the most effective community organizing groups mobilize a relatively small number of people. Unlike most labor organizing campaigns—which require gaining the support of a *majority* of members in a given workplace in order to win a National Labor Relations Board (NLRB) election—community organizing only requires that there are enough people mobilized to disrupt business as usual, to get an issue into the media, or to catalyze allies who have influence over public officials or corporate leaders. Most successful community organizing involves using a group's very limited resources in strategic ways. This approach makes it possible to win many "issue" campaigns, but it is limited when it comes to electoral politics—where you need to win a plurality of voters to achieve a victory.

Indeed, ACORN differs from many of its community organizing counterparts in terms of its strategic leap into the arena of electoral politics, not only doing voter registration and get-out-the-vote work (much of it outside its own membership base) but also supporting candidates for public office. From its early days in Arkansas, ACORN rejected the view—strongly held by many community organizing groups in the Alinsky mold—that electoral politics was off-limits. It ran its own members for office, and it endorsed candidates who had worked with ACORN on issue campaigns. ACORN has also been willing, and sometimes eager, to forge close relationships with elected officials, mostly liberal Democrats; to mobilize its members in election campaigns; and even to encourage its members to run for office. Also, because it is a national (and federated) organization, ACORN has the capacity to target resources—particularly its organizing staff—to different parts of the country when they can be helpful in key electoral races. ACORN's significant role in the 2004 and 2008 national elections (including with national coalitions), and its work on ballot referenda in key swing states, is due in large measure to its ability to coordinate its activities at the national level.

ACORN is also one of the few community groups that have successfully figured out how to combine organizing with development and "services," and to minimize the inevitable tensions that occur when the same organization engages in both. It runs a housing development nonprofit, sponsors several public charter schools, and provides mortgage and tax preparation counseling services. The IAF affiliates in New York have also combined community organizing with housing development through their sponsorship of several large-scale projects called Nehemiah.

One of the great paradoxes of contemporary community organizing is its separation from the labor movement. Based on his ties to John L. Lewis, president of the United Mine Workers union and founder of the Congress of Industrial Organizations (CIO), Alinsky originally viewed community organizing as a partnership with labor unions. In the 1930s, the people who worked in Chicago's slaughterhouses lived together in the Back of the Yards neighborhood, went to the same churches, participated in the same sports leagues, and were members of the same unions. The people who lived in that neighborhood were "citizens" and "community residents" as well as "workers." The problems they faced—such as slum housing, poverty, low wages, unemployment, dangerous jobs, and crime—were interconnected (Horwitt 1992; Slayton 1986; Fisher 1994). As a result, Alinsky viewed labor and community organizing as dual strategies for addressing the problems facing working class people in urban industrial areas. Unions helped community groups win victories concerning municipal services and jobs; community groups helped unions win victories against the meatpacking companies and other employers.

Alinsky had a tremendous influence on the next generation of community organizers. He inspired many civil rights, student, and antiwar activists and influenced organizers in the early years of the environmental movement, feminism, and consumer activism. But one of Alinsky's key strategic impulses—the connection between community and labor organizing—was noticeably absent from the upsurge of community organizing in the 1960s, 1970s, and 1980s. There were exceptions—including the work of the United Farm Workers union, the involvement of some unions in the civil rights movement, and several unions' sponsorship of community development corporations and affordable housing—but for most of this period, community organizing groups had little day-to-day contact with the labor movement.

ACORN emerged in the 1970s out of the civil rights and welfare reform movements. Initially, like the rest of the burgeoning community organizing crusades, ACORN was not closely linked with organized labor. But ACORN's leaders soon realized that a strategic alliance with unions would help improve the conditions of its low-wage members and strengthen its political influence. Accordingly, ACORN has forged strong alliances with organized labor, particularly the Service Employees International Union. These relationships have brought ACORN closer than other community organizing groups and networks to labor. (Some local IAF groups also had close ties to unions). ACORN's effectiveness in waging local and state living wage and minimum wage campaigns, and its success in the political arena in electoral campaigns, is due, to a considerable degree, to its participation in coalitions with unions. ACORN's federated structure and its close ties with organized labor make it unique in the world of community organizing.

The Changing Playing Field for Organizing

To be effective, progressives—including community organizers—must adjust their strategies to complement the broad changes in the economic, demographic, and political landscape. In recent decades, major changes have occurred in the following areas.

Militarism, Globalization, and Corporate Consolidation
We will never solve our domestic problems, or help alleviate the widespread misery in the poor nations around the world, as long as we continue to spend such a large part of our federal budget on national defense and engage in military adventures. Today, two decades after the end of the Cold War and all the talk about a "peace dividend," the United States has not significantly reduced its reliance on military spending. Indeed, the "war on terrorism" has increased federal funding for war and "homeland security."

Globalization has paralleled the deindustrialization of cities and the decline of unionized workplaces, especially in the industrial sectors. This has led to an increasing polarization of incomes and an increase in low-wage jobs ("Wal-Martization"). As a result of corporate consolidation, many decisions are made in boardrooms far removed from the affected local communities. With the decline of local corporate power structures, community groups cannot easily target local business leaders as part of grassroots organizing campaigns. For example, because of the dramatic increase in bank mergers, groups working against bank redlining no longer can confront local bank directors on their own turf. Because ACORN is federated, it can negotiate with national banks about their practices in local markets. Local unions, community groups, and environmental groups working to restrain Wal-Mart can find local organizing "handles" but must find ways to work together across the country to influence decisions made in Bentonville, Arkansas. Without some kind of national network or movement, local groups are limited in their ability to bargain with large corporations and influence federal policy.

Suburbanization and the Urban Fiscal Crisis

More than half of the U.S. population—more than half of all voters, and almost half of the poor—now live in suburbs. Suburban districts dominate Congress and many state legislatures (Swanstrom, Casey, Flack, and Dreier 2004; Berube and Kneebone 2006). However, most community organizing groups, including ACORN, are rooted in big and middle-size cities, and mostly in the low-income neighborhoods. These are areas typically represented by liberal Democrats who occupy reasonably "safe" seats in state legislatures and Congress. ACORN has almost no presence in suburban America. The progressive Left—the labor movement, community groups, women's groups, and others—needs a strategy for building a stronger base in the "swing" state legislative and congressional districts that are primarily outside cities (Egan 2006; Judis and Teixeira 2004). Moreover, deindustrialization, the exodus of high-wage jobs, and the suburbanization of middle-class residents have created a chronic fiscal crisis for cities. Most of the nation's most serious problems are concentrated in cities and older suburbs, but local governments lack the resources needed to seriously address these problems. This makes it more difficult for local governments to respond to demands by community groups for more funding for housing, police and fire protection, hospitals, schools, parks and playgrounds, and other municipal services (Dreier, Mollenkopf, and Swanstrom 2005).

Capital Mobility and the Business Climate

Whenever community organizing groups, unions, and environmental activists propose policies to make business act more responsibly—for example, living wage laws, business taxes, clean air laws, "linkage" fees on new commercial buildings that target the funds for affordable housing, and inclusionary zoning laws that require housing developers to incorporate units for low-income families—business opponents claim that those policies will scare away businesses and lead to job losses. Because our federal system allows states and localities to set many business conditions, footloose corporations can look for the best "business climate"— low wages, low benefits, low taxes, lax environmental regulations, and a "union free" atmosphere. Many state and local government officials feel that in order to attract or maintain jobs, they have to participate in "bidding wars."

Most local politicians believe that they are trapped in what they perceive to be a fiscal straitjacket. If public officials move too aggressively to tax or regulate the private sector, business can threaten to pull up stakes and take their jobs and tax base with them. They can also mobilize a sustained political assault (often with the aid of the local media) against incumbent politicians for being unfair to business. Few politicians want the reputation that because they lost the "confidence" of the business community, they drove away jobs and undermined the tax base. Corporations may be bluffing when they threaten to leave if cities enact such laws, but it is hard for local officials, unions, and community groups to know for certain. Business warnings are not always empty threats. As a result, most officials accommodate themselves to businesses' priorities, accept the "Chicken Little" scenarios, and err in favor of business. City officials have responded to their fiscal crises by becoming more "entrepreneurial"—by encouraging private investment and promoting public-private partnerships. What this means, in practice, is that cities subsidize private development, typically on terms dictated by the private sector.

Community organizations and other progressive groups have responded in several ways. They have produced studies challenging businesses' arguments and warnings that living wage laws and other regulations have serious negative consequences. For example, these studies demonstrate that strong unions are good for the economy because they increase effective demand and job creation (Flaming 2007). Studies point out that although some businesses are mobile, many are relatively "sticky" or immobile because they are tied to the local economy (Dreier 2005a, 2005b). Progressive city officials and activists need a clear sense of when business threats are real and when they are not. What characterizes progressive local governmental regimes (such as those of Mayor Harold Washington in Chicago, Mayor Ray Flynn in Boston, and Mayor Antonio Villaraigosa in Los Angeles) is their willingness to test whether businesses are bluffing and to redefine the concept of a "healthy business climate" as one that includes good jobs, affordable housing, and a clean environment.

Community organizing groups also have demanded that if local governments provide public subsidies to private companies, they should include a quid pro quo of community benefit agreements—including jobs, housing, parks—on terms dictated by community groups and (in some cases) unions. A new emphasis on accountable development—promoted by local groups like the Los Angeles Alliance for a New Economy (LAANE) and national advocacy groups like Good Jobs First—turns the entrepreneurial city on its head, pushing cities to use their leverage over land use and allocation of subsidies to require businesses to be more socially responsible. Local inclusionary zoning, linkage, linked deposit, and living wage laws illustrate this approach. The idea is somewhat modeled on the community investment agreements that community groups have negotiated with banks to resolve anti-redlining protests. One of the largest is ACORN's agreement with the developer of the Atlantic Yards megacomplex in Brooklyn, which requires the Ratner Development Company to provide jobs and affordable housing for local residents (Atlas 2005).

Immigration and Racial/Ethnic Diversity

America's neighborhoods, cities, and metropolitan areas are strongly segregated by race, but the demographic trajectories of our major metropolitan areas are more complex and diverse than ever before. The massive wave of immigration over the last four decades, and the increased suburbanization of black, Latino, and Asian populations, have changed metropolitan demographics. In its early years, starting in Arkansas, ACORN sought to build a movement that would unite the poor—black and white—around economic justice issues. As ACORN expanded into big cities, its members were comprised primarily of African Americans. In the past decade, its membership has become more diverse, with a growing number of Latinos and Afro-Caribbeans. ACORN works primarily in high-poverty neighborhoods where poor blacks and Latinos, but not poor whites, are concentrated. The urban fiscal crisis can pit black, Latino, Asian, and white communities against each other as they fight for scarce municipal resources, such as playgrounds, schools, and housing. The changing demographics of metropolitan areas challenge unions and community groups to address the reality of increasing racial diversity while seeking ways to build bridges across races and neighborhoods.

Rebuilding a Progressive Movement

Ultimately, ACORN must be evaluated in terms of its role in helping shape and build a broad progressive movement that can influence public policy. In the late 1800s and early 1900s, the Progressive movement sought to change how Americans thought about what we now call the social contract—the rights of citizens, the role of government, and the responsibilities of business to the larger society. Progressive reformers—immigrants and union activists, middle-class reformers (for example, journalists, clergy, and social workers), and upper-class philanthropists—ushered in the first wave of consumer, worker, and environmental protections.

From the 1930s through the early 1970s, the American social contract was based on the premises of the New Deal—a coalition led by the labor movement. The labor movement's strength was focused in cities, and its core constituents were immigrants and their children, African Americans, and, to a lesser extent, white southern small farmers, with allies among middle-class reformers (for example, planners, intellectuals, journalists, and social workers) and some liberals within the business community. During this postwar era, the United States experienced a dramatic increase in per capita income and a decline in the gap between the rich and the poor. The incomes of the bottom half of the class structure rose faster than those at the top.

In the 1960s, progressives hoped to build on this foundation. Representing the left wing of the Democratic Party, United Automobile Workers (UAW) president Walter Reuther had been making proposals since World War II to renew and expand the New Deal and to engage in national economic planning. He advised Presidents Kennedy and Johnson to champion a bold federal program for full employment that would include government-funded public works and the conversion of the nation's defense industry to production for civilian needs. This program, he argued, would dramatically address the nation's poverty population, create job opportunities for African Americans, and rebuild the nation's troubled cities without being as politically divisive as a federal program identified primarily as serving poor blacks.

Both presidents rejected Reuther's advice. (They were worried about alienating Southern Democrats and sectors of business that opposed Keynesian-style economic planning.) Johnson's announcement of an "unconditional war on poverty" in his 1964 State of the Union address pleased Reuther, but the details of the plan revealed its limitations. The War on Poverty was a patchwork of small initiatives that did not address the nation's basic inequalities. Testifying before Congress in 1964, Reuther said that, "while [the proposals] are good, [they] are not adequate, nor will they be successful in achieving their purposes, except as we begin to look at the broader problems [of the American economy]." He added, "Poverty is a reflection of our failure to achieve a more rational, more responsible, more equitable distribution of the abundance that is within our grasp" (Boyle 1998). Although Reuther threw the UAW's political weight behind Johnson's programs, his critique was correct. Since the 1960s, federal efforts to address poverty have consistently suffered from a failure to address the fundamental underlying issues. Most progressives have understood that the civil rights victories, such as the Civil Rights Act (1964), Voting Rights Act (1965), and Fair Housing Act (1968), were necessary but not sufficient alone to reduce poverty and inequality.

In the 1970s, the New Deal and Great Society gains were supplemented by other victories that emerged out of civil rights, women's rights, environmental and consumer activism; these victories were fueled by the growth of the Naderite network, feminism, environmental and consumer groups, and community organizing. Some 1970s victories include affirmative action, the Clean Air Act and other environmental laws, strong regulations on business regarding consumer products and workplace safety (such as the Occupational Safety and Health Act), and significant improvements in the legal and social rights of women, including reproductive freedoms. The major victories that emerged from community organizing (linked to civil rights) were the Home Mortgage Disclosure Act (1975) and the Community Reinvestment Act (1977), which resulted from the ability of groups to link local and national campaigns against bank redlining.

Many community organizations, including ACORN, were born in the 1970s in the aftermath of the civil rights and antiwar movements. They emerged at a time when the post–World War II prosperity—fueled by the rise of the United States as a global superpower, steady economic growth, and a narrowing gap between rich and poor—was coming to an end. Major U.S. corporations began an assault on the labor movement and the living standards of the poor and working classes. *Business Week* best expressed this view in its October 12, 1974, issue: "It will be a hard pill for many Americans to swallow—the idea of doing with less so that big business can have more. . . . Nothing that this nation, or any other nation, has done in modern economic history compares with the selling job that must be done to make people accept this reality."

The late 1970s saw the beginning of several trends: the rise of neoconservatism as a political and intellectual force, the dismantling of the social safety net, a dramatic decline in union membership, the chronic fiscal crisis of major cities, and the increase in the political power of big business and its political and intellectual allies. Since then, liberals, progressives, and Democrats have generally been on the defensive, seeking to protect the key components of the New Deal, the Great Society, and subsequent victories from being dismantled by the increasingly powerful right wing—led by the uneasy alliance between big business, the religious Right, and the mainstream of the Republican Party.

During the past decade, a number of separate, and sometimes over-lapping, issues have catalyzed local and national organizing groups. These include campaigns for environmental justice, living wages and community benefit agreements, immigrant rights, fair trade and opposition to sweat-shops, and opposition to the U.S. invasion and occupation of Iraq. All of these campaigns seek to redistribute wealth and power. They seek to restrain the influence of big business and force corporations to be more socially responsible. They challenge conservative ideas about the role of government.

Other campaigns—such as those for gay rights, reproductive freedom, gun control, and civil liberties (for example, opposition to the Patriotic Act)—have an uneasy alliance with movements that focus more directly on economic justice. Conservatives have been able to use these "wedge" issues to win electoral victories, but the political trajectory has not entirely been toward the Right, as the results of the November 2006 and the November 2008 elections suggest. Growing economic insecurity—what Jacob Hacker calls a major "risk shift"—has the potential for building po-litical bridges between the poor and the middle class, between residents of cities and suburbs, and between people who may otherwise disagree about "wedge" issues.

The labor movement is clearly the backbone of any effective progres-sive movement. Despite steady declines in the proportion of the labor force in unions, there is real excitement about the successes over a num-ber of major unions and a sense that a revitalization of organized labor is possible. Some of the bigger unions have laid the foundations for future growth, as recent gains in Los Angeles, Houston, and elsewhere indicate. The labor movement has been most successful where it has focused or-ganizing efforts among workers in low-wage industries, primarily among women, immigrants, and people of color. Unions that have made the most headway in recent years have forged alliances with community and church groups and emphasized mobilization and leadership among rank-and-file workers.

The exit polls of the November 2004 and November 2008 elections revealed that when voters' loyalties were divided between their economic interests and so-called moral values concerns, union membership was a crucial determinant of their votes. In November 2008, for example, 57 percent of white men favored McCain, but 57 percent of white male union members favored Obama. White gun owners cast 68 percent of their votes for McCain, but 54 percent of white gun owners who are also union members preferred Obama. Among white weekly church-goers, McCain scored a landslide, receiving 70 percent of their votes. But Obama had a slight edge (49 percent to 48 percent) among white weekly churchgoers who were union members. Similarly, 58 percent of white non-college graduates voted for McCain, but 60 percent of white union members who didn't graduate from college tilted to Obama. Over-all, 53 percent of white women cast ballots for McCain, but a whopping 72 percent of white women union members favored Obama. These num-bers show the tremendous power of grassroots organizing. Nationwide, according to Guy Molyneux (in an e-mail to the author), 67 percent of union members of all races—and 69 percent in swing states—supported Obama. They voted for him because of the unions' effectiveness at edu-cating and mobilizing members. They spent millions of dollars and built an army of volunteers who went door to door, reaching out to other members about key economic issues. Members in "safe" Democratic states staffed phone banks and made tens of thousands of calls to union-ists in key swing states. But unions today represent only 12.1 percent of all American employees. Membership has dramatically declined from the numbers a generation ago (about 35 percent of workers in the 1950s and 25 percent in the 1970s were union members) and is significantly smaller than in other affluent countries. If unions represented even 20 percent of the work force, Obama would have won by a landslide. Democrats who narrowly lost their races for Congress would have prevailed.

As the results of the 2006 and 2008 elections also suggest, the alleged shift to the Right does not adequately reflect public opinion. The propor-tion of Americans who define themselves as liberals has been declining for several decades. But this does not mean that Americans do not share most liberal values. For example, fewer women call themselves feminists now than did twenty years ago, but more women agree with once-con-troversial feminist ideas like equal pay for equal work or women's right to choose abortion. Likewise, more Americans today than twenty years ago believe that government should protect the environment, consumers, and workers from unhealthy workplaces and other dangers. Most Americans believe the federal government should help guarantee health insurance for everyone. A majority of workers support unions, and most Americans are pro-choice, want stronger environmental and gun control laws, and be-lieve that the minimum wage should be raised and that the nation should do more to combat poverty.

Conclusion

ACORN's policy agenda is in the Progressive and New Deal tradition of regulating capitalism to prevent excessive greed by pushing for tenement housing reforms, workplace safety laws, the minimum wage, aid to mothers and children, Social Security, the right of workers to organize and bargain collectively for better wages and working conditions, subsidies to house the poor, and policies that encourage banks to make mortgage loans to boost homeownership. There were clear indicators in 2006, confirmed during the 2008 election, that the nation's political mood was shifting. Voters showed that they were frustrated by the war in Iraq, by widening inequality and declining economy security, and by the Bush administration's crony capitalism. But it was still unclear whether progressives could find a coherent twenty-first century agenda to replace the New Deal and the Great Society, to counter the right-wing's "anti-government" message, and to find a way to protect and expand social democracy at home in the midst of globalization (Bai 2007).

Those who think a progressive revival is politically unrealistic should recall how depressed conservatives and Republicans grouped after 1964 when President Lyndon Johnson beat Goldwater in a huge landslide and the Democrats won huge majorities in Congress. At the time, almost every pundit in the country wrote the conservative movement's obituary. Goldwater's right-wing supporters were viewed as fanatics, out of touch with mainstream America. With the help of conservative millionaires, corporations, and foundations, they created new organizations, think tanks, and endowed professorships at universities to help shape the intellectual climate and policy agenda (Perlstein 2001). They created a network of right-wing publications and talk radio stations. They recruited new generations of college students, funded their campus organizations, and got them internships and jobs within conservative organizations and with conservative government officials and agencies. They identified, cultivated, and trained potential political candidates. They brought together the two major wings of the conservative movement—the business conservatives and the social/religious conservatives—in an uneasy but relatively stable coalition to elect conservative Republicans. Then they took over the GOP's atrophied apparatus. They helped change the political agenda. In 1980, they elected Ronald Reagan. In 2000, they helped Bush steal the election. In 2004, they helped Bush win a second term, almost fair and square. They helped conservative Republicans gain control of Congress and changed the ideological completion of the Supreme Court and the federal judiciary.

The movement built itself up from scratch, utilizing the network of conservative pastors and churches, and providing sermons, voter guides, get-out-the-vote training, and other resources to create a powerful organizational infrastructure. Separate, but overlapping with the religious Right, the National Rifle Association and the gun lobby also used its huge war chest and organizational resources to mobilize its members and their families. Moreover, the religious Right and the gun lobby are not just part of an election-day operation. They are part of an ongoing movement that provides people with social, psychological, and political sustenance on a regular basis. The rise of suburban megachurches is one example of this phenomenon.

Political victories are about more than election-day turnout. Successes on Election Day are a byproduct of, not a substitute for, effective grassroots organizing in between elections. The history of the past century shows that progress is made when people join together to struggle for change, make stepping-stone reforms, and persist so that each victory builds on the next. This kind of work is slow and gradual because it involves organizing people to learn the patient skills of leadership and organization building. It requires forging coalitions that can win elections and then promote politics that keep the coalition alive.

Over the past century, the key turning points for improving American society involved large-scale mobilizations around a broad egalitarian and morally uplifting vision of America, a progressive patriotism animated by "liberty and justice for all." These movements drew on traditions of justice and morality. They redefined the rights and responsibilities of citizens, government, and business. In the Gilded Age, it was agrarian Populism and urban Progressivism. During the Depression, it was the upsurge of industrial unionism linked to Roosevelt's New Deal. In the 1960s and 1970s, it was the civil rights, women's rights, and environmental movements, promoting a vision of how the nation's prosperity should be shared by all but not squandered for future generations.

The progressive Left has yet to figure out how to frame issues and mobilize constituencies in the early twenty-first century that can achieve sustained political and economic power. Each time there has been a political realignment, it has occurred in ways that even its strongest proponents could not have anticipated. America today is holding its breath, trying to decide what kind of society it wants to be. Liberal and progressive forces are gaining momentum, but they still lack the organizational infrastructure needed to effectively challenge the conservative message and movement. They have begun to invest in building that infrastructure—think tanks, grassroots coalitions, technology, recruitment of staff, and identification and training of candidates (Bai 2007). Some of that investment bore fruit in November 2004 (including the impressive work of the Americans Coming Together project) and in November 2006, when unions, community organizing groups, and other progressives helped elect a Democratic majority in Congress. But there is much more to be done.

Americans are used to voting for presidential candidates with backgrounds as lawyers, military officers, farmers, businessmen, and career politicians. The 2008 election was the first time they were asked to vote for someone who has been a community organizer. Of course, Barack Obama has also been a lawyer, a law professor, and an elected official, but throughout his presidential campaign, he frequently referred to the three years he spent as a community organizer in Chicago in the mid-1980s as "the best education I ever had" and as a formative period in his life. In 1985, at age twenty-three, Obama was hired by the Developing Communities Project, a coalition of churches on Chicago's South Side (affiliated with the Gamaliel Foundation network). His job was to help empower residents to win improved playgrounds, after-school programs, job training, and housing, and to address other concerns affecting a neighborhood hurt by large-scale layoffs from the nearby steel mills and neglect by banks, retail stores, and the local government. He knocked on doors and talked to people in their kitchens, living rooms, and churches about the problems they faced and why they needed to get involved to change things. For example, he organized tenants in the troubled Altgeld Gardens public housing project to push the city to remove dangerous asbestos in their apartments, a campaign that he acknowledges resulted in only a partial victory. After Obama helped organize a large mass meeting of angry tenants, the city government started to test and seal asbestos in some apartments but ran out of money to complete the task.

Through his references to his own experience and his persistent praise for organizers at every campaign stop, Obama may have helped recruit a new wave of idealistic young Americans who want to bring about change. According to all surveys and exit polls, interest in politics and voter turnout among the Millennial generation (born after 1978) increased dramatically in 2008, a direct result of the Obama phenomenon. In addition, professors reported that the number of college students taking courses in community organizing and courses about movements and activism has increased. Community organizing groups like ACORN, as well as unions and environmental groups, report that the number of young people seeking jobs as organizers spiked in the wake of Obama's candidacy. Through his own example, as well as by the vitriol unleashed by the Republicans and the right-wing attack machine, Obama increased the visibility of grassroots organizing as a career path, a means of bringing about social change, and a way to give ordinary people a sense of their own collective power to improve their lives.

During his presidential campaign, Obama often referred to the valuable lessons he learned working "in the streets" of Chicago. "I've won some good fights and I've also lost some fights," he said in a speech in Milwaukee during the primary season, "because good intentions are not enough, when not fortified with political will and political power." Although he didn't make community organizing a lifetime career—he left Chicago to attend law school at Harvard—Obama often says that his organizing experience shapes his approach to politics. After graduating from law school, Obama returned to Chicago to practice and teach law but in the mid-1990s began contemplating running for office, thinking he could use many of the same skills he learned on the streets. In 1995 he told a Chicago newspaper, "What if a politician were to see his job as that of an organizer—as part teacher and part advocate, one who does not sell voters short but who educates them about the real choices before them?" (De Zutter 1995). Since embarking on a political career, Obama hasn't forgotten the philosophical and practical lessons that he learned on the streets of Chicago and that became central to his campaign for the White House.

For example, community organizers distinguish themselves from traditional political campaign operatives who approach voters as customers through direct mail, telemarketing, and canvassing. According to Temo Figueroa, the Obama campaign's national field director, most presidential campaigns take volunteers off the street and put them to work immediately on the "grunt" work of the campaign—making phone calls, handing out leaflets, or walking door to door. Figueroa—the son and nephew of United Farm Worker union activists, and a UCLA graduate who worked as a union organizer for many years—says the Obama campaign has been different. Obama enlisted Marshall Ganz, one of the country's leading organizing theorists and practitioners, who teaches at Harvard's Kennedy School of Government, to help train organizers and volunteers. Ganz and other experienced organizers, including Mike Kruglik, one of Obama's mentors in Chicago, led campaign volunteers through several days of intense training sessions called "Camp Obama." Potential field organizers were given an overview of the history of grassroots organizing techniques and the key lessons of campaigns that have succeeded and failed. The Obama campaign enlisted hundreds of seasoned organizers, including veterans from unions, community groups, churches, and environmental groups. They, in turn, mobilized thousands of volunteers—many of them neophytes in electoral politics—into tightly knit, highly motivated, and efficient teams. This organizing effort mobilized many first-time voters, including an unprecedented number of young people and African Americans. Many of the campaign's successes were due to this grassroots organizing approach.

The influence of Obama's organizing experience was also evident in his speeches, his continued use of the UFW slogan "Yes, we can / Sí se puede," and his emphasis on "hope" and "change." His stump speeches typically included references to America's organizing tradition. "Nothing in this country worthwhile has ever happened except when somebody somewhere was willing to hope," Obama said in a speech in February 2008. "That is how workers won the right to organize against violence and intimidation. That's how women won the right to vote. That's how young people traveled south to march and to sit in and to be beaten, and some went to jail and some died for freedom's cause." Change comes about, Obama said, by "imagining, and then fighting for, and then working for, what did not seem possible before." "Real change," he frequently noted, only comes about from the "bottom up," but as president, he could give voice to those organizing in their workplaces, communities, and congregations around a positive vision for change. "That's leadership," he said.

It is unclear how Obama's organizing background will shape his approach to governing. He will have to find a balance between working inside the Beltway and encouraging Americans to organize and mobilize. During the campaign, he signaled his understanding that his ability to reform health care, tackle global warming, and restore job security and decent wages will depend, in large measure, on whether he can use his bully pulpit to mobilize public opinion and encourage Americans to battle powerful corporate interests and members of Congress who resist change. For example, in a speech in Milwaukee during the primary season, Obama talked about the need to forge a new energy policy. He explained, "I know how hard it will be to bring about change. Exxon Mobil made $11 billion this past quarter. They don't want to give up their profits easily." Another major test will be whether he will spend his political capital to help push the Employee Free Choice Act (EFCA)—a significant reform of America's outdated and business-oriented labor laws—through Congress against almost unified business opposition. If passed, EFCA will help trigger a new wave of organizing that will require enlisting thousands of young organizers into the labor movement.

Progressives within Obama's inner circle will look for opportunities to encourage his organizing instincts to shape how he governs the nation, whom he appoints to key positions, and which policies to prioritize. Meanwhile, a new generation of volunteer activists and paid organizers— inspired in part by Obama's own example—will be looking to join his crusade or to push him to translate his campaign promises into public policy. As an organization with its own membership, as part of a broader progressive coalition, and as a model of how to effectively use organizational resources, and work both inside and outside electoral politics, ACORN has an important role to play in building a movement for social and economic justice.

REFERENCES

Atlas, J. 2005. "The Battle in Brooklyn." *Shelterforce*. November–December.

Atlas, J., and P. Dreier. 2006. "Waging Victory." *American Prospect*. November 11.

———. 2008. "The GOP's Blame-ACORN Game." *Nation*. November 10.

Bai, M. 2004. "Who Lost Ohio?" *New York Times Magazine*. November 21.

———. 2007. *The Argument: Billionaires, Bloggers, and the Battle to Remake Democratic Politics*. New York: Penguin.

Barone, M. 2008. "Why Should Palin and Voters Be Reverent toward Obama's Community Organizing?" *U.S. News and World Report*. September 8.

Berube, A., and E. Kneebone. 2006. *Two Steps Back: City and Suburban Poverty Trends 1999–2005*. Washington, DC: Brookings Institution. December.

Bhargava, D. 2008. "Organizing Principles." *New York Times*. September 13.

Boyle, K. 1998. "Little More Than Ashes: The UAW and American Reform in the 1960s." In *Organized Labor and American Politics, 1894–1994*, ed. Kevin Boyle. Albany, NY: SUNY Press.

Boyte, H. 2008. "The Peculiar Attack on Community Organizing." *Minneapolis Star-Tribune*. September 8.

Breidenbach, J. 2002. "LA Story: The Coalition That Made a $100 Million Trust Fund Happen." *Shelterforce*. March–April.

Candaele, K., and P. Dreier. 2002. "Housing: An LA Story." *Nation*. April 15.

Clarkson, F. 2003. "Putting the 'Mass' in Massachusetts." *In These Times*. December 15.

DeNavas-Walt, C., B. D. Proctor, and C. H. Lee. 2006. *Income, Poverty, and*

Health Insurance Coverage in the United States: 2005. Washington, DC: U.S. Census Bureau.

De Zutter, H. 1995. "What Makes Obama Run?" *Chicago Reader.* December 8.

Dickens, G. 2008. "Matthews: Is 'Community Organizer' the New 'Welfare Queen'?" NewsBusters.org. September 9. Available at *newsbusters.org/blogs/ geoffrey-dickens/2008/09/08/matthews-community-organizer-new-welfare-queen.*

Dreier, P. 2002. "Social Justice Philanthropy: Can We Get More Bang for the Buck?" *Social Policy* 33, no. 1 (Fall): 27–33.

———. 2005a. "Builders Clucking Like Chicken Little." *Los Angeles Times.* July 3.

———. 2005b. "Can Cities Be Progressive?" *Nation.* June 15.

———. 2006a. "Growing the Minimum Wage." TomPaine.com. November 27.

———. 2006b. "Rosa Parks: Angry, Not Tired." *Dissent.* Winter. Available at *www.dissentmagazine.org/article/?article=169.*

———. 2008a. "From Organizer to Elected Official." *Nation.* September 8. Available at *www.thenation.com/directory/bios/peter_dreier.*

———. 2008b. "Will Obama Inspire a New Generation of Organizers?" *Dissent.* Spring. Available at *www.dissentmagazine.org/article/?article=1215.*

Dreier, P., and J. Atlas. 2007. "The Missing Katrina Story." *Tikkun.* January.

———. 2008. "GOP Mocks Public Service." *Nation.* September 5. Available at *www.thenation.com/doc/20080922/dreier_atlas.*

Dreier, P., R. Freer, R. Gottlieb, and M. Vallianatos. 2006. "Movement Mayor: Can Antonio Villaraigosa Change Los Angeles?" *Dissent.* Summer. Available at *www.dissentmagazine.org/article/?article=656.*

Dreier, P., J. Mollenkopf, and T. Swanstrom. 2005. *Place Matters: Metropolitics for the 21st Century.* 2d ed. Lawrence: University Press of Kansas.

Eckholm, E. 2006. "City by City, an Antipoverty Group Plants Seeds of Change." *New York Times.* June 26.

Egan, T. 2006. "'06 Race Focuses on the Suburbs, Inner and Outer." *New York Times.* June 16.

Faber, D., and D. McCarthy. 2005. *Foundations for Social Change: Critical Perspectives on Philanthropy and Popular Movements.* New York: Rowman and Littlefield.

Fine, J. 1996. "Back to Basics." *Boston Review.* February/March.

Finfer, L. 2008. "Community Organizers Are a Staple of Democracy." *Newsday.* September 10.

Fisher, R. 1994. *Let the People Decide: Neighborhood Organizing in America.* Updated ed. New York: Twayne.

Flaming, D. 2007. *Economic Footprint of Unions in Los Angeles.* Los Angeles: Economic Roundtable. December. Available at *www.economicrt.org/summa-ries/Econ_Footprint_LA_Unions_synopsis.html.*

Garnick, D. 2008. "Organizers Just Small-Time to GOP." *Boston Herald.* September 8.

Geoghegan, T. 2008. "Hey Sarah—Organize This." Slate.com. September 5. Available at *www.slate.com/id/2199473/.*

Gottlieb, R., R. Freer, M. Vallianatos, and P. Dreier. 2006. *The Next Los Angeles: The Struggle for a Livable City.* 2d ed. Berkeley and Los Angeles: University of California Press.

Hacker, J. S., and P. Pierson. 2005. *Off Center: The Republican Revolution and the Erosion of American Democracy.* New Haven: Yale University Press.

Hart, S. H. 2001. *Cultural Dilemmas of Progressive Politics: Styles of Engagement among Grassroots Activists.* Chicago: University of Chicago Press.

Horwitt, S. 1992. *Let Them Call Me Rebel: Saul Alinsky, His Life and Legacy.* New York: Random House.

Huppke, R. 2008. "Organizing a Response to the GOP." *Chicago Tribune.* September 7.

Jenkins, J. C., and A. Halcli. 1999. "Grassrooting the System: Recent Trends in Social Movement Philanthropy, 1953–1990. The Development and Impact of Social Movement Philanthropy." In *Philanthropic Foundations: New Scholarship, New Possibilities,* ed. E. C. Lagemann. Bloomington: Indiana University Press, 1999.

Jenkins, J. C., and C. Perrow. 1977. "Insurgency of the Powerless." *American Sociological Review* 42, no. 2: 249–68.

Jenkins, J. C., and B. Klandermans, eds. 1995. *The Politics of Social Protest.* Minneapolis: University of Minnesota Press.

Judis, J., and R. Teixeira. 2004. *The Emerging Democratic Majority.* New York: Scribner.

Kellman, J. 2008. "Service Changes People's Character." *Newsweek.* September 5.

Kelly, J., and T. Lee. 2008. "No Call to Belittle Community Work." *Seattle Post-Intelligencer.* September 8.

Kurtz, S. 2008. "Inside Obama's ACORN." *National Review.* May 29. Available at *nationalreview.com/?q=NDZiMjkwMDczZWI5ODdjOWYxZTIzZGIyNzE yMjE0ODI=.*

Kwon, A. D. K. 2008. "Community Organizing Defines U.S." *Syracuse Post-Standard.* September 15.

Lawrence, J. 2008. "Community Organizer Slams Attract Support for Obama." *USA Today.* September 4.

Lipsky, M. 1970. *Protest in City Politics.* Chicago: Rand McNally.

Malkin, M. 2008. "The ACORN Obama Knows." June 25. Available at *michel-lemalkin.com/2008/06/25/the-acorn-obama-knows.*

Martin, I. 2006. "Do Living Wage Policies Diffuse?" *Urban Affairs Review* 41, no. 5: 710–19.

McCarthy, J., and M. Zald. 1977. "Resource Mobilization and Social Movements." *American Journal of Sociology* 82, no. 6: 1212–41.

McKitrick, C. 2008. "Quips Sting Utah Activists." *Salt Lake Tribune.* September 6.

Micklethwait, J., and A. Wooldridge. 2004. *The Right Nation: Conservative Power in America.* New York: Penguin.

Milkman, R. 2000. *Organizing Immigrants.* Ithaca: Cornell University Press.

———. 2006. *L.A. Story: Immigrant Workers and the Future of the Labor Movement.* New York: Russell Sage Foundation.

Moran, R. 2008. "Obama's Ties to ACORN." *American Thinker.* May 29. Available at *www.americanthinker.com/blog/2008/05/obamas_ties_to_acorn_more_subs.html.*

Morris, A. 1984. *The Origins of the Civil Rights Movement.* New York: Free Press.

Morris, A., and C. Mueller, eds. 1992. *Frontiers of Social Movement Theory.* New Haven: Yale University Press.

Oliver, P. 1984. "If You Don't Do It, Nobody Will." *American Sociological Review* 49:601–10.

Paget, K. 1990. "Citizen Organizing: Many Movements, No Majority." *American Prospect* 1, no. 2: 115–28.

Parachini, L., and S. Covington. 2001. *The Community Organizing Toolbox: A Funder's Guide to Community Organizing.* Washington, DC: Neighborhood Funders Group.

Perlstein, R. 2001. *Before the Storm: Barry Goldwater and the Unmaking of the American Consensus.* New York: Hill and Wang.

Reynolds, D. 2002. *Taking the High Road: Communities Organize for Economic Change.* Armonk, NY: M. E. Sharpe.

———, ed. 2004. *Partnering for Change: Unions and Community Groups Build Coalitions for Economic Justice.* Armonk, NY: M. E. Sharpe.

Sege, I. 2008. "Community Organizers Fault Comments at GOP Gathering." *Boston Globe.* September 6.

Sidney, M. 2003. *Unfair Housing.* Lawrence: University Press of Kansas.

Simmons, L. 1994. *Organizing in Hard Times: Labor and Neighborhoods in Hartford.* Philadelphia: Temple University Press.

———. 2000. "Labor and LEAP: Political Coalition Experiences in Connecticut." *Working USA* 4, no. 1 (Summer): 19–34.

Simpson, S. 2008. "Community Organizers More Valuable Than Palin Thinks." *Hartford Courant.* September 5.

Skocpol, T. 2003. *Diminished Democracy: From Membership to Management in American Civic Life.* Norman: University of Oklahoma Press.

Slayton, R. 1986. *Back of the Yards: The Making of Local Democracy.* Chicago: University of Chicago Press.

Smock, K. 2004. *Democracy in Action: Community Organizing and Urban Change.* New York: Columbia University Press.

Social Justice Grantmaking: A Report on Foundation Trends. 2005. New York: The Foundation Center, and Washington, DC: Independent Sector.

Social Justice Philanthropy: The Latest Trend or a Lasting Lens for Grantmaking? 2005. Washington, DC: National Committee for Responsive Philanthropy.

Squires, G., ed. 2003. *Organizing Access to Capital.* Philadelphia: Temple University Press.

Swanstrom, T., C. Casey, R. Flack, and P. Dreier. 2004. *Pulling Apart: Economic Segregation among Suburbs and Central Cities in Major Metropolitan Areas.* Washington, DC: Brookings Institution.

Swarts, H. 2002. "What Makes Community Organizing Succeed?" *Snapshots.* January–February.

Weir, M., and M. Ganz. 1997. "Reconnecting People and Politics." In *The New Majority: Toward a Popular Progressive Politics*, ed. by Stanley Greenberg and Theda Skocpol. New Haven: Yale University Press.

2

Understanding ACORN
Sweat and Social Change

Wade Rathke

As I sat down to offer some thoughts about what distinguishes ACORN and its contributions over more than three decades, several things rushed through my head. What happened in 1983 or 1997 or even 1977 or 2003? If I drew a blank, was it a problem? If I did remember, then was it important? Having defined myself as ACORN's chief organizer for thirty-eight years, I have marked my time by often simply saying, "I got there first and stayed the longest." I can honestly state that I have not spent many moments mulling over the organization's past, largely because I have been absorbed in my job of realizing the organization's future. Few questions surprise me more than when outsiders, reporters, or other well-meaning inquisitors ask me to state ACORN's biggest accomplishment or most important victory. After all is said and done, the organization itself is our largest achievement.

In the Beginning

First, let us go back to ACORN's origins in 1970 in Little Rock, Arkansas. Why there? Why then? Why this? It has become almost a cliché to mention the 1960s in America. To many, that period has been trivialized as a time of youth, sex, drugs, and rock 'n' roll, but it was also a time of intense social ferment, propelled by the accomplishments of the civil rights movement earlier in the decade and the emergence of new and ambitious movements designed to end the Vietnam War, liberate women, and recognize the value of the environment. Times indeed were a' changing! For many organizers, though, the natural legacy of the rights-based movement became the transition to a critical debate about power and how power might be built and exercised in a community. The civil rights movement saw the development of many branches from this tree seeding the development of other movements based on race, identity, economic development, and alternative institutions. Another part of the dialectic, whether expressed by Saul Alinsky or Tom Hayden or Stokely Carmichael or Huey Newton, was asking what role might organization play in the empowerment of previously marginalized and disenfranchised communities.

The National Welfare Rights Organization (NWRO), founded in 1966 by Dr. George A. Wiley in a march in Ohio against welfare cutbacks, became my entry into the world of this debate. George was a civil rights veteran. As a deputy director of CORE (Congress of Racial Equality) in the mid-1960s, he brought that civil rights tradition, its lessons, and tactics to NWRO. He also brought the blending of civil rights with economic rights and the argument that the oppression of the poor had to be mediated by a sense of entitlement under law (for example, welfare rights) and that expressing a morally correct voice needed to translate into pride and power for welfare recipients rather than humiliation of circumstance and supplication for support. I had been recruited and hired as an organizer for the Massachusetts state affiliate of NWRO in June 1969 after a rally in the Boston Commons at which Wiley spoke. Since I had most recently been an organizer/activist in the student movement and antiwar movement, the idea of working to build an empowering organization that billed itself as the largest poor people's organization in America was irresistible to me. The constituency was clear and the targets were obvious and handy, so it all seemed so much more concrete with results that were equally real and measurable. I may not have known much at twenty, but I knew I wanted to build something that would last longer than the sound of the shout and holler.

In the lightning rounds that marked the times, I grew up quickly on the job, moving from founding organizer of the Springfield chapters to head organizer of the Massachusetts Welfare Rights Organization based in Boston in less than six months. Six months later I was driving into Little Rock from Boston via New Orleans to found ACORN. In that short sprint of time, I had come to a fair number of conclusions that would end up shaping ACORN for decades, many of which were counterpoints to my time with NWRO. The early years of ACORN's experience in Little Rock seemed to confirm and deepen the core commitments and values that have highlighted the organizational experience over subsequent decades:

- *Majority constituency.* We could not win enough from a minority base, even though one in seven residents of Boston were welfare recipients. The shifting times did not give us enough leverage to win. An organization genuinely needed to unite low- and moderate-income people broadly so that power could be built. Fundamentally, we would become a constituency organization of poor and working families, and it was the base rather than the organizational formation or methodology that would always define the organization, from the community organizations at the core to the branches—including services in housing counseling or tax and benefit access; or the media outlets, the labor unions, and tenants groups; or issue coalitions and campaigns.

- *Multi-issue and multiracial.* A single-issue organization was ineffective at building power because the organization's survival hung not on its own work or membership but on the vicissitudes of the particular issue and its fortunes. The initiative by Massachusetts governor Francis Sargent to impose a "flat grant" that would have raised the benefits for all welfare families in Massachusetts was a victory of sorts, but by eliminating the "special needs" campaigns we used to grow the organization, it would also haven take away our primary organizing tool, making it harder to grow and build power. Never again! Similarly, the organization needed to be multiracial and have a broader income base in order to not be stunted by any other external forces seeking to pigeonhole our ambitions or mission.

- *Power in numbers and ballot boxes.* Virtually from the beginning, ACORN broke out of the simpler ideological box that held that power was simply numbers, or feet on the street with signs waving, and adapted our constituency's basic core values that politics and power meant voting and measuring the results at the ballot box. As early as 1972 in the run-up to the "Save the City" campaign that greatly expanded ACORN's membership and base in Little Rock, the ACORN Political Action Committee (APAC) planted its marker by aggressively endorsing Doug Stephens for the Little Rock School Board. The APAC upended common wisdom by carrying Stephens to victory based on overwhelming majorities in the eastern, southern, and central wards, creating the first election victory in a generation where a candidate failed to carry the affluent 5th Ward in the Heights and Pleasant Valley. The "takeover" of the Pulaski County Quorum Court two years later in 1974 saw hundreds of actual ACORN members elected as justices of the peace, an event that made front-page headlines in the *Washington Post* even as the *Arkansas Gazette* was still working to avoid recognizing ACORN. The election of these justices of the peace signaled that ACORN was not willing to simply be a power broker but was committed to making sure that *all* the people, including lower-income families themselves, were part of its adopted motto, "The people shall rule."

- *Tactical flexibility.* My high school Latin teacher constantly parroted in each class the maxim *repetitio est mater studiorum*—repetition is the mother of study. Whether in Massachusetts or Arkansas or anywhere else, it became obvious that the more we followed a formulaic campaign and tactical design, the more likely it was for the target to be able to ignore, avoid, or sidestep our demands. We needed the ability to operate on a wide-ranging scale that could give voice to our members and their participation but also utilize the full arsenal of tactics we could assemble from research, media, and other leverage. In NWRO our dependence on "special needs" (benefits for school clothing or winter clothing or furniture vouchers) as organizing tools meant that the elimination of such quasi-discretionary benefits in favor of higher, flat grants by the state crippled the momentum and growth of the organization in Massachusetts. Importantly, in ACORN we also quickly learned, as we had piloted in Springfield, Massachusetts, that our ability to *actually* deliver the spoils of victory built power.

At any rate driving into Little Rock in 1970, I was going into a state to build a new "model" for organizing. The initial months of development were undertaken with the support of NWRO and Dr. George Wiley. Arkansas worked as a location partially because it had some conditions that I thought were important, and, significantly (compared to California and Georgia which I also considered), the leadership of the ninety-nine members of NWRO in the state at that time were open to the "ACORN experiment." There were other advantages to Arkansas. The capital city and the largest city were one and the same, and were located in the geographical center of the state, making the prospects of building statewide organization easy to imagine and practical to implement. The population was widely mixed without one group being dominant. Income was low, meaning that some issues that in more wealthy states might be only welfare issues, in Arkansas might cover a majority of the families (free and reduced-price school lunches were a good example). Arkansas was a backwater where we could wildly experiment, both succeeding and failing, while trying to build a new model in a way that might not have been possible on the East or West Coast. We had an even chance to build something exciting, effective, and different, and that was the opportunity of a lifetime.

Looking backwards, the early stages of ACORN's development seem more certain and predictable than they were at the time and might be loosely grouped in the following ways:

- *Setting the stage, 1970–1972.* The first campaigns have to be won if an organization is to survive. From 1970 to 1972 groups were organized around welfare and income-based issues to establish a base in Little Rock and North Little Rock under the ACORN banner. After an early victory winning a commitment from Governor Winthrop Rockefeller to establish a "Furniture for Families" program for lower-income families, ACORN's efforts expanded to championing free and reduced-price school lunches, free textbooks, and other programs such as the Unemployed Workers Organizing Committee (UWOC) and the Vietnam Veterans Organizing Committee (VVOC). An ACORN Service Center in North Little Rock included a food buyers' club among other things, and a very different group was built in the white, rural area of Lawson in Pulaski County. ACORN and NWRO discontinued their relationship within six months as ACORN began to expand its issues and income constituency and NWRO realized it was not comfortable with a non-welfare-recipient base.
- *Save the City campaign, 1972–1974.* ACORN more aggressively expanded its community organizing profile by building a number of groups in eastern, central, and western Little Rock around a platform of issues seeking to both embed the base in local issues and affect the city directors' election. These ACORN neighborhood organizations fought for the creation of local parks, tried to stop real estate blockbusting, pushed for more equitable distribution of community development funds and fair property tax assessments, and tried to win much needed local infrastructure improvements.
- *Protect Our Land Association, 1972–1974.* ACORN had begun to implement its expansion around the state opening offices in Pine Bluff, Fort Smith, and elsewhere. Issues around increases in utility rates for gas and electric coincided with concerns about the announcement of the construction of a huge coal-fired plant along the Arkansas River between Little Rock and Pine Bluff. In the first campaign that increased ACORN's national profile, we organized groups among the rural residents and farmers on both sides of the river in the dispersal range of the likely pollutants, forming ACORN Protect Our Land Association. Unable to stop AP&L (Arkansas Power and Light) in Arkansas before the Public Service Commission, we targeted stockholders in the company, particularly among the large institutional investors at Harvard, Yale, and other colleges where we spread the campaign, and we received great support. All of this not only won reforms in the plant size and pollution controls but also established the organization as a force both locally and nationally.
- *Quorum Court and Lifeline campaigns, 1974–1976.* The Quorum Court was the county legislative body responsible for setting taxes, most importantly, and was an archaic structure with hundreds of seats and smaller districts. Such an atomized structure favored an organizational effort that could

consolidate a slate across a broad base of districts that were electing justices of the peace in the county. Winning the majority along with our allies hastened the constitutional change that reduced the size of the legislative body to a more "modern" level. The other major electoral effort was the municipal initiative drive to win "lifeline" electric rates that would set lower prices for the first 400 kilowatts of usage to support elderly and low-income families. We won the election at the ballot box but later lost in the court challenge, based on a technicality where an electric cooperative had a few customers in the city footprint, which was hugely disappointing (Hillary Clinton was the opposing counsel in the lawsuit) but taught us many lessons for the future.

- *20/80 campaign, 1975–1980.* In 1975 ACORN opened its first affiliate outside of Arkansas in South Dakota, and it then followed quickly with chapters in the neighboring states of Texas, Louisiana, Tennessee, and Missouri. This huge expansion drive was focused on seeing ACORN in twenty states by 1980. The organization was seeking in this brief time span to be able to play a role winning a voice for the issues and interests of low- and moderate-income families in the 1980 presidential campaign. This expansion created on a national basis the modern footprint of the organization and many of its issues and campaigns. The expansion outside of Arkansas meant that in one year, 1978, ACORN finally became a corporation, created a national board and leadership structure in a first national convention in Memphis (and then a platform conference the following year in St. Louis), and moved its operational headquarters to New Orleans, where it has been for the last thirty years.

The last twenty-five years have been as significant as the first years of ACORN, but the branches of history and development are harder to categorize. In 1978–1980 the roots were laid in direct labor organizing, which has now led to the inclusion of what are sometimes called by the Service Employees International Union (SEIU) "the ACORN locals," SEIU 100 and SEIU 880. Work expanded through the squatting campaigns of the late 1970s to create the ACORN Housing Corporation development and counseling programs; relationships in Dallas, Tampa, and Little Rock created noncommercial FM radio stations in those cities; and more. The present is always a shadow of the past, and the work in the first decade of ACORN's history was seminal in this regard as well, but each decade has been rich in history and accomplishment. Nonetheless, the core organizational values and constituency have continued to trump any specific campaign or experience.

Building a Dues-Paying Membership Organization

Any search for the secrets of ACORN's success should not discount the membership and the dues each family pays. For many people, this simple component seems too obvious, too transparent, but in fact it is the critical distinguishing characteristic at the foundation of the organization. The dues program began during a confluence of terrible necessity and ideological presumption. In late 1970 as we moved in a different direction from the National Welfare Rights Organization, we had no money. NWRO had provided the early support for ACORN's work. Either we went to our members and got them to pay dues or the organization could not financially survive. We hardly survived then. My social security statements for those years are stark proof of the periods when I made $30 and $40 per week and was lucky to make over $2,000 per year. And, I was not alone! We operated from pillar to post, squatting in free office space for a couple of months here and then a couple of months there, borrowing paper and machines, and hiring away staff to provide the nucleus for our operation. We were young, and none of this seemed crazy at the time. In fact, it seemed normal. This was the way "movements" worked, so nothing seemed that strange.

But, none of us knew anything about dues. The members had to teach us about dues, and the lessons they taught were endlessly important and, at the time, very surprising. Three lessons are still tattooed on my brain and will be forever; these lessons confounded the organizers but taught me that dues were the way to go forever. Two of them are old lessons, and one is fairly new.

Carolyn Carr was the organizer who used to deal with a member in the Woodrow to Pine group in Little Rock named Lela Phillips. Even as a member, Lela used to lead the entire staff in members and dues, although she insisted on only collecting the dues on a month-by-month basis. She was as timely as a clock and would make her regular rounds in the neighborhood and collect the dues from each and every one of her members without fail. She saw collecting dues the same way that others paid their burial policies: little by little, month by month. Carolyn would talk to Mrs. Phillips about getting more in advance or in a yearly sum, but she believed it was important to see the members every month, to tell them about what was new and upcoming in the organization, and to keep them active. Sister Phillips took me to school on dues!

Another story from that period involved an organizer named Donna

Parciak, who was a VISTA volunteer we had cadged onto the early staff. In one staff meeting, while I was pressing her about dues being paid in the North Little Rock groups where she was working, she blurted out a problem that involved Dixie, a very low-income African American neighborhood where we had an active organization. It seemed that she did not think she was doing a good job there and she felt guilty about having neglected the group over the last several months while she was working on a campaign and doing more in other groups. So, what was the problem? The Dixie group continued to pay their dues and turn them into the office faithfully, even though Donna felt like she was not delivering on her job as an organizer. In Dixie, what Donna was missing was that the organization there had become theirs, not hers, and their expectations for the group and the necessity of supporting their organization with dues were different than hers. She saw them as poor people for whom dues were really a burden. They saw the dues as an organizational tithe and something they paid because it was important to support something that could only exist for them and with their support.

The last lesson bridged the decades. I was in Manila with community organizers who had been working among the urban poor there for thirty years. They had been kind enough to listen to ACORN's experience and to share their own with me, and they were honoring me by taking me to one of their most active groups, which was desperately trying to hold on to a squatted area near an old Marcos shipyard along the water. On the issue of dues, they had been attentive but skeptical. Perhaps dues could be paid by the poor in the United States, but people were way too poor in the Philippines, and, with all due respect, they said, such a thing would never work in Asia. We sat down with the local leaders in one of the groups so that I could ask them, with the help of translation, about their issues and how it all worked. As we talked, I thought I heard them refer to "their money." I asked them pointedly where they were raising the money. Were they collecting dues for the local group? Absolutely! They collected dues every month and supplemented the dues with other community fundraisers, mainly involving food. This local group might be in Manila, but we had 1,000 groups all over the United States just like it. The veteran organizers were surprised, and I hope not embarrassed, when they found that despite their ideological prejudice about what the poor would never do, the poor knew it took dues to keep the organization going, and they simply paid for what they felt was important. Just because the organizers had never discussed the issue of dues did not mean that the members in the local organization did not know their importance.

The real problem with dues is that they are hard to collect. Not hard in the sense of heavy lifting or people not being willing to pay, but hard in the sense that it requires constant, unswerving, daily, monthly, and yearly discipline. A dues collection system must be constantly maintained or it all breaks down completely. Although ACORN has found that membership dues are the lifeblood of the organization, no other organization has really adopted the system because of the maintenance it requires. As natural as a dues system is for members, many organizers, ironically, find it unnatural. Collecting money is not what many people imagine when they picture themselves as organizers. Perhaps they see themselves standing on a table addressing crowds or secluded in a back room cutting a deal, but they don't necessarily see themselves as checking off the list and counting the dollars and checks in the back room at the end of the night with a local group treasurer. Every night. Night after night. That is what is involved in a dues system and the commitment to allowing the members to own their own organization. As Lela Phillips taught us in Little Rock, if we do not ask every month on a consistent basis and prove to the members that their dues are essential to us, then we have ripped the guts out of the system itself.

Making the system work requires a large staff willing to sweat in the streets rather than a small office-bound staff. Organizers have to maintain constant communication with the members across the gamut of local activities on both the internal, local level as well as the local, citywide, and other issue-based campaigns that allow continual participation and excitement. The internally focused practice of the local ACORN groups and their additional levels of meetings and events that create the vibrant internal life of the organization is essential, rather than simply the externally based campaign and public process of the organization. There is nothing pretty or dramatic about dues, but, like lists, they are at the heart of the organization.

Like so much of the organization's history, even as we quickly gloss over more than thirty-eight years, what seems like a straight-line development is in fact much more evolutionary. That was certainly true of dues. First, there was simply instituting dues—creating the practice and getting the job done. There were constant arguments among the staff about how it could be done and among the membership about how much should be collected and who should do the collection. Secondly, there was the process of getting better at dues, which took years and years, constant mistakes and miscues, and the experience of hundreds of organizers and members. Dues were a campaign, and the process of moving the levels of dues "per organizer" was a major program that often involved organization-wide struggles pitting new staff and their inability to recognize limits against old staff and their belief that there were ceilings that could not be broken. Increased staff wages were often "sporting propositions" that exchanged the possibility of increases in pay against the realization of increased sustainability from membership dues and internal fundraising levels. These were wrenching experiences, but they forged the organization that we have today from the crucible of such common experiences. I often wonder if there was a better way, an easier way, or a more comfortable and correct course we could have taken. I know I could not find one, and I also wonder if ACORN is becoming soft around these critical questions of internal standards on things like dues and continuing to engage in the painful mistakes and process of getting better in the streets so that we can get better at every level. This dialectical process of construction and critique has allowed us to survive and thrive and is part of the story between the lines of every event, campaign, victory (and defeat), which has brought us to this point.

Leaders and organizers share a challenge. Local group democracy is rigid and exacting in its accountability, not because of deep-seated philosophical commitments to voting, but because of a shared commonality of labor that is based on the sweat equity of membership maintenance and dues collection. Members can vote with their feet and do so quickly, and organizers and leaders are bound at the hip in the tasks involved in preserving the sometimes mercurial and mysterious balance required to allow organization to stabilize and grow. Within ACORN examples are legion of the price paid by top leaders, even nationally prominent leaders, who neglected the base in their home cities and local groups. Recently, an excellent treasurer of the national organization from Dallas sustained two elections of the national board in less than a one-year period to be re-elected as ACORN's treasurer, but then was gone within three months of his last election, having failed to win a seat as a delegate from Texas. The base had changed there, and he had not attended to it quickly enough, particularly as the membership became more Hispanic in one city after another. At national board meetings, delegates regularly stand to speak and demand assurances that their offices will be fully staffed and supported so that they have assistance in maintaining their local groups' activities, and therefore their own positions.

A membership organization is not a public-interest group with an amorphous, squishy, self-described constituency, but a real-life, flesh-eating machine that must be fed constantly on activity and victory. Neither does membership activity necessarily translate into a social movement, although ACORN has many of the characteristics of a social movement. Turning the wheels of the organization is not a matter of mobilizing disparate parts of the general low- and-moderate income base we identify as our support but precisely and exactingly motivating and activating our membership base. The internal cultural clues are specific and institutionally exacting in our program. The dialectic around tenant organizing is a good example. Tenants are a central part of the ACORN base, but there is a constant internal tension about whether or not offices with extensive tenant operations are mobilizing tenants or building organization among them. Essentially, the argument is whether or not the base is stable enough to handle the internal discipline, democracy, and accountability of the organization. ACORN offices that want to push this program have to answer institutional questions that go to the heart of the internal—and financial—life of the organization.

This has been one of those classic issues in organizing where there is clearly a debate but little discussion. Partly the problem is the lack of "bright lines." With a large mass base, whether generalized or membership—or both as is often the case for ACORN's tactical turnout—mobilization must be intense and disciplined, whether for large actions, big meetings, or even elections. Traditionally and practically, few groups have been better at this than ACORN, because we mind the math and constantly are on top of the numbers. From the outside it all simply looks like people in motion, but on the inside understanding our numbers makes a difference, particularly around questions of internal governance and the interplay between the organizers and the base, or membership in our case.

A commitment to organizational practice rather than simply mobilization technique is related to issues of actual leadership decision making and direction, including supervision and oversight of staff work, as well as democratic input and process for membership. Unquestionably, building an organization slows down the response to issues and opponents, but the trade is worth it in our experience. We have proven that the organization can still move quickly to respond to opportunity and attack. Doing so within an organizational and democratic process allows ACORN to withstand more extensive attacks from opponents, as well as endure longer campaigns because of the deeper commitments and firmer decision-making apparatus intrinsic to our organizational experience.

Weak commitments to internal process inevitably involve other tensions, particularly around capacity. Tenuous relationships between the organizing and the base not tempered with real organizational experience and commitments weigh heavily on the ability of professional organizers and membership activists to retain organizing skills so that they can respond to opportunity. Additionally, there is a hidden external assumption that there are no real financial costs involved in mobilization and movement. Without a strong relationship between the benefited bases or, in ACORN's case, actual membership, there is no relationship between activity and responsibility for sustainability, which is essential over the long haul.

Sustainability is critical to social movements unless one sees social change as simply episodic and situational. There is something magical about moments of movement, but movement is not magic as much as muscle powering imagination and will. For a brief moment, perhaps, surge and sacrifice can spur social change, but the work of real change and realizing change continues to be a daily grind without shortcuts. Unfortunately, such change is so wildly outside of the interests of power and wealth that we can never believe that the bills will be paid by someone or something other than the people who are crying for the change and who put their feet in the street.

As the organization has grown, particularly with ACORN's rapid expansion over the last decade, membership dues as a percentage of overall operating income have decreased. Now only about 10 percent of the gross expenditures are covered directly by membership dues. This is somewhat ironic given that dues have also increased dramatically and the stability of the system has substantively improved because of technological improvements such as bank drafting systems. Although the bylaws and board policy have always stipulated that a certain percentage of the dues was intended for support of the national organization, in practice all dues are spent locally to support the basic office, staff, and operations. Local support is supplemented by additional "internal" income, which is membership driven and self-sustaining. Internal fundraising ranges from raffles and dinners to annual banquets and street fairs.

The bigger the office and operation, the more money seems like magic, simply appearing without the membership recognizing the work involved in acquiring resources. The smaller and newer the office, the more dues and internal fundraising are 60 to 90 percent of the overall office income. Inevitably, therefore, the older, stronger, bigger, and more powerful the ACORN operation, the more difficult the relationship between membership-controlled finances and resources that are dependent on deals, development, and staff in creating grants, contracts, and donations. Most of these resources do not lead to conflict and tension because so much of the work of the organization still flows from the community level, where the local group activities and finances are propelled by membership and grassroots leadership involvement and energy. We do face challenges internally at the higher levels of the structure. At large city, state, and national board levels, it is difficult to integrate accountability and discipline as the numbers of dollars explode so far outside of the experience of members and leaders that staff dependency has a tendency to increase. At the end of my time as chief organizer, I have not been judged as much on my ability to train members in local group dues collection as on my ability to manage an organizational family that employs more than 1,000 staff of all varieties and descriptions. Each year we raise and spend over $100 million, of which a significant part comes from dues and internal fundraising, but big chunks come from campaign support and labor and corporate partnerships. I suspect there is an organizational law of accountability that holds that the smaller the entity and the jurisdiction, the greater the accountability. The larger the entity and the more extensive the jurisdiction, the lighter the structural weight and discipline of board control. Knowing that this inverse relationship is perhaps inevitable has required a cultural commitment to more meetings, reports, and decision points to force interaction and exchange around governance between leadership and staff at the top levels. Small is not beautiful in organizing for power, so we have embraced a brave, new world with temerity but with conviction and hope that we can maintain the elements from our base all the way to the farthest reaches of the superstructure we have built on top of that very wide and deep foundation.

In the modern ACORN organization, membership dues are more deeply rooted in the "internal" financing program, where they essentially supply the tree trunk and sprout the branches of sustainable and replicable income that privileges the base, their dues payment, and their community-based fundraisers. Springing from the base are service platforms, associate and provisional membership programs with varying rates of dues and contributions, and volunteer support by members matched by their employers. Access to payroll deduction systems allows members to increase their contributions by directing donations to ACORN rather than to less connected social services. Various sustainable partnership programs are available through corporations, unions, and other institutions where the ACORN membership is able to source, distribute, and implement contact and outreach programs for multiple programs. External support will always come and go, so the long term future of the organization relies on membership participation and control, supported by dues and the internal programs that have been built as infrastructure emanating from that base and that are controlled by the democratic structure of the organization.

At the scale of current operations, the path that has been paved with dues has to be widened with other internally created and directed support.

Perhaps more important than the economic impact of membership dues is the institutional and cultural weight accorded dues and membership within ACORN. Leadership and the staff constantly privilege the base experience with membership and dues. The iconic story on the member/leader side of the organization is always the tale of the first time that someone knocked on the door of their house, and they made the decision to join the organization. The touchstone for staff is always the answer to the question of how many people attended the first neighborhood meeting in your first drive and how many members joined the organization in that first organizing drive. The cultural weight of these classic tales legitimizes ACORN bona fides and distinguishes the ACORN experience from other organizing traditions in a unique way that continues to resonate throughout the organization, whether the organizer is talking about Brooklyn, Buenos Aires, Des Moines, or El Paso. Bertha Lewis, Northeast Regional Director, recently came back from early meetings in Lagos about the prospects for an ACORN Nigeria. In making a report to 800 staff members at the Year End / Year Begin meeting in 2006, she reported on her first visit and showed photos from the trip. More than one hundred people had been at the first meeting, and more than forty had joined. ACORN may be a sophisticated, large-scale, big-budgeted operation now, but even as I age and the board and others discuss who will lead when my time is over, it is inconceivable that a successor would not be able to tell stories from the street, tales of many meetings and actions, members and leaders, and the hard work of "dues and don'ts" of community organizing that is the backbone of the work.

Other Core Principles

Of course, there were other elements in the early years that have distinguished ACORN besides its proven ability to create a separate and unique institution. Like dues and membership, most of these principles seem self-evident, but cumulatively they have built the organization.

A quick list would include these additional principles:

- *One flexible, corporate structure.* Internally, ACORN gave full representation on a completely equitable basis to all membership-based affiliates. New projects, organizations, and initiatives thus could easily be integrated into the family of ACORN organizations, whether they were radio stations, groups of unemployed or organized workers, international groups or whatever might be needed to reflect a growing and expanding organization across an extended period of time. The structure was deliberately organic and adaptable. ACORN was built for growth more than anything else, so all structural impediments found in other organizations that limit growth were eliminated. Once the hands went up in the air, the organization could be put in motion. Roberts' Rules of Order were banned. ACORN was not even incorporated until 1978. The structural rule is that if it builds power, if it adds to the whole, then it can be done. Nothing about the organizational structure is limiting; everything is expansive.

- *Nonprofit, NOT tax exempt.* Churches and colleges are tax-exempt, though in many ways I don't see why this is good public policy. But citizens' organizations of low- and moderate-income families that want to be effective and aggressive need to avoid hiding the hand that is throwing the rock. A secret of ACORN's success structurally is that we have never built a bar or governor on the membership's ability to make any decision they feel appropriate or take any action democratically chosen. Being tax-exempt means that you embrace interference from the state in exchange for precious little advantage, while hobbling the organization and its membership. It is simply a matter of time before you will find yourself as an organizer having to tell elected leaders and dues-paying members that there is something they can *not* do, because of the organization's tax status, leaving the members either looking for another organization to allow them to act or understanding that they can not really build the power that the organization advertised itself as pursuing. An organizer's job is to give membership options to allow choices for the organization to grow and win, not to wag a finger about rules that no one understands.

- *Coordinated autonomy.* Keeping the organization internally vibrant has required allowing each level of the organization as much independence of action as it needs to engage issues and members. Within the organization, however, as the work has moved past the local group or community level, it necessarily requires coordination—and therefore agreement—from all the other organizational actors at the next levels—city, state, or national. At the local group, the members can call the shots within their community. When it comes to a citywide concern, a high majority of the groups in the city have to agree to get it done with the same majority vote at each level. Reaching consensus (another way of saying a "high majority" and an important ACORN principle of operation) means that ACORN is then able to act independently at that level, assuming everything else is equal.

- *One big corporation.* One organization fits in one corporation, indivisible. So many other organizations are federations with constantly shifting components based on the vagaries of contracts for training, staffing, service, or consultation, frequently empowering the organizers, who are constantly forced to define and defend value, rather than appropriately building the organization. ACORN puts everything under one big tent and holds it together.

- *What's in a name?* From the beginning we always knew that the name was important. It had to be simple. There had to be a symbol. Any member at any kitchen table around the country would need to know how to easily draw it on a poster or at the bottom of a flyer. ACORN had to be something that any member could in fact remember. It seems that we instinctively understood what is now known as "branding," which turns out to be incredibly important in imprinting the organization and its identity in the maddening roar of so much else in the world. The organization has to stand for something, and it has to stand out. We have listened to a thousand jokes about the name and the fact that we are a bunch of nuts, and we have endured tens of thousands of comments about growing into an oak, but branding the organization has been critical in building the architecture of ACORN.

- *Finding a place for politics.* Perhaps this principle seems like a corollary to the earlier point of not being tax-exempt, but it is really much more than that. The membership understood exercising and building power within ACORN not as a philosophical concept where the power of our numbers matched the power of other people's money or some such, but as a practical program where they wanted to directly engage their own voices in the public process and be political actors where they could dare to struggle and possibly win. ACORN is nonpartisan and always has been, but it has been willing to create vehicles like political action committees for the members to act, when the majority willed it. It has also endorsed, supported, or even established and run new political formations, like the Working Families Party in New York, Connecticut, and elsewhere so that members can express their voice as loudly as possible.

- *Willingness to prove the majority.* ACORN has distinguished itself from many other organizations by its willingness to "prove its majority" and demonstrate—sometimes at considerable risk—the full level of its support. For over thirty years, beginning with the "lifeline" utility initiatives and fights to eliminate sales tax on food and medicine, and more recently with huge efforts to win minimum-wage initiatives, ACORN has built power by its willingness to absorb the risk, shoulder the weight, and win or lose at the ballot box. Almost invariably such activity has built power for the organization and increased its weight and stature among its own constituency, political professionals, and the public at large. Winning in a conclusive way, in fact, settles arguments about tactics and strategies.

- *Always protect, expand, and privilege the base.* The base is everything, and the organization always needs to synchronize every activity consistently with the base. ACORN is a *constituency-based* organization more than it is anything else, both as we self-define our work and as we present the organization in public. On the staff side, we are organizers of low- and moderate-income families, and that defines the work and the craft more than saying that we are purely community organizers, labor organizers, political organizers, media organizers, campaigners, or any other sectoral specialists within the overall project of mass-based organizing. This orientation and our commitment to it collectively and institutionally have allowed us to transcend any narrow limits and boundaries in attempting to fashion an organization large enough to serve as a vehicle for the aspirations and struggles of our members and our people.

- *Democratic process and permanent staff.* The membership vote and practice democratic process, while the staff is centralized and mission driven in order to implement the decisions of the membership. ACORN concluded early on that there would never be a magical future moment when the organization would not need staff to achieve its full measure of effectiveness and capacity. Staff could not be a transitory phenomenon but had to be permanent if the organization was to follow through on its commitment to serve and give voice to its members. The "in and out" three-year span of the Alinsky paradigm just seemed to create a concrete ceiling to the organization's ability to grow and exercise power in the name of fearing organizer dependency. Structurally, ACORN has chosen implementing more leader to staff mechanisms to assure accountability, rather than abiding by an inflexible and indefensible "rule."

An Institutional Weapon for Voice and Power

The best guide to understanding the organization and all that distinguishes and overrides these many decades of work continues to be the overreaching organizational commitment to fashioning an institutional weapon and tool for our constituency and its drive for voice and power. Within that constituency and the accountability provided by membership and the discipline required with dues, many exceptionalities and incongruities are fairly easily accommodated so that friction is reduced.

For example, ACORN is able to use a range of diverse tactical opportunities in achieving strategic objectives, which activates our base while not alienating our members. We have also proven an ability to reconcile a commitment to direct action with an increasing implementation and delivery of direct service within the same base. In more than thirty of our one hundred offices, ACORN Housing administers a housing counseling program that assists prospective homeowners. This program put 6,500 families into first-time ownership in 2006 alone and has built the largest nonprofit housing counseling program in the country. This year in 2008 the ACORN Centers (formerly ACORN Tax and Benefit Access Centers) operated from more than eighty-five of our offices and handled taxes for more than 50,000 of our families, providing more than $65 million worth of refunds, more than half of which came from the Earned Income Tax Credit (EITC) program. The IRS certified ACORN as the third largest nonprofit VITA operator in the country, after only AARP and the military. Recently, ACORN added the "benefit" access component of the program so that in more than one-third of our offices, we are able to determine and activate eligibility in an additional fifteen entitlement areas around food support, health, and education. In 2007 ACORN expanded the national ACORN Financial Justice Center into individual offices to provide more systematic financial literacy and education programs, along an array of financial services and products. These will supplement the programs already run with ACORN Housing to protect our members concerning auto loans, insurance products, general consumer financing issues, payday lending, and now foreclosure avoidance. In every recent election cycle, ACORN has registered between 500,000 (midterm years) and more than 1 million new voters (in presidential years) in the largest nonprofit effort in the country. All of this work is done through rallies, demonstrations, picket lines, press conferences, lawsuits, public meetings, street blockings, and whatever else the members decide is necessary to grab the lapels of the suits until they listen to the demands of low- and moderate-income families. ACORN has spent thirty-eight years listening to targets vacillate and say, "I could agree with much of what ACORN is trying to do, if they did it another way."

As a membership organization, ACORN simply has to deliver to its membership and do so effectively and aggressively. An outside study produced a conservative figure of over $15 billion in benefits gained from ACORN's campaigns in a ten-year period, and that was *before* the huge statewide victories raising the minimum wage. Also, the study only counted one-time results rather than the impact of recurring benefits from ongoing victories in housing, wages, and taxes. In 2007 the minimum wage increases won in Ohio, Missouri, Colorado, Arizona, and other states where ACORN was the central driver delivered more than $6 billion in wage increases to approximately 5 million low-wage workers. Since the victory increasing the minimum wage in Florida, workers have received more than $4 billion in increases. These are victories that keep on giving year after year.

Of course, one of the founding principles of ACORN was the commitment to be a broad-based, multi-issued and multitactical organization. These lessons were learned painfully in the "special needs" campaigns many of us ran so successfully in Massachusetts with the National Welfare Rights Organization. This effort built the largest state affiliate of NWRO but also left us exposed to simple public policy adjustments that could strip away the organizing handles we used to build the organization. ACORN has always tried to maintain activity across diverse fronts so that no one area of resistance can impede the overall direction and growth of the organization and membership progress.

Diversity along these lines has been essential because opposition has been consistent throughout ACORN's history, especially given the ascendancy of the right over the last decade. Websites, editorial pages of the *Wall Street Journal*, Republican Party operatives, and ideologues in Congress and elsewhere have been increasingly strident in objecting to our work. Growing larger has widened the size of target offered by the organization to our opponents, as one might expect.

Over the years our partnerships and alliances have also deepened both in defending and extending the organization. More than twenty-five years of experience in organizing our constituency at work and in workplaces has produced deep partnerships at every level, with unions for example. What began as efforts to address problems faced by ACORN members in unemployment and job seeking, largely after the Carter administration recessions in the late 1970s, first led to the creation of independent unions. Later affiliations with the Service Employees International Union produced locals that include the more than 70,000-member Local 880, which grew from pathbreaking work among home health and home daycare workers, and additional projects in organizing Wal-Mart workers, informal and immigrant workers, and contracting to organize hundreds of thousands of workers from SEIU, American Federation of Teachers (AFT), Communication Workers of America (CWA), International Brotherhood of Teamsters (IBT), and the United Food and Commercial Workers (UFCW). These relationships though, like partnerships that have evolved over decades from direct campaign activity with financial institutions (Citigroup, Chase, Bank of America, Capital One, H&R Block, and others), while providing support, services, and strength are situational and symbiotic, rather than sustaining. Unions, churches, or corporate partners will all be with ACORN as long as it serves their own interests, but they keep their distance when the fur is flying. These relationships are political, even when permanent, because they are driven by institutional interests that are autonomous and directed by self-determined instincts around survival and growth. We understand these interests because we share them. While these relationships are important and vital to ACORN yesterday, today, and tomorrow, one of the bedrock principles of our organizing is that sustainable organizations can not be built as barnacles on the docks of other institutions because once the water is rising, not everything will be saved. The raison d'être of a permanent, mass-based organization has to be within its own base and never external.

Flowing from that logic, ACORN's survival and success can only be achieved through scale. We have to maintain our membership and grow rapidly so that the organization is strong enough to withstand any assault and powerful enough to engage any target and therefore serve our membership effectively as an appropriate vehicle for righting their grievances and realizing their aspirations. This tension has been constant in the internal life of the organization: the drive for growth and the search for a calm, quiet space; or, in the ACORN vernacular, expansion versus maintenance. Only size protects the overall organizational project and only scale can allow the organization's ambitions to be achieved consistent with the membership's goals and objectives. Recent years have seen the organization open offices in more than one hundred cities in the United States and membership balloon out to more than 500,000 members. The membership categories have been enlarged for the first time to enroll members who were not organized directly through the community base, with variable options on dues payment levels and different voices in organizational governance. ACORN is trying to realistically plan to increase membership size tenfold to over 2 million members in the coming years as part of the current expansion program designed to take the organization to the next level of performance and production.

In recent years, with the organization of the separate ACORN International, the constituency commitment has passed national boundaries to see if success can be created in Canada (where there are now offices and organization in Toronto, Vancouver, and Ottawa), Peru (Lima), Mexico (Tijuana and Mexico City), Argentina (Buenos Aires), Dominican Republic (Santa Domingo), along with emerging projects in Kenya (Nairobi) and Nigeria (Lagos). ACORN International has also extended its reach in dealing with campaign targets on a more global scale, which now includes campaign and organizing offices in India (Mumbai, Delhi, and Bangalore). Growth along these lines requires huge resources and capacity, along with new innovations and methodology to staff, finance, and sustain operations.

Katrina was the perfect storm deepening all of these convictions. New Orleans quickly became a worldwide reference point for the confluence of issues around race and poverty, but for ACORN it was also a huge test of what it meant to have, for over thirty years, a membership of 9,000 in this city where we have also maintained our national headquarters. This membership saw their homes washed away and were caught in a nationwide diaspora. Our staff was split between working in our hall in Baton Rouge and in expanded, but temporary quarters, near our offices in Houston, while our leaders and members were spread all over. Every day was a struggle to survive in terrible circumstances and, as importantly, a fight to win our members and our constituency's "right to return" to the city. Almost three years later, while so many institutions in the city are still crippled and broken, including churches, unions, and public services, ACORN can show how a membership organization is really defined. We have built the first new houses in what is now the iconic Lower Ninth Ward. We have been integral in the planning process for the future, even acting as the district planner for several months in the Upper and Lower Ninth Wards. We created a home clean-out program simply because our members could not come home without it. As part of the ACORN Hurricane Rebuilding and Recovery program, volunteers from all over the country in addition to local members and staff gutted more than 3,000 houses. As a grassroots membership organization, we also were surprised and pleased to get hundreds of thousands of dollars worth of support from the Internet and hosting celebrities like Roseanne Barr, Charles Barkley, Usher, and others who came to help rebuild ACORN neighborhoods.

ACORN organized Katrina survivors all over the country to fight for support and return, including busing 500 survivors to Washington, DC, in February 2006 to lobby Congress for recovery money—finally!—an effort that received front-page coverage in the *Washington Post*. Spring saw buses of members organized by ACORN rolling in from Little Rock, San Antonio, Dallas, Houston, Atlanta, and all over Louisiana to vote in the elections in New Orleans. Actions and lawsuits pushed FEMA to deliver. Even though by 2007 we had only located and returned about half of our members, ACORN had recruited almost 3,000 new dues-paying members in New Orleans in a year as part of the recovery fight. Housing, education, community development, planning, emergency services, forcing potable water into hard hit areas for rebuilding—the list of needs was endless and constant.

As the time lengthens since the storm, parts of the New Orleans ACORN operation are still "Katrina all the time." Supporters and opponents of ACORN alike learned the full dimensions of ACORN and what it means to truly be a deeply rooted, grassroots, membership organization, and they ended up affording us a new, if sometimes grudging, respect. As an organization, we also learned something about ourselves. We could integrate all of the pieces of the operation when it counted—organizing, housing, or electoral work, research, or whatever was needed—and it only worked because the face of the membership was in front of the effort, whether that face belonged to Vanessa Gueringer, Gwendolyn Adams, or emerging Ninth Ward organizer Tanya Harris in New Orleans (recognized by CNN).

Back to the base and back to the membership in a perfect circle, moving round and round; that is the classic ACORN story of building, organizing, fighting, and winning. It turns out that it is all about the simple things done every single day, over and over, one step after another. Most days, building organization is more perspiration than inspiration. Over the decades, persistence and perseverance have been as critical in a thousand victories as the thrill of breaking through the barricades and scaling the steps to take over the stage. In times of movement, when all hell is breaking loose, unimaginable change is possible. Much of the time, and it has certainly been true for the last thirty years, the work is a slog where the reward only comes from sweat. The most important contribution can be piling one brick on top of another to build the house and simply going to work every day. In that sense, the organization has mirrored almost perfectly the values and habits of so many of our members, which has turned out to be essential to the project of building the ACORN we are today. The years go by, one after another, then the decades, and the contributions of thousands of leaders, tens of thousands of members, and hundreds and hundreds of organizers add up to quite an amazing organization that is, simply put, the fruit of their labor.

SUGGESTED READINGS

Adamson, M., and S. Borgos. 1984. *This Mighty Dream: Social Protest Movements in the United States.* Boston: Routledge and Kegan Paul.

Arkansas Institute for Social Justice. 1977. *Community Organizing: Handbook No. 2.* Little Rock: Arkansas Institute for Social Justice.

———. 1979. *Community Organizing: Handbook No. 3.* New Orleans: Arkansas Institute for Social Justice.

Bailis, L. N. 1974. *Bread or Justice: Grassroots Organizing in the Welfare Rights Movement.* Lexington, MA: Heath/Lexington Books.

Brooks, F. 2003. "Resolving the Dilemma between Organizing and Services: Los Angeles ACORN's Welfare Advocacy." *Social Work* 50, no. 3: 262–70.

———. 2007. "The Evolution of Community Organizing Campaigns at ACORN 1970–2006." Unpublished manuscript.

Delgado, G. 1986. *Organizing the Movement: Roots and Growth of ACORN*. Philadelphia: University of Temple Press.

Fisher, R. 1994. *Let the People Decide: Neighborhood Organizing in America*. Updated ed. New York: Twayne.

Kest, S., and W. Rathke. 1979. "ACORN: An Overview." In *Community Organizing Handbook No. 3*. New Orleans: Arkansas Institute for Social Justice.

Kotz, N., and M. L. Kotz. 1977. *A Passion for Equality: George A. Wiley and the Movement*. New York: Norton.

Orr, M., ed. 2007. *Transforming the City*. Lawrence: University of Kansas Press.

Piven, F. F., and R. A. Cloward. 1979. *Poor People's Movements: Why They Succeed, How They Fail*. New York: Vintage.

Rathke, W. 2005. "A Wal-Mart Workers' Association?" In *Wal-Mart: The Face of Twenty-First Century Capitalism*, ed. by N. Lichtenstein. New York: New Press.

———. 2008. "The Country Roads That Created ACORN." In *Lessons from the Field: Organizing in Rural Communities*, ed. by J. Szakos and K. L. Szakos. New Orleans: Social Policy Press.

———. 2009. *The Battle for the Lower Ninth: ACORN and the Rebuilding of New Orleans*. New York: Verso.

———. 2009a. *Citizen Wealth: The Campaign to Save Working Families*. San Francisco: Berrett-Koehler Publishers.

Rathke, W., and B. Laboistrie. 2006. "The Role of Local Organizing: House to House with Boots on the Ground." In *There Is No Such Thing as a Natural Disaster: Race, Class, and Hurricane Katrina*, ed. by C. Hartman and G. Squires. New York: Routledge.

Russell, D. 1990. *Political Organizing in Grassroots Politics*. Blue Ridge Summit, PA: University Press of America.

Staples, L. 2004. *Roots to Power: A Manual for Grassroots Organizing*. Westport, CT: Praeger.

West, G. 1981. *The National Welfare Rights Movement: The Social Protest of Poor Women*. New York: Praeger.

3

Education as a Field
for Community Organizing
A Comparative Perspective

Elaine Simon and Eva Gold

Proclaiming a "rising tide of mediocrity" in the performance of American public schools, the 1983 presidential commission report, *A Nation at Risk*, set off a strong and sustained response from educators and elected officials (U.S. Department of Education 1983). Politicians began to stir doubt about the efficacy of public institutions, and education reform began imposing standards and accountability strategies and experimenting with leadership and governance. The federal No Child Left Behind Act, signed into law in early 2002, represents the ultimate expression of the standards movement. Lawmakers and policy theorists continue to experiment with different governance models, particularly in urban settings, including state and mayoral control and the outsourcing of core elements of schooling.[1]

Whether the situation in American education was as threatening or the problem as widespread as the authors of *A Nation at Risk* suggested, there is rightful concern about the quality of urban public schools serving primarily minority and low-income students. Particularly troubling is the gap between performance in such urban schools and performance in affluent suburban schools serving primarily white students. For example, a recent report on the achievement gap shows stark differences between white and minority students and between urban and suburban school performance, and it also shows the lack of progress over time, despite the many well-intentioned efforts to close the gap (McCall et al. 2006). Thoughtful observers fault education reform efforts as being too top down and, therefore, never really gaining the commitment of practitioners responsible for implementing them at the school level. Inadequate funding for struggling schools and districts, inequitable distribution of high quality teachers, and the short time frame in which results are expected also contribute to a lack of progress (Hess 1999, 178; Cuban and Usdan 2003; Coburn 2003).

Declining public confidence in urban schools and the inability of public school professionals to turn things around has brought a variety of new actors into the school reform arena in recent years (Kronley and Handley 2003; Fruchter 2001, 2007; Lewis 2003). Nonprofit and for-profit organizations are playing distinctive roles that reflect their different theories of change and different visions for who should be involved in schools, what schools should look like, and how they should be governed (Honig 2004; Hill 2000; Simon, Christman, Hartmann, and Brown 2005). Some organizations have given up on public education and advocate taking apart large urban systems or even recommend privatization. Community organizing groups are among those external organizations working to strengthen public education by improving its quality and by making public schools more equitable, accessible, and sensitive to the diverse populations in cities.

Community organizing groups took up the challenge of education when members repeatedly raised schools as among the most pressing neighborhood issues. In 1988, New York ACORN established a schools office overseen by a citywide education committee and staffed by organizers. In the mid-1980s, the Texas Industrial Areas Foundation's (IAF) Fort Worth affiliate started a parental involvement program at Morningside School that kicked off the formation of the Alliance Schools network, which now numbers over 120 schools. When Chicago enacted a radical decentralization reform in 1988 creating Local School Councils as a powerful structure for community involvement, organizing groups in Chicago saw an entry point for addressing the education issues that troubled their members.

Research for Action carried out one among several research projects in recent years that have documented the increase in community organizing groups turning their attention to education and have described the nature of their accomplishments (Baum 2003; Shirley 1997, 2002; Warren 2001; Gold, Simon, and Brown 2002; Mediratta, Fruchter, and Lewis 2002; Mediratta, Shah, and McAlister 2008). This chapter draws primarily on data from our study, carried out between 1999 and 2001 in collaboration with the Cross City Campaign for Urban School Reform, which included a broad national survey of community organizing groups working on education and in-depth case studies of five urban groups representing different organizing traditions. Three of the groups we studied are affiliated with national networks. These include Austin Interfaith, an affiliate of the Texas IAF; Oakland Community Organizations (OCO), affiliated with the Pacific Institute for Community Organizing (PICO); and New York ACORN, affiliated with the national ACORN organization. We also studied two independent groups: the Logan Square Neighborhood Association in Chicago and the Alliance Organizing Project in Philadelphia (Gold, Simon, and Brown 2002)

Researchers have not sufficiently differentiated between the two major community organizing traditions—institution based and neighborhood based—and how their contrasting approaches to leadership, human, and social capital development affect the way they address the challenges of education reform. Many of the studies of education organizing are aimed at audiences unfamiliar with community organizing and focus on describing the general contours of its methodology and identifying what makes community organizing groups distinct from other types of education reform groups. A number of studies focus on a single case or organizing tradition. In this chapter, we look across our five cases to suggest what difference, if any, organizing traditions make in improving the quality, equity, and responsiveness of public education to low-income, minority students. This chapter explains the unique challenge of education as an issue for organizing, explores what groups are able to achieve in the face of this challenge, and situates an ACORN education initiative in a comparative study that looks across different organizing approaches.

Both organizing traditions are effective catalysts for equitable education reform that is sensitive to minority and low-income students, and both support introducing new ideas and getting past barriers to change. Sustaining these reforms, however, requires a shift in educators' fundamental assumptions about the role of parents and community-based groups in education. We found that strong leadership development, cross-sector relationships, and long-term programmatic efforts were needed to bring about such a shift. These strategies were intrinsic to the practices of institution-based groups, while neighborhood-based groups had to adapt their practices and work in coalitions in order to have an impact in education.

The Challenge of Education as a Field for Organizing

A leader of a nonprofit partner of NY ACORN, who was trying to put into context their struggle to improve city schools, characterized the field of education as organizing's Vietnam. The Vietnam metaphor vividly captures the challenge of education organizing, where winning a decisive victory, the fuel that sustains an organizing campaign, is nearly impossible. Each field in which community organizing groups work has its own logic concerning the role of the state and private interests, mechanisms for community-based groups' input, levers for influence, and what constitutes success. Each field presents challenges. Here we detail the logic and challenges of education as a field for community organizing and examine how community organizing contributes to improving public education.

Education is such a challenging field for organizing for three main reasons: its insularity from external participation and input; its embeddedness in a multilayered system of political, economic, and social systems; and recent contestation about the state's responsibility for schools as public institutions. Even as those committed to public education are working to make it more responsive and equitable, private interests are slowly and without much visibility, turning education into a public/private hybrid institution—greatly complicating the system and limiting the points of entry for community organizing.

Literature on school reform and school change has taught us that one source of schools' challenge to education organizing is their insularity, a result of their highly professionalized culture and bureaucratic organization whose reward structure is top-down rather than bottom-up (Fullan 1999; Sarason 1982, 1990). This entrenchment of school power structures means that education reform designed to make schools more inclusive of parents and community are often shallow, serving instead as "a form of public relations to create greater institutional legitimacy for current educational practices" (Anderson 1998, 571; see also Malen and Ogawa 1988 on local school councils). However, as Clarence Stone points out, schools are more open to citizens' influence in affluent areas, noting that school officials recognize the important contributions of affluent parents and respond to the formal and informal pressure they can bring. Stone sees a "disconnect" in poor communities between public institutions and the citizens they serve (2005). He and others point out that parents in low-income neighborhoods are often shut out of the schools because school professionals see them as lacking the credentials or status to contribute. Low-income parents and community members themselves may be reluctant to participate because their own experiences with the public schools have been negative or they are intimidated by the professional setting (Lareau 2003).

This history of isolation creates suspicion on both sides. Community involvement programs must overcome teachers' perceptions that community organizations are encroaching on their professional autonomy and their resentment of the additional workload that parent engagement might require (Shirley 2002). There are others who see a dark side to privileging community values. Casanova (1996) points to professionals' fear that parochial interests will prevail. Bryk and Schneider (2002) also note that unresolved conflict between parents and professionals can adversely affect school climate. The challenge for community organizing, then, is to deepen the connections between schools and communities, changing schools' receptivity to and respect for low-income, minority, or immigrant parents and to increase parents' sense of empowerment to deal with schools and to gain knowledge of what happens in schools.

Another challenge of education as a field for organizing is its embeddedness in multilayered organizational, political, and social environments. While the classroom or school is where most parents and community members first interact with the institution, much of what happens there is shaped by policies set by the larger school district. Even if community organizing groups are able to penetrate the culture of a local school, such basic features as curriculum, teacher and principal selection, budget, and student composition may not be in the purview of that school because they are determined centrally as a result of teacher recruitment practices or certification requirements. Targeting the school district also may be inadequate because the district too is embedded in a political, economic, and civic context. District funding, for example, is shaped or constrained by such external factors as the local tax base or the willingness of local political actors to commit or raise adequate funding for the schools. Residential segregation by race and class also affects equity in school resources within districts. Parents in middle-class neighborhoods can often wield disproportionate power to protect the benefits to their schools because city decision makers and boosters are desperate to keep such families in the city (Cucchiara 2006; Varady and Raffel 1995). These schools also attract more qualified teachers than neighborhood schools (Neild, Useem, and Farley 2005).

Districts are not only embedded in local city politics and subject to the consequences of class pressures, but they are also embedded in state politics, statewide rivalries, and the consequences of state-level economic and social diversity. States contribute a significant amount to the budgets of urban school districts, as much as 50 percent, but—given the disparity in tax bases between urban, rural, and suburban districts—funding formulas often create a significant funding gap between them (Education

Trust 2005). Advocates have challenged the fairness of funding formulas in several states in the last ten years; New York City's Campaign for Fiscal Equity (CFE) is among the most well known.[2] Given the embeddedness of classrooms in schools, schools in districts, and districts in states, claims at one level eventually require targeting decision makers at multiple levels of the system.

A third challenge for organizing is the shrinking public sector and how that trend manifests itself in education. As noted, dependency on property taxes to fund public schools has created a severe disadvantage for cities with declining tax bases and greater need. Subsidies from higher levels of government are declining as a proportion of the budgets in many districts. As in other public sector realms now—health care, housing, welfare—education too is seen as a field for entrepreneurship and private investment. Cities across the country are experimenting with new forms of management, which include contracting with vendors to carry out responsibilities such as curriculum development, professional training, and research, as well as contracting with private nonprofit and for-profit providers to operate schools (Christman, Gold, and Herold 2006; Henig, Holyoke, Lacerino-Paquet, and Moser 2003; Rufo-Lignos and Richards 2003). Although the federal No Child Left Behind legislation does provide important information for community organizations about student performance disaggregated by social and economic variables and has a provision for parent involvement, it also provides multiple entry points for the private sector (Kohn 2004). The research we have conducted on Philadelphia's "diverse provider" model suggests that this breakup of the public sector and contracting-out strategies ultimately make it more difficult for activist and community-based groups to find points of entry and avoid compromising their ability to remain critical and hold schools accountable (Gold, Cucchiara, Simon, and Riffer 2005).

Differences in Community Organizing Models

While community organizing groups trace their roots to the Saul Alinsky tradition originating in the late 1930s, their current forms and strategies represent significant evolution and diversification (Fisher 1994). A number of studies analyze variation within the field of community organizing (Speer et al. 1995; Appleman 1996; Swarts 2002; Wood 2002). The main line of difference among organizing groups today is in whether they organize communities through institutions—faith-based or other types of community institutions—or whether they organize through neighbor-hoods based on issues and recruiting individuals door to door. Speer and colleagues use the terms "church-based organizing" and "neighborhood-based organizing" to distinguish the two major types (1995). Appleman uses the broader term "institution-based organizing," since groups that organize through faith-based institutions also include other organizations, such as schools or unions, as institutional members. The major organiz-ing networks that use an institution-based strategy include the Industrial Areas Foundation (IAF), the Pacific Institute for Community Organizing (PICO), Gamaliel, and the Direct Action and Research Training Center (DART) (Appleman 1996; Warren and Wood 2001). In contrast, the As-sociation of Community Organizations for Reform Now (ACORN) is the only national network of groups that uses a neighborhood-based method of recruitment (see Speer et al. 1995; Appleman 1996). In addition, as our study documented, there are a number of community organizing groups that are not affiliated with networks and that may follow different major recruitment traditions. These comparative studies distinguish the theories, practices, and outcomes of the two major types of organizing approaches—faith-based or institution-based organizing, represented in our sample by IAF and PICO, and neighborhood-based organizing, rep-resented in our sample by ACORN.

At the outset, these two approaches to organizing are distinguished by their theories of how to build up a base of members. Institution-based groups focus on building relationships, capitalizing on already existing social networks (Wood 2002). This strategy identifies issues over time. Neighborhood-based organizing, in contrast, rejects the institution as a mediating vehicle, starting with individuals who live in close proximity and quickly identifying issues or campaigns as the basis for working to-gether (Delgado 1986; Speer et al. 1995). Neighborhood-based strate-gies are described as valuing tension between the organizing group and the targets of the organizing campaigns, whereas institution-based groups extend the strategy of relationship building to dealing with targets as well (Speer et al. 1995). Of course, these distinctions are idealizations, and in practice the two strategies do not follow the philosophies exactly.

As a way to analyze the work of community organizing and to com-pare groups and types of efforts, several authors have used a framework that suggests power arrangements can be altered at three different levels (Gaventa 1980; Appleman 1996; Speer et al. 1995). According to this framework, developed by Gaventa (1980) in his book about relations be-tween coal industrialists and workers in the Appalachian Valley, the first level of power is the ability to influence the allocation of resources through the power to "reward and punish powerful decision-makers" (Appleman 1996, 4). The second level of power in Gaventa's framework entails gaining a seat at the table where resource decision making occurs and thus acquiring the power to participate in setting agendas and framing issues. Achieving power at the third level results in "re-conceptualizing resource allocation and how a community thinks about itself" (Appleman 1996, 4). Achieving this level of power is the most difficult to accomplish but all community organizing groups aim to do so.

The studies that used Gaventa's framework to compare organizing groups found that most groups achieved successes at the first level of power—obtaining increased resources—and many also achieved power at the second level—gaining a seat at the table. Both the Appleman (1996) and Speer et al. (1995) studies found that altering power relations at the third level was rare, however, and that accomplishments representing the second level of power, while significant, require groups to carefully balance their inside-outside roles.

The comparative studies agree that there is a clear difference between institution-based and neighborhood-based organizing in the depth of leadership development and resulting power that these organizations build, represented by the measure of member turnout and by the level of power alteration that they achieve (Speer et al. 1995; Swarts 2002; Appleman 1996). Speer and colleagues compared the processes of the two contrasting approaches represented by institution-based and neighborhood-based organizing and their implications for organizational power and individual members' sense of empowerment. These studies found that the institution-based approach built into its organizing process many opportunities for leadership development and that leaders took a great deal of responsibility for extending the base within the institutions they belonged to. In the Speer and colleagues study, the neighborhood-based organizing group stressed "speed" and action and so was more able to respond to specific issues quickly and with less deliberation. The tradeoff was in the degree to which each altered power relations, rather than in the sense of members' empowerment (Speer et al. 1995; Appleman 1996). Using Gaventa's power framework to compare the two types of organizations, Speer and colleagues found that the institution-based strategies resulted in greater power, measured by member turnout at events and the nature of media coverage (Speer et al. 1995).

Appleman's study, while mainly focused on a comparison of institution-based groups and their outcomes using Gaventa's levels of power framework, includes an addendum that compares institution-based organizing with ACORN's neighborhood-based strategy. Her analysis echoed Speer and colleagues in finding that ACORN had lower turnout than institution-based groups but could move more quickly "to turn up the heat on targets during difficult negotiations" (Appleman 1996, 57). She notes that these two approaches represent different philosophies of power, with institution-based groups more focused on building relationships, even with targets of campaigns, and ACORN more focused on retaining the tension with targets in order to keep the upper hand in negotiations. In a sense, ACORN's philosophy suggests it aims more at power at the first level. However, as Appleman points out, in the 1970s ACORN was instrumental in passing the Community Reinvestment Act, which "shifted the debate about access to capital and corporate responsibility," an outcome that represents power alteration at the highest level of power.

Wood's comparison of an institution-based and an issue-based group echoes the findings of Appleman and of Speer and others in that he finds that institution-based groups focus on achieving changes in culture and depth of leadership development, which results in greater sustainability of changes than the issue-based group was able to achieve (Wood 2002). Similarly, Swarts's study comparing institution-based groups and ACORN finds that the institution-based groups achieve greater depth in leadership development, allowing them to develop long-term goals. ACORN's advantages, according to Swarts (2002), include the reach to a wider range of participants and the speed of their decision-making process. These findings about faith-based or institution-based organizing are also confirmed in Warren's in-depth study (2001) of IAF groups in Texas, whose strategy he sees as based on building social capital in communities, which strengthens their power through relationships.

In summary, there is much consensus in the literature on community organizing, and comparative studies on organizing networks, that contemporary institution-based organizing groups focus more on leadership development and relationship building, while neighborhood-based groups achieve less depth and power as measured by turnout but have the advantage of flexibility and responsiveness to issues and circumstances. In terms of power alteration, it is less clear which approach is more effective. Authors acknowledge that it is very difficult to achieve power alteration at the third level in Gaventa's framework, but they point to promising efforts in that direction for both types of groups because of the potential to reach a national scale through their networks and working in coalition. Institution-based groups seem to approach this type of power through their long-term strategy, while ACORN approached the third level of power with the passage of the Community Reinvestment Act at the national level, providing a toehold for local campaigns. As we discuss below, we found in our study that ACORN was more likely to work as part of a coalition with other groups, including organizing groups, to enhance its power and resources than some of the institution-based groups, particularly those affiliated with IAF, were likely to do.

Education Organizing Case Studies

The organizing groups whose work we followed in depth represent both institution-based and neighborhood-based approaches. Austin Interfaith and the Oakland Community Organizations (OCO) are affiliates of networks that use an institution-based approach to organizing. New York ACORN is affiliated with the national network that uses a neighborhood-based model. One of the independent groups, the Logan Square Neighborhood Association (LSNA), uses an institution-based approach, while the other, the Alliance Organizing Project (AOP, which is now disbanded), primarily used a neighborhood-based approach defined by school catchment area. All but AOP are multi-issue groups. Although we are comparing organizing traditions represented by the national networks, we include independent groups in our analysis because there are so many of them working in education. Their inclusion here offers another dimension for comparison. Table 3.1 summarizes the major differences in approach among the groups.

Of course, beyond the type of community organizing approach, contextual features of the city, region, and state in which community organizing groups work—including the complexity and size of the school district, existing reform policies at city and state levels, the school district governance structure, the political environment, and economic conditions—also shape their activity. Here, based on our research that ended formally in 2002, we briefly describe the groups' education organizing and accomplishments, along with salient contextual influences that shaped their definitions of the problems to be addressed.[3] In the discussion that follows the case studies, we look across the stories to understand the role that the organizing models played in shaping the groups' strategies and accomplishments, and we identify some important factors to consider in understanding these differences. We should note that our brief descriptions of five groups' education organizing efforts do not fully represent

Table 3.1. Range of organizational characteristics of the five groups

Community organizing groups	Recruitment	Network	Single- or multiple-issue
Oakland Community Organization (OCO)	Institution (faith-based)	Pacific Institute of Community Organizing (PICO)	Multiple
Austin Interfaith	Institution (faith-based, school, union)	Industrial Areas Foundation (IAF)	Multiple
Logan Square Neighborhood Association (LSNA)	Institution (school, community organization)		Multiple
New York ACORN	Membership (neighborhood-based)	ACORN	Multiple
Alliance Organizing Project (AOP)	Membership (neighborhood-/school-based)		Single— education

the complexity of their strategies and the totality of the outcomes they achieved.

Oakland Community Organizations

In 2001, Oakland Community Organizations (OCO) in Oakland, California, had thirty-one member congregations representing 40,000 low-income, minority residents. It had built its reputation over three decades as a powerful group, working on neighborhood issues such as housing, drugs, and crime prevention. In the early 1990s, OCO began working on education because its members were concerned about school overcrowding as a result of an explosive growth in new Latino and Asian immigrant populations and with their children's low scores on standardized tests. Early efforts, which included after-school programs and attempts at individual school change, introduced OCO to the possibilities and challenges of improving schools. The group concluded that it needed to find a systemwide approach.

Tying together members' concern about school overcrowding with a growing awareness of the benefits of small schools, OCO began a campaign for small autonomous schools. OCO began working with a local education reform group, the Bay Area Coalition for Equitable Schools (BayCES), to fashion a small school policy for the district and an inclusive process for school development. OCO's collaboration with BayCES and the plan for small schools filled a vacuum created by the repeated turnover in the administration of the Oakland Unified School District (OUSD) and the consequent lack of a coherent plan for reform of the city's schools. Capitalizing on his relationship with a newly appointed superintendent, the BayCES director gained entrée to district leaders and was able to forge a coequal partnership among BayCES, OCO, and OUSD, which led to the adoption of the small schools policy as a major component of the district's reform plan. The district established an office for reform to implement the policy. The small schools campaign attracted a $15 million grant from the Gates Foundation to support BayCES' work in facilitating OCO-recruited design teams made up of parents, teachers, and students in developing plans for each new school.

Oakland's small school initiative has continued to grow and thrive. An evaluation of OUSD's new small autonomous schools policy, completed in 2003, showed that the schools succeeded in the key areas of equity, teacher quality, parent involvement, student achievement, and school climate (Little and Wing 2003).[4] OCO is still pushing for more small schools and recruiting participants for design teams. As of November 2006, the OCO/BayCES/OUSD partnership was responsible for developing forty new small schools in Oakland through an inclusive process serving more than one-quarter of all the students in the school system.[5]

Among the challenges to this effort has been continued turmoil in district leadership and governance. Soon after the initiative was underway with full support from the superintendent, district budget problems led to state oversight and his replacement with a state administrator. OCO and BayCES were successful in maintaining the momentum of the small schools development process over a number of years despite these changes, with OCO working to keep parents and community members involved and ready to put pressure on the state administrator when necessary. Another PICO affiliate in California has established a statewide project that bolsters OCO's call for parent and community involvement in schools.[6]

Austin Interfaith

In the mid-1980s, Texas IAF Network affiliates began to work with public schools, developing a vision of schools with strong community involvement and a collaborative culture that would raise students' achievement.

Schools became IAF institutional members, forming a statewide network known as the Alliance Schools Initiative. To advance the network, the Texas IAF persuaded the state education agency to establish a $20 million Investment Capital Fund, which provides grants for school restructuring that incorporates community involvement. Although not limited to Alliance Schools, this funding stream provides an incentive for schools to work with Texas IAF affiliates. By 2000, the network included 118 schools serving low- to moderate-income neighborhoods in ten communities across Texas (Warren 2001; Shirley 1997).

Each of the Texas IAF groups uses a similar approach in working with schools. In order to become an Alliance School, teachers must vote to join. Each Alliance School forms a "core team" of parents, community members, and school staff that identifies and addresses important issues. Through this process of collaboration and relationship building, IAF groups seek to establish a "relational culture," where teachers and parents see and act on their mutual interests. Teachers become full members and leaders in the IAF affiliate group and, alongside parents and community members, attend IAF five-day and ten-day training in the methodology of organizing. Teachers and parents also participate together in the annual statewide Alliance Schools Conference.

With a membership among the most ethnically and economically diverse of the Texas IAF Network affiliates, Austin Interfaith is a coalition of forty-five institutions, including twenty public schools (out of one hundred schools in the Austin Independent School District), located mostly in Austin's low-income East Side.[7] (Austin Interfaith also works with a diverse set of congregations and two unions.) The initial impetus for Austin Interfaith to work with schools arose from members' concerns about low student achievement, made apparent by Texas's emphasis on testing and rating schools. Low achievement in Austin's East Side schools reinforced the geographic division among children from different backgrounds by denying access to the district's competitive science magnet program. Among Austin Interfaith's accomplishments was establishing the Young Scientists Program in a set of elementary schools that resulted in an increase from 10 to 40 percent of East Side students attending the science magnet program.

Austin Interfaith aimed to change the culture not only of the schools but the district as a whole. Over time, school staff trained and socialized in Austin's Alliance Schools formed a cadre of leaders who influenced new schools to join the network and sustained community school relations in the existing network schools. An indication of Austin Interfaith's influence on the district as a whole was the superintendent's choice of a former Alliance School teacher to lead a newly established middle school and his decision to pilot an experimental pedagogical approach in Alliance Schools.

Austin Interfaith also worked on school issues citywide through accountability sessions where its leaders put pressure on officials and electoral candidates to declare their support for issues relating to bilingual education and retaining teachers priced out of Austin's booming real estate market. Austin Interfaith also used its power of numbers to vote to assure the equitable distribution of new school facilities funded through city bond issues.

New York ACORN

Experienced in addressing housing and economic justice issues since it was founded in 1981, New York ACORN began organizing around education a few years later because school concerns continued to surface in its neighborhood meetings. At the time of our study, New York ACORN boasted over 22,000 members representing diverse neighborhoods in the Bronx, Northern Manhattan, and Brooklyn. The children of its members attended schools in half of what were then the city's thirty-two community school districts. New York ACORN established a schools office in 1988 to coordinate its work in education.[8]

New York ACORN has carried out its education organizing on a variety of fronts and at different scales over the years. Its many initiatives have focused on inequities and discrimination toward low-income, minority students across the vast, complex, and volatile New York City school system. One of its efforts documented discrimination in access to selective programs through a series of carefully researched *Secret Apartheid* reports[9] that gained wide media attention. In response to members' concerns, New York ACORN also targeted issues in individual schools, such as safety, overcrowding, assignment to bilingual programs, and facilities. The group was able to tap its contacts with influential politicians and civic leaders developed through housing and fair wage campaigns to bring visibility to the education issues and get access to powerful education officials.

New York ACORN's efforts to establish small autonomous high schools were shaped by and took advantage of the momentum in the city for small schools. Looking for access to strong high school alternatives for its members, New York ACORN extracted a promise from top school officials for it to partner in establishing several small high schools in

ACORN neighborhoods. During the time of our study, the organization was working with three new high schools in Brooklyn and Washington Heights and was pushing for the establishment of a fourth high school in the Bronx. ACORN's small school effort built on that of a group of New York City educators to establish small schools with community partners throughout the city in the 1990s. The Annenberg Foundation invested $25 million to further this strategy, and, because of its reputation for representing the interests of low-income communities, New York ACORN was invited to be a partner in the nonprofit organization established to make decisions about allocating the funds.[10]

Even as it worked as a partner with three high schools, New York ACORN's education organizing approach continued to change. Increasingly frustrated with the scale of impact that working with individual schools could achieve, New York ACORN launched a campaign to improve teaching and learning at the regional level, choosing to highlight the needs of three low-performing community school districts in the Bronx. It partnered with NYU's Institute for Education and Social Policy (IESP) to conduct research and help focus its demands.[11] New York ACORN's education organizing in the Bronx evolved over time into an ongoing partnership with several South Bronx community-based organizations and the IESP in a project to improve teacher quality known as the Community Collaborative to Improve District 9 or CC9 (Dingerson and Levner 2005).

Today, New York ACORN has begun to phase out its work with individual schools in favor of addressing education issues on a larger scale. It closed its schools office, although it still runs an after-school program in one of the high schools it established. To forward education improvement on a larger scale, New York ACORN continues to work in coalitions at the city and state levels to push for funding equity and policies to increase spending on instructional materials, lower class size, attract qualified teachers, institute early childhood education, and ensure adequate facilities. A major accomplishment a few years ago was successfully preventing the school board from awarding a contract to Edison Schools Inc., a private, for-profit education company, to take over two schools in its South Bronx neighborhoods (described in Chapter 8).

Logan Square Neighborhood Association
The Logan Square Neighborhood Association (LSNA) is an independent, institution-based organizing group started in the early 1960s by local churches, businesses, and homeowners to address neighborhood concerns

arising from rapid changes in the population of Chicago's Logan Square neighborhood. Latino families make up about 65 percent of the neighborhood's current population, replacing the primarily white, working-class population who fled the city. More recently, gentrification is bringing young middle-class professional families into the neighborhood and threatening housing affordability.

LSNA uses a democratic process to determine its agenda and to build solidarity in the neighborhood. With forty-seven institutional members, LSNA's "core committee" meets each year to devise a "Holistic Plan," ratified in an annual community meeting. In addition to improving local public schools, the plans include goals to develop youth leadership, enhance neighborhood safety, maintain affordable housing, and revitalize the local economy. While LSNA is an independent organizing group working in a single neighborhood, it looks to the Chicago-based National Training and Information Center for support in training its organizers and gaining information about other organizing efforts across the city and the country.

Chicago's 1988 school reform initiative created an important vehicle, the Local School Council, for organizing parents around education issues and gave the community a link to the schools and authority in school level decision making.[12] LSNA's first foray into education organizing was to lead successful campaigns to obtain funding to build annexes for schools experiencing overcrowding as a result of the influx of new immigrants. The schools that benefited from LSNA's efforts became active members of the organization.

Looking for other ways to strengthen school and community connections, LSNA organizers sought to address parents' isolation and lack of empowerment. To create opportunities for parents to improve their knowledge and skills and to strengthen their connection to their children's schools, LSNA developed a Parent Teacher Mentor Program, which brings parents into classrooms. LSNA also established Community Learning Centers at four schools. Over 800 neighborhood women have participated in the Parent Teacher Mentor program.[13] Graduates run the community centers and have taken on other leadership roles in Logan Square.

Although LSNA is focused on one neighborhood, more recently its parent mentor program inspired Illinois ACORN to build a statewide effort. LSNA found that many of the parent mentors became interested in pursuing careers as teachers. Illinois ACORN developed a statewide Grow

Our Own Teacher Initiative in collaboration with LSNA and a group of local colleges and is working with several school districts across the state.

The Alliance Organizing Project

The Alliance Organizing Project (AOP) had an eight-year lifespan as an independent organizing group focused solely on the issue of education in Philadelphia, Pennsylvania. Its organizing model most closely resembles a neighborhood-based approach. AOP recruited in selected neighborhoods individual parents whose children attended schools that the group targeted. It counted those schools where it succeeded in gaining a foothold as partners but not institutional members. AOP also created a citywide committee of members that focused its efforts on issues of safety, student achievement, and teacher quality.

AOP, the only single-issue group that we studied, was also unique in that the school district itself embraced it and its funding was considered part of the district's systemic reform initiative, which included among its tenets an emphasis on public engagement through parent and family involvement.[14] According to the district's own strategic plan, AOP's mission was to help in the "transformation of the relationship between every school and the parents and communities which surround it" (School District of Philadelphia 1995). The close tie to the district was not all positive for AOP. As a new organization that had to build a base from scratch, its alignment with the district caused AOP to struggle for legitimacy in its neighborhoods and with other parent advocacy groups.

AOP eventually focused its work in seven schools in two neighborhoods. AOP's safety campaigns were the direct result of the deteriorated school facilities and extreme conditions of blight and high crime in the declining city neighborhoods where it was active. AOP won increased funding from the city council for crossing guards and funding from local nonprofits and the school district for after-school programs that involved parents working with teachers to provide children a safe place during after-school hours as well as academic enrichment. In coalition with other organizing and advocacy groups, AOP tackled such citywide problems as teacher quality and inadequate state funding. AOP also banded together with youth organizing groups, city unions, advocacy, and other community-based groups to protest privatization of the district when, in 2001, there was a state takeover.

In its short life, AOP was able to energize citizen activism for improving schools, but it faced several challenges that ultimately led it to closing its doors in 2003. As mentioned, AOP experienced resistance from school administrators and other parent groups. Without an institutional base, AOP struggled to retain elementary school parents as members when their children moved on. With the state takeover, foundations lost faith in Philadelphia as a site for activism. Nonetheless, AOP's work inspired other groups to take up education organizing in Philadelphia. A coalition of groups working on teacher quality eventually contributed to a historically significant union contract and new teacher recruitment policies that have the potential to raise teacher quality for schools with primarily low-income students.

Comparison of Organizing Models and Their Impacts: What Are the Lessons for Education?

Each of the case study groups had significant concrete accomplishments—dollars brought in to the schools, more parents and community members participating actively in school improvement efforts, new schools and facilities, new policies and programs. Given the tremendous variation in the contexts and strategies of the five groups, we draw on Gaventa's levels of power framework and on other comparative studies of organizing in order to examine their achievements and to tease out what difference their organizing models made (Speer et al. 1991; Appleman 1996; Gaventa 1980).

What would power at the three levels look like applied to education? Gaining power at the first level would be measured by a group's ability to serve as a catalyst in bringing new resources to schools in the form of funds, personnel, or programs and in the reallocation of existing resources and opportunities so that they are accessible to a wider range of students. Power at the second level would entail the inclusion of community members in decision making about resource allocation and school or district planning. They may participate in existing decision-making structures or contribute to the formation of inclusive structures at different system levels. Gaining power at the second level is critical as a significant step toward assuring the sustainability of resource gains. Gaining power at the third level would mean a shift in the assumptions, discourse, and practices of educators to reflect fair distribution of resources and openness to community concerns. For authentic and sustainable change in the field of education, community organizing groups must at least gain power at the second level with a seat at the table in decision making. The long-term sustainability of reforms depends on achieving power at the third level—changing the way educators at different levels (the school, the district, the city, the state, etc.) think about inclusion and equity.

Power at the First Level: Bringing Resources
All of the groups that we studied—whether institution based or neighborhood based, networked or independent—were successful in winning new resources for schools, thereby achieving power at the first level. These new resources came from a variety of sources and took many forms. The groups were able to pressure the public sector to allocate new funds or reallocate expenditures to communities with greater need. Examples include AOP winning funds for additional crossing guards from the city budget, IAF convincing the Texas Education Agency to create the Education Investment Fund, and New York ACORN obtaining facilities and staff for new schools. Groups also assured the equitable distribution of resources for schools when they used their power to get out the vote for bond issues based on equity criteria. In addition, the groups leveraged funds from private foundations that added to the public pot—such as OCO's small schools campaign that attracted substantial funds from the Gates Foundation and ACORN's participation in attracting Annenberg Foundation funds for New York City.

By bringing new resources and directing them to the students most in need, community organizing groups addressed important concerns about equity for low-income, minority, and immigrant populations in public education. As noted in the beginning of this paper, suburban and more affluent communities have been able to garner resources for their schools using their own wealth and influence. Organizing provides a vehicle for those less well off to redirect some of these resources and begin to level the playing field in education.

Power at the Second Level: A Seat at the Table
All of the groups achieved a measure of involvement in decision making, though at different levels and to different degrees. As noted in the discussion of what makes education a challenging field for organizing, schools are both insular (particularly regarding less well-positioned constituents) and embedded in multilayered bureaucracy. For community organizing groups to achieve power at the second level, they had to break through these barriers and gain access to discussions and decision making about programs and resources for low- and moderate-income parents. Gaining power at the second level addresses equity concerns and concerns about

the quality of school community relations. The institution-based groups were more successful at gaining and maintaining such access than the neighborhood-based groups.

Unlike New York ACORN, the three institution-based groups created structures for participation in which they embedded leadership development opportunities, particularly at the school level. Examples include the core teams in Texas's Alliance Schools, LSNA's Parent Teacher Mentor program, and OCO's design teams. ACORN's model for participation was in the context of its neighborhood organizing, but this approach provided fewer opportunities for members to learn about school matters and develop relationships with school staff. The lack of structures for participation in the school meant that New York ACORN struggled to find a role as partner in the schools that it established.[15] Of the five groups that we studied, OCO was the only one able to gain a genuine seat at the table on a citywide scale with its establishment of the small schools initiative and partnership with the Oakland Unified School District and BayCES.

New York ACORN was more successful entering into agenda setting at city and state levels than at the school level because of its general reputation as a powerful community-based group with a track record of work in education. Its participation as a partner in the mid-1990s Annenberg-funded district reform effort is one example of its role in decision making at a citywide level. While New York ACORN did not build formal structures at the school level, it did serve as the catalyst in creating formal coalitions of community organizing and other community-based groups at both city and state levels for forwarding a variety of equity issues. These coalitions reflect ACORN's model of gaining influence—creating tension to coerce public officials' response to demands—and stands in contrast to the more relational approach of the institution-based groups that included officials and organizational members/leaders as part of a decision-making body. Its citywide reputation and its ability to use tension as a lever for influence did not benefit New York ACORN in trying to gain influence at the school level where relationship building is more effective at gaining legitimacy and trust.

Power at the Third Level: Shifting the Paradigm

In her assessment of institution-based organizing, Appleman (1996) noted that change in power relations sufficient to bring those in power to rethink the basis on which society's institutions value citizens is a tall order, and she gives community organizing groups credit for efforts that come within reach of such change. Among the indicators that she counted is recognition of the groups' demands by the press and public officials. Speer and others also used press coverage of the community organizing groups' ideas as an indicator of power at the third level (Speer et al. 1995).

Here we look at three types of evidence that the groups gained power at the third level: they were seen as legitimate players in the education arena; school districts (or states) adopted and carried out policies that address the problems (and solutions) that community organizing groups identified; and, finally, the larger education community embraced these programs, sustaining them through political and administrative changes.

All of the groups succeeded in being recognized as legitimate players in the education arena. The institution-based groups gained media attention through coverage of public accountability sessions and spearheading successful programs. The ability to attract attention to their issues is a strength of neighborhood based organizing (Speer et al. 1995). New York ACORN's successful *Secret Apartheid* campaigns received extensive news coverage, and newspaper editorials supported the reports' demands.

Groups also gained legitimacy through their work over time in the field. They developed expertise, connections, and reputations as powerful organizations committed to improving public education. Other reform groups and education officials also came to value them for their broad membership base necessary to garner and sustain support for education reforms. In Oakland, for example, BayCES recognized that it needed OCO's ability to gain the participation of a wide swath of the community. New York ACORN's successive efforts in the education arena—serving as a catalyst to raise awareness of inequities and addressing threats to public education and community participation—built its reputation in education reform and demonstrated its sustained commitment to improving schools and opportunities for low-income students. As a result, ACORN was invited to be the community-based partner with established education reform groups on the citywide Annenberg reform effort in the late 1990s, and it continues to play a pivotal role in several coalitions of community-based groups for education reform.

Based on the measure of whether groups were able to shape policy, OCO was the most successful of the groups we studied. OCO developed a clear programmatic initiative that could be translated into policy and made a long-term, deep commitment to its enactment. By aiming to address problems on the citywide scale, the OCO-influenced policy set the stage for wide participation of the city's students, parents, and teachers.

ACORN had mixed success in influencing policy, taking several differ-

ent paths as it searched for a vehicle and level at which to work. While the
Secret Apartheid report called attention to inequities and led to a review
of practices, its demands were not translated into official policy. Appleman
quotes a long-time ACORN organizer who, in contrasting ACORN's
approach with institution-based groups, charged that "institution based
organizing tends to build relationships with targets too early, resulting
in reducing the necessary tension for successful negotiations" (Appleman
1996, 57). While this approach is good for drawing attention and gaining power at the first level, it is not effective for sustaining a long-term
effort.

ACORN's later work to promote small high schools supported an
external citywide small schools initiative that aimed at policy change, and
the organization's work with its partner schools likely contributed to the
legitimacy of the overall initiative, which has continued to develop new
schools even though ACORN is no longer involved. ACORN renewed its
efforts in the South Bronx as part of a coalition of groups aiming to influence district policy on teacher training. By working in coalition, ACORN
supplements its strong ability to set the stage for negotiation on issues
with the programmatic strengths of some of the other groups. Certainly,
in light of the public school system's complexity and the rich array of organizing groups in New York City, it makes sense for community organizing groups to work together to gain power at the third level, if they hope
to change fundamentally thinking about the distribution of resources and
community involvement (Mediratta and Institute for Education and Social Policy 2001).

As with New York ACORN, AOP's influence on policy, although enacted long after its demise, turned on its work in coalition with other
groups that complemented its strengths. AOP served as the catalyst in
defining and bringing forward the issue of teacher quality.

The most convincing proof that a group has achieved power at the
third level is evidence that the larger community embraces the new or
changed policies and programs, sustaining them through political and administrative changes. This criterion is the most difficult to meet, but we
found that where groups built participation structures and where these
structures invited a wide range of actors to learn about each other and develop a sense of common purpose, such change was most likely to happen.
An institution-based strategy, with its investment in educating and developing members' leadership and building relationships to create a common understanding among differently situated actors, was best suited to
creating communitywide agreement on interests and goals. In our cases,

certainly Austin Interfaith was successful in building locally (and Texas IAF across the state) a large cadre of people deeply committed to the Alliance School philosophy and knowledgeable about new ways to structure a school-community environment. When we were finishing our formal research in Austin, there were some indications that the larger school district valued the Alliance Schools approach and that the growing number of staff and community members dedicated to this way of thinking might form a critical mass in that medium-sized district.

There is strong evidence of wide community acceptance of the small-schools approach that OCO has shepherded. Its strategy has a number of features that contributed to the small schools initiative gaining such wide support. OCO had a long-term commitment to a well-defined initiative that was translated into policy and actually implemented. OCO was also able to forge strong relationships across sectors in Oakland—partnering with the nonprofit and public sectors and getting the teacher's union on board. OCO also incorporated into the initiative opportunities for developing strong leaders among its church-based members and the teachers involved in planning new schools. The small schools policy came to life for one-quarter of the children in Oakland, gaining wide acceptance from the community. That the initiative has continued and grown through several changes in school governance and leadership at the district level is further evidence that the community has embraced as a reform strategy small schools that serve all of Oakland's children.

From our observations, there were fewer opportunities for in-depth leadership development and relationship building in the neighborhood-based groups' efforts than in the more programmatic strategies used by the institution-based groups. However, New York ACORN's work in education did not conform strictly to the model portrayed in the literature on neighborhood-based organizing, and it reveals ways in which New York ACORN adapted its organizing to meet the demands of the world of education. For example, in contrast to the description that Speer and colleagues offer of neighborhood-based groups' approach to the research phase of an organizing campaign, New York ACORN devoted extensive resources and time to this phase in its education campaigns in order to marshal evidence that would be convincing to an audience of school professionals. In doing so, the research phase served as an opportunity to educate and build leadership among members who participated in the thorough inquiry required to document unequal access to programs. In addition, as our research was winding down, New York ACORN was beginning to experiment with formal structures for school planning that would more directly involve parents in decision making with school staff. In a similar fashion, although AOP recruited on a neighborhood basis, it also incorporated an eclectic set of tactics that confounds strict categorization. For example, it forged a programmatic strategy that built parent leadership with its after-school program and endeavored to build strong relationships with school principals and teachers.

Changing assumptions and, thereby, the on-the-ground practice, of school professionals and the larger community about the value of parents' and community members' viewpoints and where to direct resources is challenging. It requires a depth of understanding and commitment that can only be developed through a long-term effort and significant investment in the people responsible for carrying out reforms. These strategies were intuitive to the institution-based groups, which focused on building relationships with school officials (as well as public officials and powerful civic actors) and embedding leadership development of their members into long-term programmatic efforts. While these strategies are not emphasized in the standard repertoire of neighborhood-based groups, we found that New York ACORN and AOP adapted to the challenges of education organizing by incorporating into their work some of the strategies usually associated with institution-based groups to gain power at this third level. They also relied on working in coalitions, complementing their own strengths with their partners' abilities to develop and sustain programmatic approaches and to build power in numbers. To adequately assess their achievement of power at the third level, it would be important to track the work of these groups over a long period, assessing the breadth and sustainability of shifts in policy and practices.

Summary

Regardless of organizing model, community organizing for education reform is particularly effective at achieving power at the first level, the power to bring pressure that yields new resources for schools and distributes resources more fairly. Often community organizing groups serve as catalysts to increase equity, overcoming the challenges of entrenched educational bureaucracy or policy churn as well as interest group politics that favor more affluent constituents. To sustain such changes, community organizing groups have also demonstrated their ability to gain power at the second level, by getting a seat at the table to set the agenda. Institution-based groups were particularly successful at gaining entrée to decision making because they were more likely to set up structures for participation that also provided opportunities for members to become knowledgeable about education issues and to develop relationships with school professionals. The institution-based groups were more successful at reaching power at the third level because they were more likely to create long-term programmatic efforts that also provided opportunities for leadership development across sectors and among different stakeholders. We saw evidence that New York ACORN adapted its organizing strategy to meet the challenge of working on education issues by taking up more long-term efforts and working in coalition to complement the strengths and limitations of the neighborhood-based organizing approach for education reform.

Conclusion

As a field for organizing, education presents several challenges. Its insularity as a result of being highly professionalized and bureaucratic makes it particularly difficult for low-income, minority, and immigrant populations to penetrate. Its embeddedness in a multilayered system that is fundamentally political makes it difficult to identify clear targets or sustain local efforts. And its contested status, bringing new forms of governance and evaluation, makes it difficult for organizing to find solid levers of influence. Even in the face of these challenges, organizing groups can point to successes among their efforts to improve education. Their approach to education reform is particularly effective in gaining the first level of power, bringing new resources that are equitably distributed. Across traditions, community organizing is effective as a catalyst for change and in putting pressure on public officials to meet community members' demands.

Gaining power at the second and third levels requires a set of strategies that institution-based groups emphasized more than neighborhood-based groups. Power at the second level, or gaining a seat at the decision-making table, requires strong community-based leaders and strong relationships within and across differently positioned stakeholders, often developed in the context of formal structures for participation. Gaining power at the third level—changing the paradigm—requires long-term, well-defined initiatives that can be translated into policy and that educators and the community at large understand and embrace. Both traditions of organizing were able to meet these challenges to some degree, although doing so required more adaptation on the part of the neigh-

borhood organizing groups, which emphasize raising issues and bringing pressure to respond to demands rather than widespread leadership
development, relationship building, and sustained commitment to a particular programmatic initiative. The neighborhood-based groups adapted
their strategies and worked in coalition to meet the demands of education organizing. The institution-based groups were better able to sustain
changes over time because they built strong leadership and relationships
across sectors.

Because of the multilayered character of education as a field, achieving power at the third level requires attention to scale, and while the
groups we studied could point to change at the classroom, school, or
district levels, conventional practices and pressures from higher levels of
the system means that these accomplishments require constant tending
unless community organizing can affect state or even federal policy. Our
research pointed to the advantages of network membership for reaching
higher levels of impact. The networked groups had a statewide, or, in the
case of ACORN, a nationwide support system that could provide money,
training, ideas, and audiences on a larger scale. Emerging independent
organizing groups focused solely on education at the local level, such as
AOP, must rely on working with networked and multi-issue groups for
larger-scale impacts.

Another issue that bears mentioning is the threat to community organizing's basic principles of having to create long-term programmatic
initiatives necessary for sustaining their efforts in education. Organizing
groups themselves generally do not design or run programs but rather
maintain an independent stance that enables them to hold public agencies accountable for carrying out such programs. Success in the education arena, however, required them to take some role in program initiatives. Groups resolved this dilemma in different ways, with LSNA unique
among our case study groups in actually operating programs. OCO managed its role by partnering with a nonprofit school reform organization to
run the small schools design process, retaining only the role that suited it
best—organizing parents, teachers, and community members and facili-
tating their involvement.

Our formal study ended in 2002. Although we have tried since then
to keep up from a distance with the groups' work, more detailed follow-
up on their efforts and outcomes would help to confirm or modify the
observations we have made here. Although the groups have been working
in education for many years, they have continually refined their strategies
for addressing the continuing challenges of education reform. In particu-

lar, understanding how community organizing has fared in the era of No Child Left Behind, which had not taken hold fully during the period of our study, is important for future research on education organizing. Youth organizing has also grown rapidly in the past few years, and research on these groups can offer another perspective on the role and effectiveness of independent, single-issue groups.

Our research contributes to understanding the nature of education as an arena for community organizing and offers a comparative perspective, connecting scholars who have studied organizing in other arenas with a growing number of scholars in the field of education who have become interested in the role of organizing in education reform. We also hope that this analysis will be useful to organizing groups considering a foray into education organizing.

Earlier, we cited the comment that education was organizing's Vietnam. Do the findings here suggest that education reform is unwinnable for community organizing and should be avoided at all costs? This analysis suggests that the achievements of community organizing for education reform are comparable to those in other fields, as treated in other comparative studies that used Gaventa's power framework. Engineering a fundamental shift in how a community thinks about itself, or power at the third level, is most difficult to achieve. The gains in resources and participation in agenda setting among groups engaged in education organizing are impressive but require a great deal of ongoing attention. Our findings suggest that community organizing is essential to authentic and equitable change in education, and groups are developing strategies that will assure the sustainability of their efforts. Community organizing is uniquely suited to move a broader public to understand the issues and to regain confidence that it is possible and worthwhile to engage in the project of improving public education.

NOTES

1. Only Chicago implemented a form of community control in the late 1980s, but that effort was confounded by the imposition of mayoral control in 1995. More recently, Chicago is experimenting with private management of schools.
2. Although the incoming governor of New York state pledged to follow through on the directions of a lower court judge who determined that the New York City schools needed $5.6 billion more annually, the New York Supreme Court ended appeals, agreeing to provide only an additional $2

billion. See D. Herzenhorn, "New York Court Cuts Aid Sought for City Schools," *New York Times*, November 21, 2006. As a result of tightening city and state budgets throughout 2007 and 2008, school funding is an ongoing issue.

3. For an in-depth case study of each group, see the Research for Action website, *www.researchforaction.org*. We include each case study in the references.

4. The new small schools are serving students from the most overcrowded and lowest performing schools and are more successful in attracting and retaining credentialed teachers than comparison schools. Small schools involve parents in ways that go "well beyond having mandated parent representation on the official School Site Council" and other school bodies (Little and Wing 2003, 2), maintain parent involvement even at the middle and high school levels, and have fewer incidences of graffiti and vandalism. Most importantly, the new small schools are exceeding expectations for academic achievement. New small schools are more likely than comparison schools to increase their academic performance index (API). Students in the new small schools who were at the lowest performance levels are more likely to increase their performance to the middle range. Attendance ranks these schools at the top of the district. Finally, 100 percent of the seniors in the new small high school that opened in 2001 graduated, "far surpassing district averages" (3).

5. As described on the Youth and Education page on the OCO website, *www.oaklandcommunity.org/issues_youtheducation.htm*.

6. The Sacramento Area Congregations Together spurred statewide legislation that funds a Parent-Teacher Home Visit project to increase communication. The PICO National Network website provides more information about the Parent-Teacher-Home Visit project, see *www.piconetwork.org/casestudies/Parent-Teacher-Home-Visit-Project.pdf*.

7. Schools are at different stages of engagement as Alliance Schools. There were twenty schools active at the time of our study in the early 2000s.

8. Shortly after we finished our research in 2002, a new mayor reorganized the New York City schools, dismantling the thirty-year-old system of community school districts and centralizing the system under mayoral control.

9. The three reports published by New York ACORN are *Secret Apartheid: A Report on Racial Discrimination against Black and Latino Parents and Children in the New York City Public Schools* (1996); *Secret Apartheid II: Race, Regents, and Resources* (1997); *Secret Apartheid III: Follow-up to Failure* (1998).

10. The nonprofit organization set up to administer the Annenberg Foundation grant was called New York Networks for School Renewal.

11. NYU's Institute for Education and Social Policy is now the Community Involvement Project of the Annenberg Institute for School Reform at Brown University.

12. See Bryk et al. 1998 and Katz 1992 for details on the 1988 Chicago School
    Reform plan and Local School Councils.
13. As of 2002, there were 840 graduates of the Parent-Teacher Mentor
    Program (Blanc, Brown, and Nevarez-La Torre 2002).
14. Philadelphia was one of five urban districts to be awarded funding from the
    Annenberg Foundation in 1995 for school reform, and it received a $50
    million matching grant. From 1995 to 2000, AOP was included in this
    reform effort and raised some of the matching funds.
15. Toward the end of 2002, staff at New York ACORN were working to
    establish cooperative decision-making structures for curriculum at the school
    level.

REFERENCES

Anderson, G. L. 1998. "Toward Authentic Participation: Deconstructing the
    Discourses of Participatory Reforms in Education." *American Educational
    Research Journal* 35, no. 4: 571–603.
Appleman, J. 1996. "Evaluation Study of Institution-Based Organizing for the
    Discount Foundation." Available at *comm-org.wisc.edu/papers97/appleman.
    htm.*
Baum, H. S. 2003. *Community Action for School Reform.* Albany: SUNY Press.
Blanc, S., J. Brown, and A. Nevarez-La Torre, with C. Brown. 2002. *Strong
    Neighborhoods, Strong Schools: Case Study: Logan Square Neighborhood
    Association.* Chicago: Cross City Campaign for Urban School Reform.
Bryk, A. S., and B. L. Schneider. 2002. *Trust in Schools: A Core Resource for
    Improvement.* New York: Russell Sage Foundation.
Bryk, A. S., P. B. Sebring, D. Kerbow, S. Rollow, and J. Easton. 1998. *Charting
    Chicago School Reform: Democratic Localism as a Lever for Change.* Boulder,
    CO: Westview.
Casanova, U. 1996. "Parent Involvement: A Call for Prudence." *Educational
    Researcher* 25, no. 8: 30–32, 46.
Christman, J. B., E. Gold, and B. Herold. 2006. *Privatization "Philly Style":
    What Can Be Learned from Philadelphia's Diverse Provider Model of School
    Management?* Philadelphia: Research for Action.
Coburn, C. 2003. "Rethinking Scale: Moving beyond Numbers to Deep and
    Lasting Change." *Educational Researcher* 32, no. 6: 3–12.
Cuban, L., and M. Usdan. 2003. *Powerful Reforms with Shallow Roots: Improving
    America's Urban Schools.* New York: Teacher's College Press.
Cucchiara, M. 2006. "A 'Higher Class' of School Reform: Urban Revitalization,
    Middle-Class Parents, and Public Schools." Paper presented at the annual
    meeting of the American Educational Research Association, San Francisco.
    April 8–12.

Delgado, G. 1986. *Organizing the Movement: The Roots and Growth of ACORN.* Philadelphia: Temple University Press.

Dingerson, L., and A. Levner. 2005. *A True Bronx Tale: How Parents and Teachers Joined Forces to Improve Teacher Quality.* Portland, OR: Grantmakers for Education.

Education Trust. 2005. *The Funding Gap 2005: Low Income and Minority Students Shortchanged by Most States, A Special Report by the Education Trust.* Washington, DC: Education Trust.

Fisher, R. 1994. *Let The People Decide: Neighborhood Organizing in America.* Updated ed. New York: Twayne.

Fruchter, N. 2001. "Challenging Failing Schools." *Shelterforce Online.* Available at *www.nhi.org/online/issues/118/Fruchter.html.*

———. 2007. *Urban Schools, Public Will: Making Education Work for All Our Children.* New York: Teachers College, Columbia University.

Fullan, M. 1999. *Change Force: The Sequel.* Philadelphia: Falmer Press.

Gaventa, J. 1980. *Power and Powerlessness: Quiescence and Rebellion in an Appalachian Valley.* Urbana: University of Illinois Press.

Gold, E., M. Cucchiara, E. Simon, and M. Riffer. 2005. *Time to Engage? Civic Participation in Philadelphia's School Reform.* Philadelphia: Research for Action.

Gold, E., and E. Simon, with C. Brown. 2002. *Strong Neighborhoods, Strong Schools: Case Study: Oakland Community Organizations.* Chicago: Cross City Campaign for Urban School Reform.

Henig, J. R., T. Holyoke, N. Lacerino-Paquet, and M. Moser. 2003. "Privatization, Politics, and Urban Services: The Political Behavior of Charter Schools." *Journal of Urban Affairs* 25:337–54.

Hess, F. M. 1999. *Spinning Wheels: The Politics of Urban School Reform.* Washington, DC: Brookings Institution Press.

Hill, P. T., C. Campbell, J. Harvey, and P. Herdman. 2000. *It Takes a City: Getting Serious about Urban School Reform.* Washington, DC: Brookings Institution Press.

Honig, M. I. 2004. "The New Middle Management: Intermediary Organizations in Education Policy Implementation." *Education Evaluation and Policy Analysis* 26, no. 1: 65–87.

Katz, M. B. 1992. "Chicago School Reform as History." *Teachers College Record* 94, no. 1: 56–72.

Kohn, A. 2004. "Test Today, Privatize Tomorrow." *Phi Delta Kappan* 85:568–77.

Kronley, R., and C. Handley. 2003. "Reforming Relationships: School Districts, External Organizations and Systemic Change." Paper prepared for School Communities That Work: A National Task Force on the Future of Urban Districts. Providence, RI: Annenberg Institute for School Reform.

Lareau, A. 2003. *Unequal Childhoods: Class, Race, and Family Life*. Berkeley and Los Angeles: University of California Press.

Lewis, A. C. 2003. "Community Counts." *Phi Delta Kappan* 84:179–80.

Little, J. W., and J. Y. Wing. 2003. *An Evaluation of the Effectiveness of Oakland Unified School District's New Small Autonomous Schools (NSAS) Policy (2000–2003)*. Oakland, CA: New Small Schools Partnership, OUSD, BayCES, and OCO.

Malen, B., and R. T. Ogawa. 1988. "Professional-Patron Influence on Site-Based Governance Councils: A Confounding Case Study." *Educational Evaluation and Policy Analysis* 10, no. 4: 251–70.

McCall, M., C. Hauser, J. Cronin, G. G. Kingsbury, and R. Hauser. 2006. *Achievement Gaps: An Examination of the Differences in Student Achievement and Growth*. Lake Oswego, OR: Northwest Evaluation Association.

Mediratta, K., and the Institute for Education and Social Policy. 2001. *Community Organizing for School Reform in New York City*. New York: Institute for Education and Social Policy, New York University.

Mediratta, K., N. Fruchter, and A. C. Lewis. 2002. *Organizing for School Reform: How Communities Are Finding Their Voice and Reclaiming Their Public Schools*. New York: Institute for Education and Social Policy, New York University.

Mediratta, K., S. Shah, and S. McAlister. 2008. *Organized Communities, Stronger Schools: A Preview of Research Findings*. Providence, RI: Annenberg Institute for School Reform at Brown University.

Neild, R. C., E. Useem, and E. Farley. 2005. *The Quest for Quality: Recruiting and Retaining Teachers in Philadelphia*. Philadelphia: Research for Action.

Rothman, R. 2002. "Intermediary Organizations Help Bring Reform to Scale." *Challenge Journal* 6, no. 2: 1–7.

Rufo-Lignos, P., and C. E. Richards. 2003. "Emerging Forms of School Organization." *Teachers College Record* 105, no. 5: 753–81.

Sarason, S. B. 1982. *The Culture of the School and the Problem of Change*. 2d ed. Boston: Allyn and Bacon.

———. 1990. *The Predictable Failure of Educational Reform: Can We Change Course before It's Too Late?* San Francisco: Jossey-Bass.

School District of Philadelphia. 1995. *Children Achieving Strategic Action Design, 1995–1999*. Philadelphia: School District of Philadelphia.

Shirley, D. 1997. *Community Organizing for Urban School Reform*. Austin: University of Texas Press.

———. 2002. *Valley Interfaith and School Reform: Organizing for Power in South Texas*. Austin: University of Texas Press.

Simon, E., J. B. Christman, T. A. Hartmann, and D. C. Brown. 2005. *Crafting a Civic Stage for Public Education Reform: Understanding the Work and*

Accomplishments of Local Education Funds. Washington, DC: Public
    Education Network.

Simon, E., and E. Gold, with Brown, C. 2002. *Strong Neighborhoods, Strong
    Schools: Case Study: Austin Interfaith.* Chicago: Cross City Campaign for
    Urban School Reform.

Simon, E., and M. Pickron-Davis, with C. Brown. 2002. *Strong Neighborhoods,
    Strong Schools: Case Study: New York ACORN.* Chicago: Cross City
    Campaign for Urban School Reform.

Speer, P. W., J. Hughey, L. K. Gensheimer, and W. Adams-Leavitt. 1995.
    "Organizing for Power: A Comparative Case Study." *Journal of Community
    Psychology* 23:57–73.

Stone, C. 2005. "Civic Capacity: What, Why, and Whence?" *The Public Schools,*
    ed. by S. Fuhrman and M. Lazerson. New York: Oxford University Press.

Swarts, H. J. 2002. "Shut Out from the Economic Boom: Comparing
    Community Organizations' Success in the Neighborhoods Left Behind."
    Working Paper, Nonprofit Sector Research Fund. Aspen, CO: Aspen
    Institute.

U.S. Department of Education, The National Commission on Excellence in
    Education. 1983. *A Nation at Risk: The Imperative for Educational Reform.*
    Washington, DC: U.S. Department of Education.

Varady, D. P., and J. A. Raffel. 1995. *Selling Cities: Attracting Homebuyers
    through Schools and Housing Programs.* Albany: State University of New York
    Press.

Warren, M. 2001. *Dry Bones Rattling: Community Building to Revitalize
    American Democracy.* Princeton, NJ: Princeton University Press.

Warren, M., and R. L. Wood. 2001. "Faith-Based Community Organizing: The
    State of the Field." Available at *comm-org.wisc.edu/papers2001/faith/report.
    htm.*

Wood, R. L. 2002. *Faith in Action: Religion, Race, and Democratic Organizing
    in America.* Chicago: University of Chicago Press.

4

From Redlining to Reinvestment
Economic Justice Advocacy, ACORN, and the Emergence of a Community Reinvestment Infrastructure

Gregory D. Squires and Jan Chadwick

A community reinvestment infrastructure has changed the way banks do business in urban and rural areas of the United States in recent decades. A longstanding tradition of redlining and racial discrimination is giving way to more equitable access to credit, particularly in the home mortgage market. Residents of low-income communities and racial minorities in particular, long excluded from the nation's credit markets, have far greater access to mortgage money and the homeownership opportunity this brings. A major factor in this evolution has been the creation of several national networks of advocacy groups, which, along with their many local member chapters, have utilized a variety of tools to democratize access to capital.

The emerging community reinvestment movement reflects a broader commitment to economic justice and the role of neighborhood-based advocacy in pursuing justice on a variety of issues. An underlying assumption is that fundamental inequities determine who gets what and why in American society and that those inequities can be ameliorated. A critical related assumption is that low-income communities and racial minorities who are the primary victims need to take the lead in pursuing the remedies. Among the issues that have been the subject of such campaigns are health care and health insurance, the minimum wage and living wage proposals, environmental racism, gender equity, and a range of public services (for example, education, police protection, transportation). Some groups focus on a single issue while others are multiple issue organizations. The community reinvestment movement has brought together many of these organizations to pursue fair and equitable access to credit.

Among these groups are the Association of Community Organizations for Reform Now (ACORN), the Center for Community Change (CCC), the National Community Reinvestment Coalition (NCRC), the National Fair Housing Alliance (NFHA), the National Training and Information Center (NTIC), and others. Despite occasional turf battles and personality conflicts, they constitute a relatively new and critical force for fair lending. They have educated consumers about how to utilize credit and their rights to credit under the law. They have carried out sophisticated research documenting the uneven distribution of financial services. These groups have worked with major media outlets to expose discriminatory lending practices and have pressured legislators and regulatory agencies to enact and enforce new rules providing for fairer access to financial service. And they have worked in partnership with some lenders. In essence, they have organized effectively to combat redlining and discrimination and encourage reinvestment in traditionally underserved communities.

To illustrate, between 1993 and 2004 the share of all conventional home purchase loans going to low- and moderate-income communities increased from 11.6 to 15.6 percent. The share going to African Americans grew from 5.2 percent to 10.8 percent, and for Hispanics the increase was from 4.7 to 6.6 percent (Federal Financial Institutions Examination Council 2001, 2005). One result is that homeownership among African Americans grew from 42.3 to 48.8 percent and for Hispanics from 41.2 percent to 49.7 percent. Whites exhibited a much higher rate in both years, 73.2 percent and 76.0 percent, respectively, but homeownership for all groups continues to grow (U.S. Census Bureau 2004; National Association of Realtors 2005). Redlining and racial discrimination in the allocation of credit have certainly not disappeared. For many today, a greater problem may be that some forms of credit have been too readily available. The terms and conditions under which credit is available often result in charges that exceed the risks posed by some borrowers. Many of those communities that had long been denied access to capital have suffered more recently from predatory lending practices, leading to record foreclosure rates and a range of other costs to local communities and the nation's economy generally.

This chapter examines some of the specific tactics and campaigns that ACORN and similar organizations have engaged in to further the goal of fair access to credit and to address continuing challenges of redlining, racial discrimination, and, more recently, predatory lending. Following a brief discussion of the ACORN model of community organizing, we examine how that model has been applied to fighting redlining and, later, predatory lending. We conclude with observations regarding next steps for continuing efforts to increase capital on fair and equitable terms.

The ACORN Model

ACORN's approach to community organizing lends itself well to identifying and responding to financial services issues. It combines the conflict strategy of Saul Alinsky with that of Fred Ross and the Community Services Organization in California, who emphasize door-to-door organizing tactics (Fisher 1994, 148). ACORN uses grassroots community organizing strategies to achieve policy change through direct action, negotiation, legislation, and voter participation, and utilizes neighborhoods as the training ground from which to later develop larger citywide, state, and national campaigns to effect justice. One difference between some Alinsky-style movements and ACORN is that ACORN has not mobilized around a single issue or single constituency but rather has found its success in the mass organization of both low- and moderate-income people around multiple issues that are of direct concern to all these individuals (Fisher 1994, 148; Hurd and Kest 2003).

In *The Logic of Collective Action*, Mancur Olson argued that individuals will only mobilize around self interest and that one way to encourage this is for an organization to provide "material incentives" to join (Olson 1965). In developing its model of organizing, ACORN acts on this theory by recruiting and organizing members around issues of specific self-interest as well as recognized community interests. While local ACORN organizers have ideas about issues that should be confronted, they seek in the initial stages of neighborhood organizing for the issues to come from the community itself—thus providing a self-interest incentive for individuals to join (Delgado 1986).

Under the ACORN model, an organizer goes into targeted low- and moderate-income neighborhoods and queries residents door-to-door in order to determine the issues about which they are most concerned. The residents are then rallied around these issues. The organizer's expertise helps this group determine strategies to confront the particular issue(s), and a campaign is planned. One of ACORN's fundamental beliefs has been that it is the *process* of organizing that is often more important (at least in the beginning) than the issue(s) people are organizing to address. The organizing itself has the ability to help people see how collective action works, that it does work, and that they are able to have their particular interests addressed (Delgado 1986).

The organizer is highly significant to ACORN's success but at the same time has a limited role. Officially, the role of the organizer is to provide technical assistance and resource development. In practice, however, it is the organizer who usually decides how and who to mobilize, what resources the organization requires from the constituents in order for it to succeed, and what organizational structure will best serve the group's goals. While neighborhood residents make major contributions to ACORN's ultimate success, it is the organizer who initiates the process, coordinates the work, maintains the schedule of events, and orchestrates interests, issues, energies, and goals. Without the organizer's initiative to enlist members (either personally or with previously enlisted members), virtually no one would join. Few individuals join ACORN without being asked. When asked to join, they are also asked directly to pay dues and actively participate. Some commit only after being approached several times (Russell 1989). One early neighborhood leader admitted to "not being a joiner of groups" but joined a neighborhood chapter after being approached by an organizer. He gave the woman a dollar, and since he had invested he went to the first meeting, where he was elected leader (against his own wishes) and soon began leading protests (Adamson and Borgos 1984, 119).

Beginning in the late 1970s when local chapters joined to create a national "People's Platform" and then demonstrated outside the Democratic midterm convention in Memphis, the previously multistate association began to transform into a unified national organization. While some members were dissatisfied with the inclusion of a national agenda and infrastructure, most saw the transformation as a necessary step to advance their agenda (Adamson and Borgos 1984, 124). Consequently, ACORN is faced with a classic problem of many national organizations: the desire of a national professional staff to control the decision-making process while maintaining local member participation.

In order to maintain a focus on grassroots organizing (the recruitment and training of local leaders and the identification of local issues), the formal structure of the organization was designed to ensure control and participation by local members. Consequently, the ACORN board of directors is made up of representatives elected from state chapters, who are first elected from city and local chapters (Russell 1989; Delgado 1986, 199–200). Each local chapter of ACORN is still able to focus primarily on issues of greatest concern to local members. At the same time, through its national infrastructure, ACORN is able to connect problems in one community with those in other areas, identify national trends, and plan campaigns to address corporate and government activities at all levels.

Through this structure, ACORN has identified the concrete difficulties their members and the communities they are from have confronted (and continue to confront) in efforts to secure home mortgage loans and other financial services. In turn, these dynamics have led to ACORN becoming a national leader in organizing efforts to change banking practices, first, in efforts to stop redlining and make credit available and, subsequently, in efforts to combat predatory lending and make credit available on more equitable terms (Kest 2006).

Redlining and the Struggle for Reinvestment

A critical step in efforts to combat redlining was passage of the federal Community Reinvestment Act (CRA) in 1977. This statute places on federally regulated depositories (for example, banks and savings and loans) an affirmative obligation to ascertain and be responsive to the credit needs of their entire service areas, including low- and moderate-income neighborhoods (Marsico 2005; Immergluck 2004; Sidney 2003; Squires 1989, 2003). ACORN and other community reinvestment advocacy groups have utilized this law to generate more than $4 trillion in new loans for traditionally underserved communities (National Community Reinvestment Coalition 2005a).

Under the CRA, federal financial regulatory agencies—the Federal Reserve Board (Fed), the Office of the Comptroller of the Currency (OCC), the Federal Deposit Insurance Corporation (FDIC), and the Office of Thrift Supervision (OTS)—are required to consider a lender's CRA record whenever a lender submits an application to purchase or merge with another institution or make almost any significant change to its business practices. Regulators generally apply a three-part test examining the lending, investment, and service activities of the financial institutions under their supervision and make those evaluations available to the general public. Regulators can deny such applications, though they rarely do so, on CRA grounds. But the CRA gives third parties, often community organizations, the opportunity to comment on and challenge these applications. Regulators have on occasion delayed consideration of such applications, asking the lender and challenging party to try to resolve their differences. These delays cost lenders money and, therefore, provide leverage to those submitting challenges. ACORN and others have utilized this process to negotiate with many lenders.

These challenges often depend on public information made available by the Home Mortgage Disclosure Act (HMDA), which requires most lenders to reveal the race, gender, and income of all mortgage applicants, the census tract in which the home is located, the type of loan for which the applicant has applied, whether the application was approved or denied and, as of 2004, some pricing information on selected high-cost loans. The information made available under HMDA and the leverage provided by the CRA have led to significant changes in the way financial services are provided.

ACORN has long utilized its practice of mass protests as a principal method for "encouraging" banks to meet their CRA responsibilities. For example, in the late 1980s in Minneapolis, 200 protesters tied a red ribbon around Twin Cities Federal (TCF) Bank's downtown headquarters, and about fifty people went to the bank president's office and demanded to talk. Following these actions, ACORN and the Joint Ministry Project were able to negotiate an agreement with TCF for the bank to target $65 million for low-income and minority borrowers (Sidney 2003). In addition to these traditional protests, ACORN and its counterparts have developed more sophisticated methods of research and advocacy (Sidney 2003, 116).

In the early 1980s community development corporations (CDCs), city officials, unions, ACORN, and other community organizations began drawing attention to local bank lending records and pressuring several banks to increase their lending in low- and moderate-income and minority neighborhoods. In 1985 ACORN and Local 100, the Service Employees International Union (SEIU), challenged an application by Hibernia National Bank in New Orleans to acquire a bank in Lafayette, Louisiana. Their research showed that in 1984 Hibernia provided just 4.6 percent of its home mortgage loan dollars to borrowers in black neighborhoods and 32 percent to those in white areas, although blacks accounted for 60 percent of the city's population. While half the population of New Orleans lived in low- and moderate-income census tracts, only 10.5 percent of Hibernia's mortgage loan money went to these neighborhoods. The Federal Reserve Board held its first public hearing in the South over this challenge; it was only its third hearing overall in response to CRA challenges. Hibernia's application was blocked for eight months before the Fed issued its order—the longest delay to that date in the history of CRA challenges. The Fed ordered Hibernia to increase its home lending to low- and moderate-income areas and directed it to make $2 million annually in FHA and Veterans' Administration (VA) guaranteed mortgage loans specifically in low- and moderate- income census tracts. It was also ordered to meet with ACORN and other community groups to work on a complete reassessment of community credit needs (Brown 1988).

Also in the mid-1980s, ACORN, along with local CDCs, negotiated strong CRA agreements with two local banks in Philadelphia, Fidelity Bank and Continental Bank. In 1982 Fidelity Bank made only twelve mortgage loans in majority black census tracts, but by the end of the first year after the agreement, Fidelity had become the main lender in low-income neighborhoods in Philadelphia, providing $18.35 million to targeted census tracts, most of which were majority black. In 1985 Continental Bank had made only fifteen housing loans in black majority census tracts, but eleven months after the agreement, nearly $4.8 million in housing related loans had been made in these same areas with an additional thirteen small business loans totaling $400,000 (Brown 1988).

While challenges under the CRA have continued into the early 2000s, by the late 1980s the nature of community reinvestment advocacy tactics had changed somewhat. Groups that had protested banking practices began pulling back from their efforts to shame local banks and began operating programs in conjunction with banks. ACORN created the ACORN Housing Corporation (AHC) in 1986 to provide one-on-one mortgage loan counseling, first-time homebuyer classes, and other assistance to help families obtain affordable mortgages through lending partnerships with banks, often developed through CRA agreements. Today, the AHC assists between 8,000 and 9,000 families a year to acquire mortgage loans. Altogether it has helped more than 45,000 families to become first-time homeowners. In addition, the AHC has rehabilitated more than 850 vacant and abandoned housing units (Kest 2006; ACORN 2006).

Since 1977 community reinvestment groups have often pressured legislators and regulators to strengthen the CRA and other fair lending laws or to minimize proposed weakening of these rules. At the 1988 congressional oversight hearings to determine if CRA covered lenders had fulfilled their obligations, representatives from ACORN, NTIC, CCC, Woodstock, and other fair housing and fair lending groups testified that regulators were failing to effectively enforce the law. These hearings led to passage of the 1989 Financial Institutions Reform, Recovery, and Enforcement Act (FIRREA), which included significant changes in the

CRA. FIRREA required that CRA evaluations and ratings, previously held confidential, be made public. Additionally, the criteria for evaluating banks were changed from focusing on process issues (for example, how often bank officials met with community groups) to considering outcome measures of the actual loans, investments, and other services provided throughout a lender's service area, although small lenders, those with assets below $250 million, have generally been subject to a more streamlined review that focused on their lending activity (Sidney 2003, 60; U.S. Senate Committee on Banking, Housing and Urban Affairs 1988).

At these same hearings, community reinvestment advocates, including ACORN, broadened their focus from the behavior of local banks to the role that the secondary market played in exacerbating redlining problems. Government Sponsored Enterprises (GSEs), including Fannie Mae and Freddie Mac, along with private mortgage insurers (PMIs) had underwriting requirements limiting the number of mortgages they would purchase or insure in low-income areas, thus discouraging lenders from originating loans in these neighborhoods. For example, ACORN testified that a minimum loan requirement (often $30,000) eliminated housing in many low-income and particularly minority areas where the value of housing often fell below these thresholds. And often the GSEs and PMIs refused to consider income derived from part-time work, public assistance, or freelance work, which often adversely affected low-income and minority borrowers (U.S. Senate Committee on Banking, Housing and Urban Affairs 1988). Complaints began to focus on how the growing secondary market firms had created "an unleveled playing field that worked to the detriment of more diverse, mixed-use urban neighborhoods" (Immergluck 2004). Advocacy around the GSE issues led eventually to GSE low- and moderate-income lending goals set in the Federal Housing Enterprises Financial Safety and Soundness Act of 1992, after urging by such groups as the Center for Community Change, the National Low Income Housing Coalition, ACORN, the Consumer's Union, the Enterprise Foundation, and the Local Initiatives Support Corporation (Fishbein 2003). For example, lending goals for 2008 call for the GSEs to make 56 percent of their purchases for loans to households with incomes below the median for their metropolitan area and 39 percent for loans to residents in low- and moderate-income tracts with high minority populations (U.S. Department of Housing and Urban Development 2005).

Arguing that the CRA is no longer needed, that it creates massive reporting burdens, and that the CRA is nothing more than "blackmail," financial service providers have tried to scale back, if not eliminate, the CRA since the time it was enacted. In recent years these efforts have met with some success (Bradford and Cincotta 1992; Squires and O'Connor 2001). But it is clear the damage would have been far worse in the absence of advocacy efforts by community reinvestment proponents.

In 2004 the four federal financial regulatory agencies proposed new rules that would raise the small bank threshold from $250 million to $1 billion, weakening the CRA exam for several institutions. The community reinvestment advocacy network led the fight against these changes, calling on their members and member agencies to send comment letters to regulators. NCRC generated 2,280 comment letters to the regulators opposing the changes, while the banking industry generated just 1,600 letters supporting them. In its campaign, NCRC sent repeated e-mail messages to its members and other community reinvestment advocates. Several of the messages included model letters people could tailor to their own organization, along with addresses of each of the regulatory agencies where the letters were to be sent. In the end, three of the four agencies withdrew this proposal but replaced the investment and service tests with a weaker community development test for lenders with assets between $250 million and $1 billion. The new rule applied to 1,508 midsized banks that control $679 billion in assets. These banks account for almost 19 percent of all banks regulated by these three agencies and almost 8 percent of their assets (Taylor 2005).

Although the new regulations scale back the CRA, they are an improvement over the original proposals. After two years and four rounds of comment letters (NCRC members generating over 12,000 comments during those years), the advocacy network was able to prevent even worse changes. According to NCRC, "a regulatory official at an FDIC board meeting observed that drastic weakening of CRA exam requirements beyond the final ruling would have been contrary to the several thousand comment letters the agencies received. Thus, if the three agencies had gutted CRA, they would have run afoul of the Administrative Procedures Act according to the regulatory official" (National Community Reinvestment Coalition 2005c). Following this action, however, OTS raised its threshold for small banks to $1 billion and eliminated the mandatory investment and service tests for all lenders (National Community Reinvestment Coalition 2005b). Though this change affected just 11 percent of all savings and loans regulated by OTS, they account for $1.1 trillion or 87 percent of all thrift industry assets (Taylor 2005). The agency subsequently announced its intent to revise its CRA regulations to bring them into conformance with the Fed, FDIC, and OCC (U.S. Department of the Treasury 2006). But clearly, the CRA remains under attack.

Predatory Lending: Redlining in Reverse

The most prominent financial services consumer issue of at least the past decade has been predatory lending. Focusing on communities long victimized by redlining practices, many lenders have utilized high-pressure tactics to encourage lower-income, minority, and elderly homeowners to borrow money for home purchase and refinancing on unfair and exploitative terms, charging interest rates and other fees much higher than warranted by the risk posed by these borrowers. Such practices have cost victimized families at least $9.1 billion per year (Stein 2001, 2), forcing many into default and causing them to lose their homes. Not only are individual families affected, but entire neighborhoods experience greater foreclosure rates, higher crime, and lower property values as a consequence of these predatory practices. Cities, in turn, generate fewer property tax revenues. Just as community advocacy groups responded to redlining, many are also taking on predatory lending in efforts to assure access to credit on fair terms in traditionally exploited communities (Immergluck 2004; Squires 2004).

ACORN began encountering the problem of predatory lending through its door-to-door organizing efforts in the 1990s. Organizers found a growing number of homeowners who had been taken advantage of by predatory lenders and were at risk of losing their homes. Since then, ACORN has focused much of its energy on exposing and curbing the predatory practices of subprime lenders, increasing community awareness of predatory practices, and mobilizing community members against predatory lenders (Hurd and Kest 2003). Subprime loans are loans that are higher priced than conventional or prime loans for borrowers with blemishes on their credit records. Such loans do make credit available to some borrowers who would otherwise not be able to obtain a mortgage. But it is in the growing subprime market where predatory practices are occurring and such lending provides no benefit for the borrowers.

After gathering stories from so many of its members about predatory practices, ACORN released a national report in 2000 entitled "Separate and Unequal: Predatory Lending in America." This report analyzed U.S. Department of Housing and Urban Development (HUD) and HMDA data on subprime lending and documented the increase and concentration of subprime lending in low-income and minority communities. Following this report, ACORN began building a strong constituency of predatory lending victims, employing a variety of techniques to pressure lenders, investors, and policymakers to halt this abusive practice (Hurd and Kest 2003).

The base of ACORN's campaign is hundreds of predatory lending victims who have shared their stories with community members, political representatives, industry officials, and the media. ACORN's model of organizing enables workers to find victims of predatory lending through their normal methods rather than relying on victims coming forward voluntarily. Additionally, because of its door-to-door organizing methods and its high profile in low-income communities, ACORN has the ability to educate through its network of members, often reaching people unlikely to be found by any other method. This base of predatory lending victims is then mobilized into crowds of victimized borrowers and other ACORN members who demonstrate in communities to increase general awareness of the issues (and ACORN's role in addressing them), rally on the steps of city halls where anti–predatory lending legislation is being considered, and protest at the offices of predatory lenders themselves (Hurd and Kest 2003).

The first lender that ACORN directly negotiated with on predatory lending issues was Ameriquest, one of the nation's largest stand-alone subprime lenders. The negotiations were promulgated by an active campaign, beginning in 1999, of demonstrations, pickets, and sit-ins at Ameriquest offices throughout the country. In March 2000, more than 400 ACORN members from around the country stormed the Washington, DC, office of Salomon Smith Barney, which purchases loans from Ameriquest. Later that same day, these same members took over an Ameriquest office and occupied it for over an hour until Ameriquest's president called from California and agreed to meet and negotiate changes in the company's lending practices (Perkins 2000). ACORN also filed complaints with state attorneys general, the Federal Trade Commission, and the U.S. Department of Justice (Hurd and Kest 2003). In July 2000, ACORN signed one of the first agreements of its kind with Ameriquest to make subprime loans available to borrowers on "fair terms." The agreement had three major components. Ameriquest agreed to invest $360 million in an ACORN pilot program to be implemented in ten cities; the program was to make subprime loans with no prepayment penalties or credit insurance, a limit on points and fees at 3 percent of the loan amount, interest rates below the market standard, and loan counseling for every potential borrower. Ameriquest also adopted a set of corporate best practices to apply to all its business operations and agreed to join with ACORN in developing and supporting federal and state legislation to set new standards throughout the rest of the industry (Hurd and Kest 2003).

Along with other community advocacy groups, ACORN also joined the fight against Household Financial. ACORN's campaign included outreach and organizing to find victims of Household's predatory lending practices, documenting victim's experiences, holding demonstrations at the company's offices in more than forty cities around the country, organizing an extensive media campaign, promoting a shareholder resolution, filing class-action lawsuits, getting Wall Street analysts to understand the possible legal and public relations consequences of Household's policies, and advocating for regulatory and legislative reforms. ACORN's campaign also included demonstrating at Best Buy headquarters and local stores, with the goal of pressuring Best Buy to end its relationship with Household, who managed Best Buy's credit card. In addition, Best Buy shoppers were warned that their credit information was being turned over to Household, which would then try to sell them credit insurance or high-priced loans (Hurd and Kest 2003; Hurd, Donner, and Phillips 2004).

In 2001, ACORN organized victims and members to demonstrate at Household's annual shareholders meeting. ACORN was able to pressure city councils in St. Louis, Los Angeles, and Chelsea, Massachusetts, to divest their pension funds of all Household investments. They also used their labor connections to encourage the AFL-CIO to pressure Household to change its practices by threatening to divest their union pension holdings of Household investments (Hurd and Kest 2003).

Because of these organizing tactics, along with those of other community groups and the national advocacy community, some success was achieved in 2001 when Household announced that it would no longer sell single-premium credit insurance (a product that increases the cost of a loan throughout the life of that loan) on mortgage loans. However, many of Household's predatory practices continued. In 2002 more than 2,000 ACORN members rallied in the front yards of homes of Household's CEO and four of its board members in Chicago, passing out flyers to the neighbors warning them of loan sharks in their communities. Finally, in 2002, a consortium of state attorneys general announced a $484 million settlement with the company. This money was for restitution as well as injunctive relief committing the company to improved lending practices in the future (Hurd and Kest 2003).

The battle over predatory lending is hardly over. The mortgage melt-down that has been front-page news continues to threaten many homeowners, neighborhoods, and the economy generally (Anderson and Thomas 2007; Bajaj 2008; Creswell and Bajaj 2007). The Bush administration proposed voluntary initiatives, the Federal Reserve has issued regulations limiting some of the problematic practices, several bills have been introduced in Congress, and a controversial bailout or rescue plan (known as the Troubled Asset Relief Program or TARP) has been launched. But the mortgage, foreclosure, and broader economic crises persist. Some victims are being compensated, thanks in part to rescue funds established by some advocacy groups to help families refinance their predatory loans with more reasonable terms of credit. Many observers, including most financial service providers themselves, condemn at least the more explicit exploitative practices and credit (or at least pay lip service to) the advocacy community for bringing these issues to light. Further progress, no doubt, will depend on further advocacy (Atlas, Dreier, and Squires 2008).

The Future of Reinvestment

Significant progress has been made in democratizing access to capital, in large part because of the emergence of a community reinvestment infrastructure spearheaded by ACORN and several "sister" organizations. By educating consumers, conducting research, utilizing the mass media, pressuring lawmakers and regulators, and on occasion collaborating with financial service providers—that is, by effective organizing and advocacy efforts—neighborhoods long starved for credit are beginning to find it readily accessible. But the victories have not come easily, and they are not necessarily permanent. If mortgage money is far more readily available today, often it is on exploitative terms. Predatory lending is the primary current battle in financial services today. And the types of organizing and advocacy efforts that have succeeded in increasing access to capital will be essential for assuring it is available on fair and equitable terms.

Some prominent voices have argued that the days of organizing are over. Community reinvestment, it is said, is a sophisticated business, and it is time for community groups to basically sit down and "do deals" with financial service providers. Larry Lindsay, former Federal Reserve Board governor and economic policy advisor to President Bush patronizingly said, "The protest banner can still be held reverently in our box of mementos, along with the love beads and peace signs." But, he continued,

"These are the two faces of community development: noisy protest and quiet accomplishment. . . . One can act one way at age 20 and another at age 40. It is called growing up" (Lindsay 2000). In their acclaimed book *Comeback Cities*, Grogan and Proscio praised the CRA but then ridiculed those "with a preference for confrontation over visible results" (Grogan and Proscio 2000). But such observations miss the critical link between confrontation and results. The NTIC's Shel Trapp responded to a similar sentiment twenty years ago when he was told "confrontation was good for the '60s, but this is the age of partnership." He replied that "In all the partnerships we formed, we first had to get the attention of our opponents. Translated, that means we've had to confront them" (Trapp 1986, 13–14).

A critical feature of the fights against redlining and predatory lending has been the involvement of diverse constituencies—neighborhood organizations, church groups, labor unions, fair housing and civil rights advocates, affordable housing proponents, and others. Building on those coalitions may become even more important to beat back efforts to dilute the CRA and weaken community reinvestment efforts generally (Dreier 2003). All stand to benefit by continuing this struggle. Many neighborhoods still need greater access to capital. The congregations of many faith-based groups are often the residents of these neighborhoods. Housing affordability problems are particularly acute for many members of labor organizations and working families generally. Civil rights and affordable housing advocates need access to capital on fair and equitable terms to further their objectives. Self-interest, along with a mutual concern for traditionally underserved communities, may well trigger even broader and more effective coalitions in the future. Skilled, experienced community reinvestment groups, like ACORN, will likely be critical to nurturing such advocacy for years to come. An infrastructure is in place to continue the reinvestment struggles. But it, too, needs continued reinvestment.

Frederick Douglass may well have best captured the central dynamic for continuing the evolution from redlining to reinvestment when, more than one hundred years ago, he famously observed, "If there is no struggle there is no progress. . . . Power concedes nothing without a demand. It never did and it never will" (Blassingame 1985, 204).

REFERENCES

ACORN. 2006. "ACORN Housing Corporation." Available at *www.acorn.org/ index.php?id=1573*.

Adamson, M., and S. Borgos. 1984. *This Mighty Dream: Social Protest Movements in the United States.* Boston: Routledge and Kegan Paul.

Anderson, J., and H. Thomas. 2007. "Why a U.S. Subprime Mortgage Crisis Is Felt around the World." *New York Times.* August 31.

Atlas, J., P. Dreier, and G. D. Squires. 2008. "Foreclosing on the Free Market: How to Remedy the Subprime Catastrophe." *New Labor Forum* 17, no. 3: 18–30.

Bajaj, V. 2008. "If Everyone's Finger-Pointing, Who's to Blame?" *New York Times.* January 22.

Blassingame, J. W., ed. 1985. *The Frederick Douglass Papers.* New Haven: Yale University Press.

Bradford, C., and G. Cincotta. 1992. "The Legacy, the Promise, and the Unfinished Agenda." In *From Redlining to Reinvestment: Community Responses to Urban Disinvestment,* ed. by Gregory D. Squires. Philadelphia: Temple University Press.

Brown, M. 1988. *Hearings on the Community Reinvestment Act.* 100th Cong., 2d sess., Senate Hearing 100–652. U.S. Senate Committee on Banking, Housing and Urban Affairs. March 22 and 23.

Creswell, J., and V. Bajaj. 2007. "Mortgage Crisis Spirals, and Casualties Mount." *New York Times.* March 5.

Delgado, G. 1986. *Organizing the Movement: The Roots and Growth of ACORN.* Philadelphia: Temple University Press.

Dreier, P. 2003. "The Future of Community Reinvestment: Challenges and Opportunities in a Changing Environment." *Journal of the American Planners Association* 69, no. 4: 341–53.

Federal Financial Institutions Examination Council. 2001. *Reports—Nationwide Summary Statistics for 2000 HMDA Data: Fact Sheet.* Table 7. Available at *www.ffiec.gov/hmdaadwebreport/nataggwelcome.aspx.*

———. 2005. *HMDA National Aggregate Report.* Table 4.2. Available at *www.ffiec.gov/hmcrpr/hm00table7.pdf.*

Fishbein, A. J. 2003. "Filling the Half-Empty Glass: The Role of Community Advocacy in Redefining the Public Responsibilities of Government-Sponsored Housing Enterprises." In *Organizing Access to Capital: Advocacy and the Democratization of Financial Institutions,* ed. by G. D. Squires. Philadelphia: Temple University Press.

Fisher, R. 1994. *Let the People Decide: Neighborhood Organizing in America.* Updated ed. New York: Twayne.

Grogan, P. S., and T. Proscio. 2000. *Comeback Cities: A Blueprint for Urban Neighborhood Revival.* Boulder: Westview.

Hurd, M., L. Donner, and C. Phillips. 2004. "Community Organizing and Advocacy: Fighting Predatory Lending and Making a Difference." In *Why the Poor Pay More: How to Stop Predatory Lending,* ed. by G. D. Squires. Westport, CT: Praeger.

Hurd, M., and S. Kest. 2003. "Fighting Predatory Lending from the Ground Up: An Issue of Economic Justice." In *Organizing Access to Capital: Advocacy and the Democratization of Financial Institutions*, ed. by G. D. Squires. Philadelphia: Temple University Press.

Immergluck, D. 2004. *Credit to Community: Community Reinvestment and Fair Lending Policy in the United States.* Armonk, NY: M. E. Sharpe.

Kest, S. 2006. (Executive Director, ACORN). Interview with Jan Chadwick. February 21.

Lindsay, L. B. 2000. "Community Development at a Crossroads." *Neighborworks Journal* 18 (Winter): 54–55.

Marsico, R. D. 2005. *Democratizing Capital: The History, Law and Reform of the Community Reinvestment Act.* Durham: Carolina Academic Press.

National Association of Realtors. 2005. *Homeownership.* April 27.

National Community Reinvestment Coalition. 2005a. *CRA Commitments.* Washington, DC: National Community Reinvestment Coalition.

———. 2005b. "NCRC Disappointed by Federal Ruling Weakening CRA." Press Release. Washington, DC: National Community Reinvestment Coalition.

———. 2005c. "NCRC Mobilizes Massive Opposition to CRA Weakening: Final Ruling Issued." *Reinvestment Works.* Summer.

Olson, M. 1965. *The Logic of Collective Action: Public Goods and the Theory of Groups.* Cambridge, MA: Harvard University Press.

Perkins, B. 2000. "ACORN Pressures Crack Ameriquest." *RealtyTimes.* Available at *realtytimes.com/rtcpages/20000727_safeguards.htm*.

Russell, D. M. 1989. *Political Organizing in Grassroots Politics.* Lanham, MD: University Press of America.

Sidney, M. S. 2003. *Unfair Housing: How National Policy Shapes Community Action.* Lawrence: University Press of Kansas.

Squires, G. D., ed. 1989. *From Redlining to Reinvestment: Community Responses to Urban Disinvestment.* Philadelphia: Temple University Press.

———, ed. 2003. *Organizing Access to Capital: Advocacy and the Democratization of Financial Institutions.* Philadelphia: Temple University Press.

———, ed. 2004. *Why the Poor Pay More: How to Stop Predatory Lending.* Westport, CT: Praeger.

Squires, G. D., and S. O'Connor. 2001. *Color and Money: Politics and Prospects for the Community Reinvestment Movement in Urban America.* Albany: SUNY Press.

Stein, E. 2001. *Quantifying the Economic Cost of Predatory Lending.* Durham, NC: Coalition for Responsible Lending.

Taylor, J. 2005. Comment letter to the Federal Reserve Board, Federal Deposit Insurance Corporation, and Comptroller of the Currency. May 6.

Trapp, S. 1986. *Blessed Be the Fighters.* Chicago: National Training and Information Center.

U.S. Census Bureau. 2004. *Housing Vacancies and Homeownership: Annual Statistics 2001.* U.S. Census Bureau, December 2. Available at *www.census. gov/hhes/www/housing/hvs/annual01/ann01ind.html.*

U.S. Department of Housing and Urban Development. 2005. *HUD's Regulation of Fannie Mae and Freddie Mac.* January 11. Available at *www. hud.gov/offices/hsg/gse/gse.cfm.*

U.S. Department of the Treasury. 2006. "Community Reinvestment Act— Interagency Uniformity." *Federal Register* 71, no. 226: 67826–31.

U.S. Senate Committee on Banking, Housing, and Urban Affairs. 1988. *Hearings on the Community Reinvestment Act.* 100th Cong., 2d sess. March 22 and 23.

5

Community Organizing Theory and Practice
Conservative Trends, Oppositional Alternatives

James DeFilippis, Robert Fisher, and Eric Shragge

ACORN is an example of an organization that is working against the current. It has over many years sustained its stance as an organization that contests inequalities, and it mobilizes through its organizations people directly affected to struggle against those inequalities. It is part of a minority of community organizations that have continued in this tradition. In contrast, many community-based efforts have abandoned these traditions, learned to accommodate to the changing context, and as a consequence have become depoliticized, highly professional service providers and local developers, supported in these roles by government and private foundations. Some readers may not even consider such work as community organizing, for these groups stand outside the major neo-Alinskyite networks and related smaller efforts (Fisher 1994). But they do include such community-based efforts as social service providers, community development corporations, economic development initiatives, and the like, which are most vulnerable and open to corporatized funding pressures. Nevertheless, even the large community organizing networks are affected by pressures of moderation and incorporation. In this chapter, we will examine some of these transitions, present and critique some of the ideas that have supported it, and then look comparatively at alternative organizing practices that help efforts sustain their challenges to the wider contemporary political economy and its moderating pressures on progressive social change organizations.

This study argues that most community-based efforts have adapted to the moderating pressures of our constrained context for social change. An emphasis on "the bottom line," building "partnerships" with local businesses and corporations, developing "relationships," and focusing on "community assets" has narrowed conceptions of community activism, for example, squeezing out conflict models from the community organizer's arsenal of strategies and tactics. Moreover, most contemporary models of community building and development focus exclusively on the local internal community, not the economic, political, and social decisions that rest outside the community and create community needs and concerns. There is a greater emphasis on social consensus, as opposed to conflict, and service provision as opposed to action. In our previous work, we have analyzed the growing moderation of community organizing and development in the current neoliberal context (Fisher and Shragge 2000; DeFilippis, Fisher, and Shragge 2006). Others have come to similar conclusions. For example, Saegert (2006) argues that in contrast to older models of community activism, the newer approaches emphasize "relationships, coalitions, and consensus building and voluntary, often entrepreneurial action. . . . Community building added a human, relational and civic component. . . . Unlike power organizing, it emphasized cooperation, mutual gain among different sectors of society" (275). In her critical discussion, she elaborates: "Community builders downplay differences in self or group interest and structural and historical factors that create and maintain economic and political inequality. . . . They seek to nurture a broad range of overlapping social networks within which different combinations of individuals and organizations can reach a consensus about the achievement of particular goals" (279). In their discussion of Community Development Corporations (CDCs), Gittell and Vidal (1998) argue that local organizations have disengaged from fighting at the national level and focused on local politics in order to achieve concrete and sustainable outcomes. Their definition of resident commitment includes "commonly described measures of social capital, such as loyalty to community, and levels of trust and cooperation among residents" (24–25). Certainly, there are positive results and progressive adaptations to the pressures of moderation (Saegert, Thompson, and Warren 2001), but the corporatization of the nonprofit world has reached deeply into the CBO (community-based organization) sector, and none are immune to its pressures (Fabricant and Fisher 2002).

Community in an Age of Neoliberalism

Because community efforts and theories about them are always specific to a particular time and place, analysis of theory and practice must situate the work in the varied economic, political, social and cultural sites that generate it. Paradoxically, at the very moment that communities are more burdened and constrained, they have also become increasingly salient and popular sites for responding to and struggling with the world they have been handed (Fisher and Karger 1997; Pendras 2002). This paradox has led to a turn toward efforts at the community level in arenas and practices as far ranging as public school reform, crime prevention, and social service delivery efforts, as well as efforts to democratize social, political, and cultural practices. Community is promoted as an alternative to conservative state policies and bureaucratic programs. Even Ed Chambers, the lead strategist for the Industrial Areas Foundation (IAF), among the most significant community organization efforts in the United States and one that shares much in common with ACORN, reflects the new emphasis on the community sector when he discusses the virtues of "civil society." "Civil society is the most important level of institutions. Its power is generational. It's where values and traditions are instilled and fostered. The state and the market came later and exist to support it. Civil society trumps the state and market in value, but most people don't think of it that way. . . . Civil society is the political conscience and benchmark of democracy" (Chambers 2004, 61).

To their credit, new communitarian theorists such as Etzioni, Elshtain, Putnam, Sandel, Kretzman and McKnight, and Eichler employ new nomenclatures of social capital, community capacity, assets building, and consensus organizing in order to move contemporary discourse away from an emphasis on the deficits and failings of individuals and families and toward more collective causes and solutions at the community level. They respond to a clear decline of collective behavior since the mid-1970s and seek to counter the extreme individualism and privatism of the past generation with work that emphasizes the value of greater public engagement. They focus on developing participation and enabling people to take more control of their lives and communities. The impacts of such extended social networks on community and individual well-being has been well documented (Fabricant and Fisher 2002; Saegert, Thompson, and Warren 2001).

Nevertheless, almost always the singular emphasis of community building theorists and initiatives is on community connection as the cause and solution to local problems. To their detriment and to the detriment of the larger movement for economic and social justice, there is rarely any attention to macro structural factors or macro power relations that control the flow of resources to or away from poor communities. Take, for example, the case study of a community building initiative called Neighborhoods of Opportunity, set in four communities contiguous to downtown Chattanooga, Tennessee, and funded by the local United Way, the city, and three foundations. Fraser, Lipofsky, Kick, and Williams (2003) document how the overreliance on neighborhoods and civil society, as well as the failure to address the basic causes of community decline rather than issues of social capital, dramatically limited the impact of this effort. The authors concluded that the community-building model constrained the valuable work done by Neighborhoods of Opportunity to organize residents to act collectively on neighborhood concerns, to develop and support local leadership, and to promote the organization (417–45). As Shragge puts it, "The concept of capacity-building and related processes of community development is not the problem; it is the context in which they are practices that is key" (2003, 123). Kubisch and others (2002) make a similar finding. Contemporary community building needs to look outside the local and broaden the problem analysis, find powerful allies, engage public and private sectors, and rethink biases and assumptions inherent in community building approaches.

Seeking Social and Economic Justice: Working against the Grain

If community-building efforts are in general too constrained in theory and practice to effect social change beyond the local community, then what would more effective practice models look like? What organizations are doing impressive work at the local level and beyond? Despite the larger tendencies of weakening political demands and shrinking perspectives, significant efforts in Anglo-American communities still exist. They provide examples of community-based organizing efforts that: (1) have not lost sight of the goals of social and economic justice for people in their communities; (2) recognize that justice within communities can only come from changes in the larger political-economy; and (3) are organizing in ways that extend beyond the community to try to realize greater justice within the community. What follows are practice examples that demonstrate possibilities of oppositional community organizing in the current difficult and complex political economy. These examples present effective, if imperfect, community initiatives. They present alternatives to more narrow and moderate community-building efforts. Of course, the three organizations are not meant to be a definitive list of effective contemporary organizing. They are offered here as illustrative examples of organizations that incorporate the three critical dimensions discussed above.

Moreover, the cases below are chosen because they reflect broader themes around the contradictory connections between communities and the larger world. Many organizations that are involved in contemporary community development see the local as central and have few relationships or dealings outside of it. In contrast, the organizations we discuss understand the importance and the limits of local work and try to find ways to go beyond it, either through coalitions, chapter structures, or international networking. Another dimension of their practice is to bridge the long-standing split between labor and community organizing. With changes in the structure and organization of work and labor markets, new community-labor strategies emerge with community organizing processes and organizations, particularly in immigrant communities finding new ways to promote improvements in working conditions. Finally, community development has become the dominant form of practice over the past twenty years, and this can range from service planning to housing provision. There are, however, exceptions that have combined development and organizing. They work on issues that mobilize residents and at the same time support development projects.

We have included three cases below. Each highlights particular themes or dimensions from the discussion above, but they all present a variety of common approaches, such as their analysis of contemporary political economy and their commitment to progressive social change through popular mobilization. The Fifth Avenue Committee (FAC) in Brooklyn, New York, highlights the issue of development and organizing. ACORN illustrates direct local organizing within a national organization with a national focus. Finally, the Immigrant Workers Center (IWC), in Montreal, Quebec, provides an example of organizing on labor issues through the community.

Fifth Avenue Committee

One of the ongoing problems with much of the work that has been written on community is its tendency to fall into dualistic thinking: organizing or development, consensus or conflict, community or labor, local or larger-scale.[1] This way of thinking limits the potential scope and range of community-based efforts for social change. Organizations certainly work in several different arenas and in a variety of ways. They organize and do development. They can be collaborative and consensual but unafraid of conflict. And they act on different scales—community, city, state or province, and global. They do so because they understand that the nature of community is one of complex relationships that manifest themselves in different kinds of interactions and that also transcend the local. The Fifth Avenue Committee (FAC) is one such organization.

The FAC emerged in the 1970s in Lower Park Slope in Brooklyn, New York. Lower Park Slope, unlike its wealthy neighbor (Park Slope) to the east, faced many of the same problems of systematic disinvestment and decline evident in so many urban neighborhoods in the United States in the 1970s. The presence of the affluent adjacent neighborhood, however, meant that from its founding the FAC understood that the organization's work could never be limited to just improving the community. It understood the threat of displacement from gentrification and the contradictions that emerge from improving things in an area where improvement is also a threat. The FAC's ability to simultaneously do organizing and development comes from an openness to this contradiction. Thus the original mission statement stressed maintaining social and economic diversity in the neighborhood—although that language was removed from its mission statement in the late 1990s and replaced with a simpler, and in many ways more radical, call for social and economic justice in the neighborhood. In the last thirty years, the FAC has become one of the largest and most dynamic community organizations in New York City. Its work reads like a motley mix of services, housing construction, retail development, and organizing. Most important for us here, however, is the persistence of development and organizing in its work.

Like many CDCs, housing is probably the largest component of the FAC's work. Since 1979, the FAC has developed a set of neighborhood properties, including supportive housing developments and straight rental units. But the organization has primarily stressed other forms of development, like mutual housing associations (MHA) or limited-equity co-ops, both of which allow the development to be sheltered from the vagaries of the flows of capital that constitute the real estate market. This housing development has taken place alongside a set of housing organizing struggles. The FAC first began to address issues of displacement pressures due to rent increases and gentrification in the late 1970s and early 1980s, but as the process of gentrification accelerated in the second half of the 1990s, these efforts became a more coherent and organized campaign. The "Displacement Free Zone" (DFZ), as the campaign is known, is a roughly one hundred-block area that is larger than the immediate neighborhood of Lower Park Slope—a recognition that the pressures facing the neighborhood are shared by those adjacent to it. Tenants in the zone who are facing evictions due to rent increases contact the FAC. The first step is negotiation with the landlord. When that does not work, the "negotiations" become increasingly noisy and confrontational. This approach often includes bringing vanloads of people to the landlord's house to picket or have a street party (or a bit of both).

While the FAC organizes confrontationally, it is also working with members of the state legislature to pass a bill that would offer landlords a tax credit if they own a building that is not governed by rent regulation laws and they agree to rent their units at below market rent to a low- or moderate-income household. The Community Stability Small Homeowners Tax Credit, as it is called, has passed the state assembly a couple of times but has not yet passed the state senate. Finally, the FAC also engaged in a protracted fight in the early 2000s to have inclusionary specifications in the rezoning of Fourth Avenue. In this effort, the FAC failed. But importantly, with the lessons of that experience guiding it, the FAC has since played a major role in similar fights in Williamsburg/Greenpoint in Brooklyn and Chelsea in Manhattan, and in both cases of rezoning, there were strong inclusionary zoning components. Despite not being "in" either of these neighborhoods, FAC was vital to the success of these efforts. While none of these development projects or organizing tactics is going to alter the basic character of domestic property as a capitalist commodity, they do alter the logic that governs the commodity exchange.

Addressing housing issues is a typical part of what CDCs do, but the FAC is also involved in issues of labor, labor markets, and workplace justice. First, in perhaps the issue that hits closest to home for CDCs, the FAC has been leading an effort to build a collaboration between labor unions and CDCs to insure that the affordable housing that CDCs construct is built with union labor and pays prevailing wages, which has almost never been the case in New York (Ciezadlo 2003). Second, in the 1990s, as "welfare reform" was occurring in Washington, a particularly punitive interpretation of the law was being imposed on low-income New Yorkers by then-mayor Rudy Giuliani. Organizing efforts sprung up around the city in opposition to the mayor and his welfare policies. One of the primary campaigns to emerge from this came from the FAC and its splinter organization, Families United for Racial and Economic Equality (FUREE). FUREE is a group of women on, or formerly on, public assistance, organizing for economic justice in the realm of public welfare policy. Their most significant campaign put pressure on the city government to improve the pay and working conditions of the workers taking care of the children of the women leaving welfare for employment.

Finally, the FAC is a leading organization in a city-wide effort to transform how local economic development is understood and done in the city. This effort, called Re-Defining Economic Development in New York (RED-NY), has been explicitly broad in focus and long-term in vision—transcending particular neighborhoods, issues, and momentary struggles or efforts.

The FAC has maintained its efforts in both organizing and development because it has fundamentally understood that community development without organizing is never going to change the larger political and economic contexts in which communities exist. Nor is it ever going to address the long-term needs and interests of low-income people in the community. In fact, it may actually undermine those needs and interests.

Immigrant Workers Centre

Workplace organizing has historically been the concern of unions, while local work "reproduction" issues have been the priority of community organizing. The emergence of community-based labor organizing is a relatively new practice bridging this older divide. One reason it has emerged is because neoliberalism and globalization have destabilized the labor market and made traditional forms of union organizing difficult, if not impossible. It is estimated that there are approximately 130 community-labor centers of this type across the United States (Fine 2005). These are mainly in immigrant communities and work with those closest to the bottom of the labor market. These centers are an important innovation in the field of community organizing, focusing on issues of labor outside of the workplace. Gordon describes these centers as seeking "to build the collective power of their largely immigrant members and to raise wages and improve working conditions in the bottom-of-the-ladder jobs where they labor" (2005, 280).

The Immigrant Workers Centre (IWC) in Montreal is a relatively new example of the community labor approach being put into action in Canada. It was founded in 2000 by a small group composed of Filipino-Canadian union and former union organizers and activist and academic allies. The idea of the center grew out of the experience of the two founders, who had worked as union organizers. They observed that much of their recruitment and education to support a union drive had to take place outside of the workplace and, apart from their homes, there were few places where this could happen, particularly in a collective way. Thus the idea of the center was to provide a safe place outside of the workplace where workers could discuss their situation.

The activities of the IWC cover individual rights counseling, popular education, and political campaigns that reflect the general issues facing immigrant workers, such as dismissal, problems with employers, or, sometimes, inadequate representation by their unions. Labor education is a priority, as are targeting organizations in the community and increasing workers' skills and analysis. Workshops on themes such as the history of the labor movement, the Labour Standards Act, and collective organizing processes have been presented by many organizations that work with immigrants as well as at the IWC itself. The Skills for Change program teaches basic computer literacy, while incorporating workplace analysis and information on rights. There is also an ongoing linking of immigrant workers' struggles with other social and economic struggles; building alliances is a priority, particularly with other immigrant organizations and social movements active on issues concerning refugee claimants. In addition, the IWC supports union organizing in workplaces where there is a high concentration of immigrant workers.

Campaigns are viewed not only as a way to make specific gains for immigrant workers but also as a way to educate the wider community about the issues that they face. For example, the first campaign, in 2000, was to prevent deportation of a domestic worker who was in Canada on a limited government program to import domestic labor. In addition to winning the campaign, the issue of importing laborers as indentured servants was brought into the public sphere, and many community organizations and unions became involved in this issue. Because many immigrant workers do not work in unionized shops, the Labour Standards Act provides one of nonunionized workers' few recourses against their employers. Along with many other groups in Quebec, the IWC became involved in a campaign to reform the Labour Standards Act in 2002. The IWC brought to the campaign specific concerns, including the exclusion of domestic workers from this act and the difficulty of accessing information on workers' rights. In 2003, several victories were won, including the coverage of domestic workers by the reformed Labour Standards.

The IWC has also initiated a campaign on issues related to the North-to-South relocation of production and the resulting job loss and factory closures in Montreal. The spring of 2003 saw the closing of three recently organized factories employing immigrant workers. Using union-busting techniques, the companies laid off workers, who then came to the IWC for help. Organizers initiated actions to sensitize workers and the wider public. One of these actions was directed at the Montreal Jazz Festival, a large buyer of T-shirts manufactured by one of the companies, Gildan. The IWC demanded that the festival adopt an ethical buying policy in response to Gildan's labor practices, locally and in their factories relocated in Honduras.

As the IWC has become better known, workers come for advice and support on specific problems and issues. The organization sees this as a way to encourage and support people in standing up against their bosses but also as a basis on which to build wider campaigns. The case of a live-in domestic worker who became ill in her employer's house and was unable to work was the beginning of the IWC's most recent campaign. This worker was accompanied to make a claim with Quebec's workplace health and safety agency to ask for compensation while she could not work. She was told that as a domestic worker she did not fit the definition of a "worker" and therefore was not covered. The IWC's research found out that three provinces in Canada (Ontario, British Columbia, and Manitoba) protect domestic workers from workplace injury or illness. In conjunction with two other organizations, the IWC, in March 2006, launched a campaign demanding that these workers be covered. It has been supported by more than seventy organizations, including the large union federations.

Another aspect of the IWC's work has been helping organize cultural events with political content. The IWC sees cultural events as contributing to recruitment, building connections to other groups, and promoting a critical social analysis. Cultural activities have been used to discuss the politics of labor. The lesson is that cultural work is a tool for recruitment, alliance building, and political education. The first event was an International Women's Day event organized in 2001. A coalition of immigrant women of diverse origins organized a cultural event, panels, and a march to emphasize their concerns and show international solidarity. International Women's Day has become an annual event and through its success has increased the profile and the issues faced by immigrant women within the wider women's movement in Quebec. May Works, a community/union festival celebrating labor struggles through the arts, launched its first events for May Day in 2005. The IWC initiated the festival, which found collaboration from trade unions and the wider activist community.

The IWC and similar centers see individual service as a key way to attract people to their organizations, and often the issues brought in contribute to building collective action and campaigns (Delgado 1996; Gordon 2005). Because individual problems are based in a workplace, they are often shared by others and form the basis for collective action. Also, for an individual to step forward to challenge a boss about working conditions is an act of courage and is inherently political. Campaigns for policy change grow out of individual experiences, such as the campaign to cover domestic workers under health and safety legislation described above. For community organizing in general, working with individuals can be a beginning point to initiate collective action.

Organizations like the IWC recognize that it is impossible to organize directly in the workplace because of the precarious nature of many immigrant workers' jobs Therefore, the target of their campaigns has been the state, and they have been demanding improvements in conditions for everyone at the bottom end of the labor market. Policy-oriented campaigns demand improvements in labor standards or extend coverage of health and safety laws. The lesson here is that the state—whether municipal, provincial/state, or national—plays a central role in shaping social and economic conditions and should not be abandoned as a target through a renewed focus on community development.

ACORN

Because all of the chapters in this book discuss different dimensions of ACORN, we mention here briefly how its model of organizing contributes to the general arguments of this chapter. ACORN's perspective and practice transcends boundaries that limit other community efforts. The focus is always on building the organization, building greater power, and mobilizing more people and funding. Their work is not constricted by dualisms, for example, community or national-based organizing, service delivery or social action, grassroots or electoral activism, and so on. Even with obvious limits, resulting from the tension between running local and national organizations (Boyte 1980; Stern 2003), ACORN's local-national structure addresses the parochialism that undermines most contemporary, as well as historical, community organizations. For our purposes, what is so valuable in the ACORN example is that it demonstrates a contemporary community organizing effort that blends democratic localism with a national organization structure in order to gain necessary power and influence in a globalized context and with globalized corporations. In a nutshell, ACORN blends the advantages of community with that of a broader engagement around economic justice issues. They address head on the contemporary contradictions in the political economy, and they do so in a national organization grounded in local communities. They are committed to engaging in an oppositional politics that struggles for power at multiple spatial levels against private as well as public targets.

Discussion

What can be learned from these brief examples? The first point to recognize is that the leadership of each organization, whether the staff, board, or its members, has a strong, explicit commitment to the struggle for social and economic justice. This starting point shapes how each organization approaches and carries out its work. Given the transitions in the wider context and the consequent drawing of community organizations into limited service and development roles (DeFilippis, Fisher, and Shragge 2006), the naming of their politics is essential in maintaining their stance. They all stand in opposition to dominant values and power relations, while working to extend and protect social and economic rights. They also believe that the power to do this is gained through organizing people, either within their own organizations or through wider alliances.

In contrast to most community organizations, those we selected are outward looking, insofar as their efforts have a focus that includes and goes beyond the local. Integrated into their practice is an analysis of the context of their work. This includes an understanding of the changing political economy as representing new barriers and opportunities for advancing the causes of their organizations. These organizations begin their practice with local work, which is the starting point because it affords the opportunity to build a base and a membership. It is through local work that a group begins to reach a constituency and build collective action. But groups are not constrained by the local. They connect with similar organizations in other places, join wider social movements or form alliances with diverse groups, or develop their own national organizations. This approach, which transcends the local level, was an important characteristic of all of these organizations. Social and economic problems cannot be addressed in any substantial way solely through local work. Going beyond the local is a central aspect in the struggle for social and economic justice.

Another dimension of an outward-looking perspective is the connection with broader social movements, such as the labor, women's, or environmental movements. ACORN grew out of the struggles of the 1960s and 1970s and continues to see itself as shaped by those politics. Others maintain connections to movements as they develop and participate in their activities. Movements inherently transcend place, and this relationship enlarges local engagement and brings it into a broader context. They build a national organization or work in alliances or coalitions with other organizations within and beyond the community. The goals of the organizations thus move into wider social and political arenas, which link local and wider concerns.

Moreover, all of the organizations understand that conflict is central to their practice. This understanding is expressed in several ways. First, in their practice, they define opposition and mobilize against it. The specific tactics can vary from street-level actions to lobbying officials, but at the core there is an "us versus them" dynamic in place, at least on the specific issues being addressed. Second, conflict is expressed through the analysis of social issues. These organizations understand that power and interest is central and issues exist because of basic inequality of power. Organizing is a means of challenging this structural power, whether it is based on class, gender, or race. In contrast to organizing traditions that hide beliefs behind the mask of pragmatism, this organizing approach implies making explicit an ideology, even a Left populist ideology, in community-based efforts. The challenge for these organizations is sustaining this stance over time, that is, keeping their vision over the long-term. All three examples combine a social justice vision with concrete successes on the ground. These elements are mutually reinforcing; one does not work without the other.

Another way that organizations have achieved success and maintained their political critique is through the presence of strong leadership. This leadership is not authoritarian or antidemocratic; rather, a core group (staff, board members) plays a leadership role within the organization and is committed to maintaining its vision and politics. Leadership needs continuity, so there must be a conscious process of recruitment and training in order to retain and build vision. However, a tension exists between leadership and preserving the organizations' political culture and flexibility to respond to new situations and changing social and economic contexts. Both ACORN and Fifth Avenue have been around long enough to understand that changing contexts need new action plans while their core values and wider politics remain central and constant.

A lesson that emerges from the case studies is that the organizations do not get stuck within the traditional models—usually presented in the literature as action and development (Rothman 1968; Shragge 2003). Different approaches are interwoven to build the wider orientation and actions of the organization. These include connecting service provision with political education, advocacy, and action. These build off each other and are not treated in a linear fashion; that is, service provision can lead to a campaign or it can be developed as a consequence of a victory. As we discussed in the practice of the IWC, education is ongoing and can occur through individual work, formal workshops, and informal processes, including mentoring leaders. The approach recognizes the importance of using more inward-focused community building and tying it to wider strategies of social and political action.

We see the case studies as demonstrating the possibilities that community organizations can contribute to the process of social transformation. The elements we identify as critical to contemporary organizing are operationalized with varying degrees of success in the three organizations discussed. These "rules" summarize the approach we have taken in this chapter. They are not easy directions to put into practice. The organizations we have examined apply them imperfectly in a climate in which too many other efforts have lost these perspectives.

NOTES

Earlier versions of parts of this chapter first appeared as "Neither Romance Nor Regulation: Reevaluating Community," *International Journal of Urban and Regional Research* 30, no. 3 (September 2006): 673–89; and "What's Left in the Community," *Community Development Journal* 44, no. 1 (2009): 38–52.

1. It should be noted that perhaps the only thing that critics like Randy Stoecker (1997) and celebrators like Paul Grogan (Grogan and Proscio 2000) agree on is that organizing and development are incompatible goals and that development has long since overtaken organizing in the work of CDCs in the United States.

REFERENCES

Boyte, H. 1980. *The Backyard Revolution*. Philadelphia: Temple University Press.

Ciezadlo, A. 2003. "Invisible Men." *City Limits*. May.

Chambers, E. 2004. *Roots for Radicals*. New York: Continuum.

DeFilippis, J. 2004. *Unmaking Goliath: Community Control in the Face of Global Capital*. New York: Routledge.

DeFilippis, J., R. Fisher, and E. Shragge. 2006. "Neither Romance nor Regulation: Re-Evaluating Community." *International Journal of Urban and Regional Research* 30, no. 3 (September): 673–89.

Delgado, G. 1996. "How the Empress Gets Her Clothes: Asian Immigrant

Women Fight Fashion Designer Jessica McClintock." In *Beyond Identity Politics: Emerging Social Justice Movements in Communities of Color*, ed. by J. Anner, 81–94. Cambridge, MA: South End Press.

Etzioni, A. 1993. *The Spirit of Community: Rights, Responsibilities, and the Communitarian Agenda*. New York: Crown.

_____, ed. 1995. *New Communitarian Thinking: Persons, Virtues, Institutions, Communities*. Charlottesville: University Press of Virginia.

Fabricant, M., and R. Fisher. 2002. *Settlement Houses under Siege: The Struggle to Sustain Community Organization in New York City*. New York: Columbia University Press.

Fine, J. 2005. "Community Unions and the Revival of the American Labor Movement." *Politics and Society* 33, no. 1: 154–99.

Fisher, R. 1994. *Let the People Decide: Neighborhood Organizing in America*. Updated ed. New York: Twayne.

Fisher, R., and H. Karger. 1997. *Social Work and Community in a Private World*. White Plains, NY: Longman.

Fisher, R., and E. Shragge. 2000. "Challenging Community Organizing: Facing the 21st Century." *Journal of Community Practice* 8, no. 3: 1–20.

Frank, F., and A. Smith. 1999. *The Community Development Handbook: A Tool to Build Community Capacity*. Ottawa: Human Resources Development Canada.

Fraser, J., J. Lipofsky, E. Kick, and J. P. Williams. 2003. "The Construction of the Local and the Limits of Community Building in the United States." *Urban Affairs Review* 38, no. 3: 417–45.

Gilchrist, A. 2003. "Community Development in the UK—Possibilities and Paradoxes." *Community Development Journal* 38, no. 1: 16–25.

Gilmore, R. W. 1998. "Globalisation and U.S. Prison Growth: From Military Keynesianism to Post-Keynesian Militarism." *Race and Class* 40, no. 2/3: 171–88.

Gittell, R., and A. Vidal. 1998. *Community Organizing-Building Social Capital As a Development Strategy*. Thousand Oaks, CA: Sage.

Gordon, J. 2005. *Suburban Sweatshops: The Fight for Immigrant Rights*. Cambridge, MA: Belknap Press of the Harvard University Press.

Haughton, G. 1999. "Community Economic Development: Challenges of Theory, Method, and Practice." In *Community Economic Development*, ed. by G. Haughton, 3–22. London: Stationery Office, Regional Studies Association.

Jessop, B. 2002. "Liberalism, Neoliberalism, and Urban Governance: A State-Theoretical Perspective." In *Spaces of Neoliberalism: Urban Restructuring in North America and Western Europe*, ed. by N. Brenner and N. Theodore, 105–25. London: Blackwell.

Joseph, M. 2002. *Against the Romance of Community*. Minneapolis: University of Minnesota Press.

Koehler, B., and M. Wissen. 2003. "Glocalizing Protest: Urban Conflicts and Urban Social Movements." *International Journal of Urban and Regional Research* 27, no. 4 (December): 942–51.

Kretzmann, J., and J. McKnight. 1993. *Building Communities from the Inside Out: A Path toward Finding and Mobilizing a Community's Assets.* Chicago: Acta.

Kubisch, A., et al. 2008. "Strengthening the Connections between Communities and External Resources." In *The Community Development Reader*, ed. by J. DeFilippis and S. Saegert, 319–26. New York: Routledge.

Lake, R., and K. Newman. 2002. "Differential Citizenship in the Shadow State." *GeoJournal* 58:109–20.

Lemann, N. 1996. "Kicking in Groups." In *The Urban Community*, ed. by W. A. Martin. Saddle River, NJ: Prentice Hall.

Marquez, B. 1993. "Mexican-American Community Development Corporations and the Limits of Directed Capitalism." *Economic Development Quarterly* 7 (August): 287–95.

Mathew, B. 2005. *Taxi: Cabs and Capitalism in New York City.* New York: New Press.

Mayer, M. 2003. "The Onward Sweep of Social Capital: Causes and Consequences for Understanding Cities, Communities, and Urban Movements." *International Journal of Urban and Regional Research* 27, no. 1: 110–32.

McKnight, J. 1995. *The Careless Society: Community and Its Counterfeits.* New York: Basic Books.

McKnight, J., and J. P. Kretzmann. 1999. "Mapping Community Capacity." In *Community Organizing and Community Building for Health*, ed. by M. Minkler, 157–72. New Brunswick, NJ: Rutgers University Press.

Panet-Raymond, J., and R. Mayer. 1997. "The History of Community Development in Quebec." In *Community Organizing: Canadian Experiences*, ed. by B. Wharf and M. Clague, 29–61. Toronto: Oxford University Press.

Pendras, M. 2002. "From Local Consciousness to Global Change: Asserting Power at the Local Level." *International Journal of Urban and Regional Research* 26, no. 4: 823–33.

Popple, K., and M. Redmond. 2000. "Community Development and the Voluntary Sector in the New Millennium: The Implications of the Third Way in the UK." *Community Development Journal* 35, no. 4: 391–400.

Powell, F., and M. Geoghegan. 2004. *The Politics of Community Development.* Dublin: A. and A. Farmar.

Putnam, R. 1996. "The Strange Disappearance of Civic America." *American Prospect*, no. 24 (Winter).

Putnam, R. D. 2000. *Bowling Alone: The Collapse and Revival of American Community.* New York: Simon and Schuster.

Rothman, J. 1968. "Three Models of Community Organization and Macro Practice Perspectives: Their Mixing and Phasing." In *Strategies on Community Organization*, ed. by F. Cox, J. L. Erlich, J. Rothman, and J. E. Tropman, 3–26. 4th ed. Itasca, IL: Peacock.

Saegert, S. 2006. "Building Civic Capacity in Urban Neighborhoods: An Empirically Grounded Anatomy." *Journal of Urban Affairs* 28, no. 3: 275–94.

Saegert, S., J. Thompson, and M. Warren, eds. 2001. *Social Capital and Poor Communities*. New York: Russell Sage.

Sandel, M. 1998 (1982). *Liberalism and the Limits of Justice*. 2d ed. Cambridge: Cambridge University Press.

Shragge, E. 2003. *Activism and Social Change: Lessons for Community and Local Organizing*. Toronto: Broadview.

Stern, S. 2003. "ACORN's Nutty Regime for our Cities." *City Journal* (Spring). Available at *www.city-journal.org/printable.php?id=1040*.

Warren, M. 2001. *Dry Bones Rattling*. Princeton: Princeton University Press.

PART II

ACORN
Case Studies of Recent Work

6

ACORN and the Living Wage Movement

Stephanie Luce

As early as 1997 Robert Kuttner called living wage campaigns "the most interesting (and under-reported) grass roots enterprise to emerge since the civil rights movement" (Kuttner 1997). By 1999, observers noted that the city-based campaigns were creating the foundation for a new social movement, and employer organizations were calling the living wage movement a serious threat. As of 2008, it seems clear that the living wage movement has been one of the most successful policy efforts of the last several decades.

One of the reasons for that success—indeed, perhaps one of the definitions of success—is that the movement has been truly a grassroots effort. No one national organization has run the movement, and no one model of campaign has dominated. Instead, in every city the campaigns take their own form, shaped by a particular congruence of community organizations, unions, faith-based groups, students, and workers. Yet there is one organization that stands out as instrumental to the success of many of the campaigns—ACORN. ACORN has been organizing in low-income communities for the past thirty-five years and in the last decade has played a key role in many of the living wage campaigns and the larger movement.

This chapter examines the various contributions ACORN has made to the living wage movement. The material is based on interviews with ACORN staff, other living wage activists, and my own personal observations as a participant in the living wage movement over the past dozen years. The chapter offers an assessment of the campaign outcomes for workers covered by living wage ordinances and the organizations involved in the movement, including ACORN. I argue that ACORN has made a significant contribution due to its ability to fight for higher wages for its own members and also its willingness to assist other organizations do the same.

The Living Wage Movement

The modern living wage movement had its start in Baltimore, Maryland, in 1994, when clergy members and union leaders pressured their city council into adopting an ordinance requiring any firm receiving public dollars for service contracts to pay their employees a living wage. A *living wage* at the time was defined as an hourly wage high enough to bring a full-time worker with a family up to the federal poverty line. While it was obvious that the federal poverty line is not a real living wage, the victory was crucial in providing a substantial raise to low-wage workers.[1] At the time, the federal minimum wage was $4.25 per hour, and the Baltimore law would bring the wage up to $7.70.

The term *living wage* was not new. Neither was the idea of attaching wage standards to public money. It is the idea behind the Davis-Bacon "prevailing wage" laws attached to federal and some state and local public dollars spent on construction work, as well as the federal Service Contract Act.[2] It was also pushed in earlier years by local activists in a few cities who demanded that public subsidies have minimum requirements attached to them. But the Baltimore campaign was the first to bring together a visible grassroots campaign, the demand that local governments find solutions to working poverty, and the term *living wage*. The idea quickly spread to other cities, where activists saw a campaign that could bring together a wide range of supporters and that could win.

Over the next decade activists around the country launched living wage campaigns, resulting in more than 140 victories by 2008. The ordinances were not the same everywhere, but most required employers holding service contracts with a city to pay their workers a wage close to the federal poverty line. Some also applied to employers receiving public subsidies for economic development and those operating concessions on city-owned property, such as airports and ports. Some ordinances also directly covered city and county employees, and in 2006, a tribal council in Sandia Pueblo, New Mexico, passed the first Pueblo minimum wage, setting a minimum of $8.18 an hour for all workers.

The living wage is not always defined as the same amount. Some ordinances set it at the hourly rate needed for a full-time worker with a family of four to meet the federal poverty threshold. In some cities, the living wage was set at 110 percent or 120 percent of the poverty threshold. The majority of ordinances indexed the wage rate so that it would rise automatically each year with the cost of living. Many of the ordinances also included a provision that required employers who did not provide health benefits to pay their workers an additional hourly wage premium.

ACORN and Living Wage Campaigns

ACORN members and staff have been fighting on economic issues for several decades. In the 1980s, many of its campaigns were aimed at corporate accountability and job creation, demanding that companies receiving tax breaks be required to create jobs and to give first preference in hiring to low-income or unemployed community members. But ACORN realized that job creation wasn't enough: if all the new jobs paid minimum wage, workers would still be in poverty. According to Steve Kest, Executive Director of ACORN, it was "an easy leap into living wage campaigns"—attaching a living wage demand onto the corporate accountability ordinances such as first source hiring agreements (Kest 2005).

According to ACORN staff member Jen Kern, the organization also had other motivations to be involved in the campaigns. First, it was clear that the living wage concept was popular with most people (as evidenced in consistent public polling support for higher minimum wage laws) and with many organizations. The campaigns offered a chance to build coalitions with new allies or strengthen existing partnerships. ACORN was particularly interested in working in coalition with labor unions.

Second, the campaigns provided a chance for ACORN to grow its base. Living wage campaigns provided an opportunity to talk to potential members in the community. Kest notes that wages had always been an issue with members and potential members, and therefore the living wage concept was a natural fit. The campaigns also offered ACORN a chance to demonstrate their power through rallies, public meetings, delegations to meet with legislators, and media coverage.

Finally, fighting on the wage issue made sense at the time. By the early 1990s, the real value of the federal minimum wage had fallen significantly below its historic high. Both the Republican and Democratic parties had been reluctant to increase the minimum wage, so by the end of the 1980s, it was at $3.35 per hour, the lowest it had been in real terms since 1955, and approximately 29 percent below the value needed for a full-time worker with a family of four to meet the federal poverty line (Luce 2004). By the early 1990s, almost a third of all American workers were earning an hourly wage below that amount.

ACORN's initial involvement with a living wage campaign came in

1995, right after the Baltimore victory. At the time, ACORN was active in a burgeoning political party effort called the New Party. The New Party was building chapters around the country, many in cities where ACORN served as a base. In 1995, the New Party and ACORN launched living wage campaigns in Minneapolis and St. Paul, Minnesota. The campaign was run as a ballot initiative and was grossly outspent, ending in defeat. But the coalition pushed the cities to establish a Joint Twin Cities Living Wage Task Force to develop recommendations on establishing a living wage in the cities. The St. Paul City Council unanimously adopted the recommendations of the Task Force in January 1997, and the Minneapolis City Council followed in March 1997. Both cities now require any firm receiving $100,000 or more for economic development assistance to pay their employees an hourly rate equal to 110 percent of the federal poverty line for a family of four (or 100 percent of the poverty line if they provide health insurance). They also require that at least 60 percent of new jobs created through the subsidies be given to residents of the city. In addition, the Minneapolis policy prohibits the city from privatizing services at a lower wage than is currently paid to city employees performing the work. Moreover, firms that agree to remain neutral in union organizing campaigns, offer card-check recognition, or provide workplace access during nonwork hours to union organizers receive preference in obtaining economic development assistance (City of Minneapolis 2005).

Around the same time as the Minneapolis and St. Paul campaigns, ACORN helped launch campaigns for a citywide minimum wage in Houston and Denver. These ballot initiatives, like the initial Minneapolis campaign, were greatly outspent and eventually defeated. But ACORN staff devoted a lot of energy to these efforts and saw in them great potential to build the organization and work with new allies. Jen Kern was a full-time national campaign staff for ACORN at this time, meaning that she worked on various initiatives. But by the summer of 1996, she was spending a great deal of time on living wage work. By 1997, ACORN was getting a lot of calls from activists around the country interested in getting involved in living wage work. It was clear that there was enough interest in living wage campaigns to sustain a full-time job. Kern was shifted to focus full time on living wages. In 1998, ACORN decided to establish the Living Wage Resource Center, with Kern as its full-time staff person. Her job was to strategize on ACORN's living wage work and assist its living wage campaigns but also to provide technical assistance to non-ACORN campaigns. This latter piece was unique for ACORN, as well as within the world of organizing.

The Living Wage Resource Center (LWRC) officially debuted at a conference in Boston in 1998. ACORN brought together representatives from campaigns around the country to talk about the burgeoning movement and strategies to win. By this time ACORN had run and won a "traditional" living wage ordinance in Boston and had a citywide minimum wage campaign underway in New Orleans.

The LWRC meant that ACORN would now play a greater role in the larger movement. Not only was ACORN directly involved in a number of the campaigns, but it was now providing resources to all campaigns. Kern worked with David Reynolds, a labor educator at Wayne State University, to create a living wage campaign manual that included the basics of running a campaign. She worked with ACORN staff to establish a website that became known as the official track record of campaign victories and ongoing campaigns. She read all related research, for and against living wage ordinances, and helped explain it to activists and summarize it for the media. She spent hours on the phone and e-mail, as well as face to face with people, helping activists build coalitions, develop campaign strategy, locate necessary resources and research, conduct their own research, interpret city code, talk to city councilors and the media, convert "no" votes to "yes" votes, and win a campaign.

In addition, Kern and the LWRC also sponsored national living wage campaign conferences. The first one was held in Boston in 1998, a second in Baltimore in 2000, and a third in Baltimore in November 2003. The conferences brought together hundreds of activists from scores of campaigns around the country. By 2003, the movement was broad enough to support different tracks: workshops for beginners just starting campaigns, workshops on implementation for those who had already got an ordinance passed, and workshops on next steps beyond the campaigns to keep the coalition together and fighting for economic justice.

Kern has relied on her own experience as ACORN national campaign staff, as well as the expertise of ACORN organizers, to advise campaigns around the country. She recommends that coalitions follow basic guidelines to build a campaign that will win and accomplish other goals, such as demonstrating political power and building organizations. The best campaigns, argues Kern, utilize both an "inside track" and an "outside track." The inside track refers to the lobbying efforts directed at moving the city council to vote for the proposed ordinance. The campaign should build delegations to meet one-on-one with each city councilor. Each visit with a council member has two purposes. First, the delegation should gather information, assessing where that councilor stands on the ordinance and how strong his or her support or opposition is. Second, visits are meant to pressure and persuade the councilor to vote for the ordinance and to urge fellow councilors to do the same. In order to persuade, the delegations should demonstrate to the city council member the depth of the coalition. Delegations might involve prominent leaders from the community, especially those from a councilor's district or ward. The delegation should also make sure the councilor knows the full list of groups and individuals supporting the campaign. Hopefully, that list of supporters grows with each visit. Councilors must see that their constituents want the living wage passed, and they must understand that there will be political repercussions for failing to support the ordinance (Luce 2004).

In addition to the inside track, living wage campaigns should pursue the outside track—the work done in the community. Kern (2003) argues that an inside track is not enough on its own: even if you could get an ordinance passed only by talking to legislators, you wouldn't want to, because you would miss out on the opportunity to build coalitions, do public education, and demonstrate your power as a coalition. Most likely, she proposes, you will need to build a coalition with power in order to get a solid ordinance with teeth passed. Kern works with campaigns to develop a strategic plan, involving escalating tactics. Early in the campaign, the coalition might focus on educational activities and on nonconfrontational tactics, like sending postcards to elected officials. A next step might be door knocking with a cell phone in hand, asking residents to support the campaign and to call their councilors right there. From there, a coalition may hold rallies outside council members' homes or public actions, and even participate in civil disobedience.

One of the strengths, and challenges, for living wage campaigns is that the different organizations involved in the campaign often come in with a preference or history in either inside or outside tactics but not both. For example, many labor unions have become used to a model of lobbying elected officials and avoiding more direct action. Some unions may try to avoid public activities that could embarrass mayors or councilors whom labor groups consider allies. On the other hand, student groups may have little experience going to City Hall to talk to legislators and may prefer to engage in more confrontational approaches. The challenge of the coalition is to bring the strengths and experiences of the different groups into one campaign. The Living Wage Resource Center has been a key factor in getting various organizations on board for a coordinated campaign. In addition, ACORN brings its own particular organizing strengths to the campaigns. According to Steve Kest, one of the contributions ACORN can make is that, "given who we are, how we do the work, and who are members are, we are able to put our members front and center leading the campaigns, testifying and lobbying—not just to trot them out, but to be real leaders" (Kest 2005). Kest says that there are other groups involved in living wage campaigns who also involve their members, but "this is something that grows directly out of our organizing approach" (Kest 2005).

Some Examples

In this section, I describe three different living wage campaigns: the Chicago "traditional ordinance" campaign led by ACORN and labor unions; the Florida statewide minimum wage campaign also led by ACORN; and the living wage campaign in San Diego, where another organization led a "traditional ordinance" campaign and ACORN played an important role as a coalition partner. I choose these three cases as examples of the different kinds of living wage campaigns in which ACORN has been involved. I also discuss the role that the LWRC has played in a few campaigns where ACORN was not a part of the campaign on the ground.

Chicago
One of the early campaigns that ACORN initiated took place in Chicago. In the summer of 1995, Chicago ACORN and the Service Employees International Union Local (SEIU) 880 (which began as an independent union affiliated with ACORN and has maintained a close relationship after affiliating with SEIU) put together a steering committee of groups interested in pursuing a living wage campaign. This included a total of sixty organizations, including the Chicago Coalition for the Homeless, the American Federation of State, County and Municipal Employees, the International Brotherhood of Teamsters, and the United Food and Commercial Workers. The committee proposed to require service contractors and recipients of economic development financial assistance to pay their workers a living wage of $7.60 per hour. Ballot initiatives are only advisory (nonbinding) in the state, so the coalition had no choice but to push for the wage increase through city legislation.

The campaign pursued both "inside" and "outside" tactics. Activists engaged in systematic meetings with the fifty-member Aldermen of the Chicago City Council, assessing their positions and asking them to sign on in support of the campaign. In each visit, the coalition attempted to demonstrate its power and the size of its support by bringing in voters from the aldermen's wards and community and labor leaders representing large organizations. The "outside" campaign involved public actions to gain media attention and demonstrate the power of the coalition. In December 2005, the campaign organized a kickoff rally at a Teamster Hall, and more than 750 people showed up. At this event, thirteen aldermen publicly endorsed the living wage. From there, the campaign escalated their mobilization efforts, holding more and larger rallies, door-knocking, and sending letters from labor leaders and a Catholic cardinal to Mayor Richard M. Daley. When SEIU held its national convention in the city, delegates marched in the street in support of the campaign, and AFL-CIO president John Sweeney met with Mayor Daley.

Eventually, twenty-six of the fifty aldermen agreed to cosponsor the proposal, and another ten agreed to vote in favor. The issue was introduced to the council in May 1996, with over 500 supporters in the audience. However, Mayor Daley announced publicly that while he supported the concept, he would veto the living wage ordinance. This decision was particularly important because, unlike in other cities, the Chicago mayor holds strong power over the city council. Daley claimed that the city could not afford the ordinance, based on a chamber of commerce study. In response, the campaign stepped up its visibility. Organizers held direct actions on Farley Candy and Whole Foods—companies receiving tax breaks or holding city contracts but paying below the proposed living wage. David Reynolds, a labor educator at Wayne State, and Jen Kern detail some of the actions in their living wage manual (Reynolds and Kern 2002):

> On a Teamster building across from the 1996 Democratic Party National Convention, the campaign unfurled a huge sign trumpeting the Living Wage. Activists successfully sued to gain access to Navy Pier in order to picket the Mayor while he welcomed the Democratic delegates to the city. The campaign organized a "tours of shame" for delegates to visit low-wage paying recipients of local corporate welfare. *Streetwise*, a paper sold on the streets by the city's homeless, ran a special Living Wage issue. (Reynolds and the ACORN Living Wage Resource Center 1998)

In the end, the campaign decided to put the issue to a vote, even without the mayor's support. They wanted to do this to put each alderman on public record and to use that vote in pushing for greater accountability in future elections. In 1997, two years after the coalition formed, the issue came to a vote. The mayor wanted to avoid public accountability for the aldermen falling into line with him, so living wage supporters attempting to enter city council chambers to witness the vote were told they could not enter because it was already full. A handful of supporters who had gotten inside sent out word that there were plenty of open seats. At this point, the hundreds of locked-out living wage activists attempted to push through, and police arrested six prominent organizers. In the end, only seventeen of the aldermen voted in favor, with thirty-one against and two abstentions.

However, the coalition's work had built a solid base of support for the living wage in the community, established stronger ties between coalition members, and strengthened some aldermen's commitment to living wage issues. Living wage supporters continued to work together on related issues in the city, securing some victories. They began to build a "Payback Time" campaign for the 1999 elections, to punish the aldermen who had voted against the ordinance. With the lead of the New Party, the activists went ward by ward to get petitions signed in support of a living wage. "Living Wage Score Card" posters were printed and hung in the neighborhoods of the most vulnerable aldermen, showing the community how their aldermen voted and encouraging people to vote against those who voted no on the living wage. Candidates began feeling pressure. In 1998, the mayor and aldermen considered giving themselves a large raise. Living Wage supporters saw an opportunity to put the living wage squarely in the public eye, highlighting the hypocrisy of a council that would give itself raises but not pass a living wage ordinance for low-wage workers. The city council turned around and passed the ordinance unanimously.

The initial success in Chicago spurred a successful living wage campaign in the broader Cook County area, as well as living wage proposals at the state level. It also led to a successful campaign by Illinois ACORN president and retired postal worker Ted Thomas. Thomas had never been in office before but was elected alderman for the fifteenth ward, based on his support for the living wage. He defeated eleven other candidates in the primary, including Mayor Daley's chosen candidate. Since the initial victory in 1998, the living wage campaign came back together in 2002 to raise the wage to $9.05 and add annual indexing, and again in 2006 to pass a "Big Box" living wage, which would have required all large retailers (such as Wal-Mart and Target) to pay ten dollars an hour. The Big Box ordinance was eventually vetoed by Mayor Daley, but the campaign resulted in several major victories, including a sea change on the board of aldermen in the following election, when voters selected the largest number of newly elected pro–living wage and pro-labor aldermen in recent history.

Florida

By 2002, the living wage movement had momentum, despite the impacts of the economic recession, 9/11, and the Iraq war. But by this time it was also clear that the movement needed to expand. Over one hundred cities, including most of the major ones, had already passed traditional ordinances. To cover more people, the movement needed to pursue new strategies. Citywide minimum wage laws were not allowed in every state, depending on home rule, and furthermore some states were attempting to pass new legislation outlawing local living wage laws. Living wage advocates decided it was time to pursue more statewide minimum wage campaigns.

States have always had the ability to pass their own state minimum wage laws with wage levels surpassing the federal standard. In fact, the first minimum wage legislation in the country was passed at the state level, starting with Massachusetts in 1912. But by the early 1990s, the federal minimum wage stagnated, and many states had also failed to raise their own minimum wages. The living wage movement helped spark momentum for activists to start campaigning to increase their minimum wage levels. For example, the ACORN national living wage conferences held workshops on statewide minimum wage campaigns. In the mid-1990s a few states raised their wage levels through ballot initiative (such as California and Washington) or through the state legislature (such as Massachusetts). Living wage activists decided to increase the number of states with minimum wage laws, and to use the campaigns as a way to turn out voters for the heated 2004 presidential election. ACORN worked with attorney Paul Sonn of the Brennan Center for Justice at the New York University School of Law to find which states would allow for ballot initiatives.

ACORN was the major organization behind the 2004 campaign to establish a statewide minimum wage law in Florida. The campaign was run as a ballot initiative to amend the state constitution, setting a state minimum wage starting at one dollar above the federal level and indexed to rise each year with inflation. ACORN worked with a community and labor coalition called Floridians for All to first collect almost 1 million signatures to qualify for the ballot and then called for voters to pass the initiative.

In general, it is not hard to convince voters to raise the minimum wage. The U.S. public has fairly consistently supported a higher minimum wage in polls. However, when it comes time to vote, minimum wage opponents easily outspend the proponents, sometimes making for an unequal competition. Business interests (the retail association in particular) in Florida raised large sums to combat the initiative, called Amendment 5. In the months before the November election, the state was hit hard by a series of four hurricanes. Living wage opponents created a television commercial against the measure: it showed footage of the four hurricanes and suggested Amendment 5 would be the equivalent of a fifth hurricane hitting the state, leaving children without care and abandoning the elderly to die on the streets.

Despite the extensive campaign against it, Amendment 5 prevailed on election day, with 71 percent of voters in favor. Indeed, it won in every single county in the state, even the ones going handily to George Bush. Economist Robert Pollin argues in his book *Contours of Descent* that John Kerry would now be president of the United States if he had only been willing to associate himself with Amendment 5 (Pollin 2005b). Pollin notes that Amendment 5 received 1.1 million more votes from Florida voters than did John Kerry, and that Kerry needed only 400,000 of those votes to reverse the outcome of the state's presidential vote, and therefore the country's.

How did Amendment 5 fare so well, despite the strong opposition from employer organizations and the lack of strong endorsement from major political candidates? In part, the issue itself is persuasive with voters. But it takes organization to get the issue to the public. ACORN and the coalition ran an extensive campaign to educate voters. In a ten-day, fifteen-city bus tour, ACORN members, Reverends Jesse Jackson and Al Sharpton, state senator Tony Hill, and others urged Floridians to vote in favor of Amendment 5. ACORN also helped coordinate large-scale rallies with speakers such as Michael Moore and Roseanne Barr. On the day of the election, ACORN ran get-out-the-vote efforts in thirteen cities, with over 1,600 volunteers.

San Diego

The San Diego living wage campaign was initiated by the Center for Policy Initiatives and the Interfaith Committee on Worker Justice. It was launched in a public rally in the summer of 2003. ACORN was relatively new in the area and joined the coalition as a member after the campaign was underway. In this role, ACORN contributed by collecting postcards from its members in favor of the campaign, doing turnout for meetings, and having a member testify to the city council. In addition, the local ACORN helped the campaign through enlisting the resources of the Living Wage Resource Center.

The coalition had to struggle to get the issue to a vote: the mayor has power to set the city council agenda, and so he simply refused to schedule it for a hearing. Living wage activists therefore not only had to convince council members to vote in favor of the ordinance but had to refer to a rarely used clause in the city charter in order to force the issue to a vote (Conlan 2005). Four council members signed on, and the issue finally came before the city council in April 2005. After a six-hour meeting, the city council passed the ordinance by a five-to-four vote. The ordinance requires contractors to pay ten dollars an hour with health benefits, or twelve dollars an hour if they don't provide heath benefits.

Living Wage Resource Center

In addition to the campaigns listed above, ACORN has played a major role in the living wage movement by assisting campaigns through the Living Wage Resource Center. Jen Kern notes that, from the beginning, the LWRC was set up and funded to assist campaigns whether a local ACORN chapter was involved or not. That means that the majority of living wage campaigns in the country have had at least some interaction with Kern.

For example, the Reverend Rebekah Jordan has worked closely with Kern over the last several years to establish a living wage campaign in Memphis, Tennessee. Her organization, the Mid-South Interfaith Network for Economic Justice, began in the year 2000 (Jordan 2005). At that time, the local labor council had heard about the living wage movement and was interested in starting a campaign (Jordan 2005). They gathered some information, but the campaign did not take off. Once Jordan started work, she ordered the living wage manual through ACORN and called Kern with follow-up questions. From there, they began regular communication to establish and run the Memphis campaign. Jordan says that the area in which Kern has been the greatest help is in thinking up a strategic plan. "There is a tendency to just use things in the campaign that you've heard about from other campaigns, but that might not work for us here," says Jordan. "Jen came here and helped us connect our campaign to the larger national movement, but also helped us craft ideas of how to move our campaign when specific challenges come up." This work involves assistance with research or putting the campaign in touch with other organizers from other campaigns. For example, when the Memphis campaign "hit a major roadblock" and found that city council members would not even meet with them, Kern put Jordan in touch with Gyula Nagy, organizer from the Alexandria, Virginia, living wage campaign. The Alexandria campaign had faced a similar situation: when they first announced their living wage proposal, the city council was unanimously opposed. Nagy helped develop the idea of a "Council-Meter," to assess each council member on their position on the living wage ordinance and assess the opportunities to move them to a more favorable position. When the Memphis group felt they would benefit from talking to other Southern cities campaigns, Kern put them in touch with Cindia Cameron of the Atlanta living wage coalition. Jordan adds that she went to one of the Baltimore living wage conferences and saw that the LWRC "is really what it is supposed to be. It is the best place to go to find things out" (Jordan 2005).

Cindia Cameron, Organizing Director for 9to5, National Association of Working Women, based in Atlanta, has a similar perspective. When she first started talking about the idea of an Atlanta living wage campaign, a colleague who had had positive experiences working with ACORN in the Denver campaign suggested Cameron start by calling Jen Kern (Cameron 2005). Cameron says that the LWRC helped the Atlanta campaign in two ways. First, Kern provided technical assistance by connecting the Atlanta activists to all the resources they needed. Through Kern, Cameron got access to academics Robert Pollin, Mark Brenner, and Stephanie Luce and to legal assistance from Paul Sonn. She got data and information about previous campaigns and made connections with other living wage activists. "We just don't have the resources to do that kind of thing on our own," says Cameron. "As a small community organization we couldn't just hire a lawyer on our own to help figure out the legal requirements" (2005). Cameron notes that the LWRC makes for an efficient use of resources for the movement as a whole.

Cameron adds that her connection with Kern "made us really smart. It made us really credible. We could walk into a meeting with City Council members and answer their questions" (2005). In addition, Kern helped the Atlanta campaign walk through some of the issues that were likely to come up and provided guidance about which issues were important. "We saved ourselves a huge amount of time, not having to track down data that wasn't really relevant," said Cameron. Some activists in the coalition were used to approaching campaigns as organizers, but not all members of the coalition had that experience. "Jen and Gyula [Nagy] were able to come in and say, 'This is what we've learned from other campaigns,' which was very helpful for getting everyone in our coalition to think strategically." Bringing in outsiders to facilitate can be useful in this process.

The Living Wage Resource Center has also worked with activists running campaigns in Vermont (what they call livable wage campaigns). Ellen David-Friedman is an organizer with the National Education Association (NEA) in Vermont. She has a long personal history with ACORN, being a fellow undergraduate and friend of a number of future ACORN organizers. She also attended an ACORN training in Little Rock early in her organizing life. She met up with ACORN again through her work on livable wage campaigns. Jen Kern came to Vermont in the late 1990s, to attend a Livable Wage conference. Kern assisted on some of the traditional livable wage campaigns in the state but also began working with David-Friedman to use the livable wage concept to "fuel dozens of collective bargaining battles with unionized, low wage school support staff workers" (David-Friedman 2005). The idea was to fight for livable wages for a portion of the union's members who were receiving very low wages. David-Friedman explains: "With teacher membership still massively dominant (in my home affiliate for example—Vermont-NEA—support staff comprise only about 25% of membership), it took a certain amount of steady gumption, good will and keen skill to raise the livable wage issue high on the organization's agenda. Since Jen is a missionary (with due apologies for unintended implications), and since she is both very smart and very relationally skilled, I had the joy of observing her win over hearts and minds" (2005).

David-Friedman and Kern were successful in convincing the NEA locally and nationally to take up the living wage campaign. "Now, after just a few years, we can observe that the NEA has thoroughly committed itself to the program of living wages for education support staff members," says David-Friedman. "The national organization provides staff, research, grants, publicity, organizing and training to support state and local affiliates." This achievement was due to the hard work of talented and committed organizers like Ellen David-Friedman herself, but she also credits the LWRC's contribution: "Jen brought an integrity and clarity of purpose that helped many of us guide things in this direction; a benefit which will now flow to many, many thousands of low wage workers."

While Kern is the public face of the Living Wage Resource Center, she is quick to point out that her contributions are not hers alone but the culmination of the best of the lessons learned from ACORN organizers around the country. These lessons come from living wage campaign organizing as well as other ACORN campaigns that have helped the organization develop sophisticated approaches to working with the media, planning public actions, lobbying, and building community support. Kern is usually on her own in her day-to-day work with campaigns but gets significant support when needed from her ACORN colleagues.

Outcomes

ACORN has clearly been a major force in the living wage movement. By 2008, living wage activists had won over 140 campaigns around the country. Of these, ACORN was a leading force in fourteen and a significant coalition partner in another six. The LWRC played a significant role in an additional fifteen campaigns (Table 6.1). However, there are only a handful of remaining campaigns in which the LWRC had no contact, and it continues to play a strong role in a number of ongoing campaigns.

In addition to the "traditional ordinances," ACORN played a large role in the effort to pass statewide minimum wage laws. By 2006, thirty-

Table 6.1. ACORN influence in city and county living wage campaigns

ACORN-led	ACORN as major coalition partner	LWRC played major role
Albuquerque, NM	Detroit, MI	Alexandria, VA
Boston, MA	Orlando, FL	Bloomington, IN
Chicago, IL	Philadelphia, PA	Brookline, MA
Cook County, IL	San Diego, CA	Buffalo, NY
Denver, CO	San Francisco, CA	Cambridge, MA
Hempstead, NY	San Jose, CA	Manchester, CT
Minneapolis, MN		Marin County, CA
New Orleans, LA		Memphis, TN
New York, NY		Missoula, MT
Oakland, CA		Montgomery County, MD
Pine Bluff, AR		Pittsburgh, PA
Sacramento, CA		Santa Barbara, CA
St. Louis, MO		Santa Fe, NM
St. Paul, MN		Suffolk County, NY
		Westchester County, NY

one states had passed statewide minimum wage increases through ballot measures or legislative action. ACORN was instrumental in many of these, including the legislative efforts in states such as Massachusetts and Michigan, and ballot initiatives in states such as Florida, Missouri, and Arizona. The success of these campaigns created enough pressure on Congress to pass an increase in the federal minimum wage at the beginning of 2007.

Kern has also assisted the university campus movement for living wages. The national living wage conference in Baltimore hosted a meeting for campus activists, and students have constantly relied on Kern as a resource for running their own campaigns, conducting research, and networking with other campus activists.

Gains from the Living Wage Movement

In addition to getting ordinances passed, what have been the achievements of living wage activists? This aspect of the living wage movement is harder to measure, as few cities keep records of the number of workers covered under living wage ordinances. The existing research shows that the monetary gains for the average covered worker can be significant (Pollin and Luce 1998; Howes 2005; Brenner 2005; and Reich, Hall, and Jacobs 2003). For example, a recent study found that the Los Angeles living wage ordinance has increased pay for about 10,000 jobs (Fairris, Runsten, Briones, and Goodheart 2005). For the initial 8,000 affected, the average pay raise was about 20 percent, or $2,600 per year. Subsequent workers have received about a $1,300 per year raise. While opponents claim living wage raises will go to wealthy workers and teenagers, the study found that most of the affected workers are from poor or low-income families and that only 4 percent are teenagers.

In another recent study, Mark Brenner and Stephanie Luce found that covered workers earning below the living wage in Boston in 1998 experienced significant increases to their wages due to the ordinance (Brenner and Luce 2005). Hourly wages rose, on average, by 23 percent, while annual income rose by an average of $10,000, from $16,990 to $26,990 a year. This significant boost to annual income resulted from a higher hourly wage but also an average increase in hours worked. In Boston, it appears that some employers adjusted to the living wage by converting part-time employees to full-time.

In my own work (Luce 2004), I attempt to provide a rough estimate of the money won in higher wages through living wage campaigns. A conservative estimate suggests that as of mid-2004, as much as three-quarters of a billion dollars was redistributed from firms, city governments, and consumers into the paychecks of low-wage workers, at an average of $3,000 per year per worker. Of course, this increase in income would not translate into a $3,000 net gain, as workers must pay taxes and may lose out on eligibility for selected public services. However, this crude exercise shows the potential redistributive power of the living wage movement, even when coverage is relatively low. If we include the impact of statewide and federal minimum wage increases, the coverage expands dramatically.

In addition to the specific outcomes for covered workers, many agree that the living wage movement has had a larger impact on how the term is used and perceived by the general public. Steve Kest says, "We've contributed to the whole popularization of the concept of living wage. It was nowhere on the agenda ten years ago; now, everyone talks about it." The term *living wage* now has political relevance. In addition, Kest notes that ACORN has helped promote the "notion that the wage floor should be decided by democratic process rather than imposed by a privatized corporate process" (2005).

Building ACORN
ACORN has experienced a lot of growth in the last decade. It's difficult to say what the source of the growth is, but it is likely that the living wage movement has contributed. Steve Kest notes that ACORN has delivered increased wages to a lot of workers: "The numbers from the living wage campaigns aren't as large as we'd like, but if you add in the minimum wage campaigns it becomes a significant income transfer to low-wage workers" (2005). Certainly, this change has helped ACORN's efforts to build its membership. Jen Kern adds that living wage ordinances themselves are not enough to transform the conditions that lead to low-wage work: "We don't just think poor people should get programs, we think they should join ACORN and get a collective voice to contest for power for their own community" (Stone 2005).

In addition, Kest notes that the living wage is a significant issue for the organization. He says that there are a few issues, such as redlining and voter mobilization, that people now associate with ACORN. Kest argues that the living wage is now one of the top three issues that he thinks the group is known for, and that "this has created an extremely positive image for us, in the eyes of our members, allies, potential allies, funders, and others" (2005).

Some activists note that they had not heard of ACORN until they got involved in a living wage campaign; others had a vague idea but little interaction with the group. Others in the living wage movement have developed ongoing relations with ACORN and individuals, such as academics and lawyers like Robert Pollin and Paul Sonn. For example, Pollin, an economist, says that he knew little about ACORN when he first got involved in conducting living wage research more than ten years ago (2005). In 1998, Jen Kern contacted him about doing a study of the citywide living wage proposal in New Orleans. Pollin had already done a study of the proposed living wage ordinance in Los Angeles, but he had not been involved in the actual campaign. He went to New Orleans in 2000 for an economics association meeting, and ACORN arranged for him to speak to the campaign there about the living wage. Pollin thought he would address a small meeting just for organizers and policy people and was surprised to find it was a large public event in a black church. He was impressed by the size of the crowd as well as the liveliness of the event. For him, this anecdote stands out in his memory as capturing the vibrancy of the New Orleans campaign.

Paul Sonn provides legal assistance to living wage campaigns through the Brennan Center for Social Justice. His work is closely connected to the work of the Living Wage Resource Center, as he and Kern often work together to assist campaigns. "I've worked with Jen on probably a dozen or more living wage or minimum wage campaigns," says Sonn. "It's been one of the most rewarding partnerships of my professional life. The commitment, energy and smarts that Jen brings to her work are incredible and have played a major role in enabling this movement to succeed and grow" (Sonn 2005). These new relationships are important because they provide ACORN access to experts and resources for future campaigns.

More significantly, ACORN has built and solidified relationships with other organizations. The living wage movement has been the key to building relationships with groups such as Working Partnerships in San Jose, the Center for Policy Initiatives in San Diego, the Tenant and Workers Resource Center in Alexandria, the Boston Labor Council and the statewide AFL-CIO in Massachusetts, and the National Educational Association in Vermont and nationally.

The Living Wage Resource Center has been a successful strategy for ACORN. Kest notes that the organization is "replicating that strategy to a greater or lesser degree in other areas such as predatory lending and voter work" (2005). The resource center model allows ACORN to provide resources to support their own campaigns internally, as well as to provide external assistance. So far, those new resource centers do not have the size and scope of the LWRC, but the model, developed and refined through living wage work, is effective.

Building a Movement

As Rebekah Jordan and Cindia Cameron point out, the Living Wage Resource Center helped them build stronger campaigns as well as develop ties with other activists around the country. New relationships—both within the campaigns, as well as in the larger movement—have been sustained in many places. The Atlanta campaign was successful in 2003 in getting the city council to increase direct worker wages to $10.50 per hour, providing raises of $400 to $4,000 per year for approximately 650 city employees, and in 2005 this wage was indexed to the Consumer Price Index. They were successful in getting the city council to pass a preference program for living wage employers in city service contracts by a vote of thirteen to one in January 2005. However, the state legislature, pressured by Delta Airlines, passed a statewide preemption bill two months later. Despite this, Cameron still believes the campaign was successful: "We got a majority of the city council to agree that $10.50 an hour was the wage that employers should pay." In addition, the campaign built a coalition of one hundred endorsing groups, representing over 200,000 people. Today, that coalition is ongoing. There are eight to ten groups that regularly participate in the group at some level and another ten to twelve that can be called on when needed. "This is a coalition of groups that had not worked together before," says Cameron (2005). "We now have a long-term, ongoing coalition addressing issues related to working poverty." The Georgia Living Wage Coalition, with active local organizations in three additional cities, has been building support for a statewide Good Jobs First bill, and is engaged in a campaign to raise the state minimum wage.

Jordan believes that the many campaigns around the country would not be working together so much without the LWRC: "Jen answers things directly but also refers you to the people you need to talk to" (2005). It is clear that ACORN played a large role in building a movement for living wages over the past decade.

Conclusion

After fourteen years of organizing, living wage supporters had won local ordinances in over 140 cities and counties, living wage policies in a handful of universities, citywide minimum wage laws in several cities, and statewide minimum wage increases in thirty-one states. In the spring of 2007, the U.S. Senate voted to increase the federal minimum wage, from $5.15

to $7.25 over three years. Approximately 13 million workers—about one out of every eleven employed persons in the country—saw their wages go up in July 2007.

What is next for the living wage movement? With so many victories, is there room to move forward? Living wage activists relish the success but see many opportunities for further work. The federal minimum wage and most of the state minimum wages are not indexed to inflation, meaning that the struggle to make the wages closer to a living wage is ongoing. There are also ongoing efforts to make sure that the living wage and minimum wage policies are enforced. In addition, living wage campaigns have undertaken new kinds of campaigns aimed at improving conditions for low-wage workers. These include new kinds of wage policies, such as the "Big Box" ordinances and other industry-specific policies, as well as ordinances that provide health care for employees. ACORN has now launched a broad effort to pass paid sick days ordinances in cities and states.

Over the past decade, the living wage movement and ACORN have developed a mutually beneficial relationship. While the movement is larger than any one organization, ACORN has been an integral part of its growth. ACORN chapters have helped run major "traditional ordinance" campaigns in places like Chicago and Boston, initiate the idea of citywide minimum wage campaigns in cities like New Orleans and Denver, and spark a renewed effort to raise statewide minimum wages in states like Massachusetts and Florida. The Living Wage Resource Center has been a backbone of the movement, providing technical assistance, strategic planning, networking, access to information, and a place to gather and analyze lessons and stories of various campaigns. Jen Kern has assisted the vast majority of living wage campaigns, directly and indirectly. Today, the interest in living wage campaigns has spread beyond the initial constituency, moving to college campuses and other countries, and Kern provides critical support to those as well. "The ACORN Living Wage Resource Center has made a tremendous difference in providing living wage and minimum wage activists the advice and technical support they need to run and win campaigns," says Paul Sonn. "Jen's extensive experience with campaign strategy and ability to provide help with messaging, policy questions and even research make her an invaluable resource, especially for smaller campaigns" (Sonn 2005).

At the same time, the living wage movement has had a significant impact on ACORN. According to its executive director, the movement has become one of the top three issues for which the organization is known. The campaigns have developed relationships with scores of new allies and generated reams of positive press for the group. While it is difficult to gauge actual numbers, there is no doubt that ACORN members have benefited directly from higher wages through the campaigns and won indirect benefits as well, such as through living wage–related unionization efforts.

In the final assessment, it is perhaps the opponents of the living wage movement who have had the most to say about ACORN's influence. A *City Journal* writer said, "ACORN has managed to get enacted into law in city councils proposals that the U.S. Congress would laugh off the stage" (Stern 2003). ACORN has been able to combine a large membership base, relationships with allies, and years of community-based organizing experience to play a key role in the movement for economic justice. Its contribution to the living wage movement is testimony to its foresight and power.

NOTES

The author thanks Matthew Luskin and two anonymous reviewers for their comments on this chapter.

1. For more on the adequacy of the federal poverty guidelines for measuring poverty, see Constance F. Citro and Robert T. Michael, eds., *Measuring Poverty: A New Approach* (Washington, DC: National Academies Press, 1995).

2. The Service Contract Act was passed in 1965 and requires any employer holding a service contract with the U.S. government or District of Columbia to pay the prevailing wage and benefit package of the locality, or the rates in any predecessor contractor's collective bargaining agreement. Contracts for less than $2,500 are exempt.

REFERENCES

Brenner, M. D. 2005. "The Economic Impact of the Boston Living Wage Ordinance." *Industrial Relations* 44, no. 1: 59–83.

Brenner, M. D., and S. Luce. 2005. "Living Wage Laws in Practice: The Boston, New Haven and Hartford Experiences." Amherst, MA: Political Economy Research Institute.

Cameron, C. 2005. Interview with the author. December 2.

City of Minneapolis. 2005. "Minneapolis Living Wage and Responsible Spending Ordinance." Ordinance 2005-OR-103.

Conlan, M. G. 2005. "San Diego Passes Living Wage Law, 5–4." *Zenger's Newsmagazine*. Available at *sandiego.indymedia.org/en/2005/04/108334. shtml*.

David-Friedman, E. 2005. E-mail correspondence with author. December 3.

Fairris, D., D. Runsten, C. Briones, and J. Goodheart. 2005. "Examining the Evidence: The Impact of the Los Angeles Living Wage Ordinance on Workers and Businesses."

Howes, C. 2005. "Living Wages and Retention of Homecare Workers in San Francisco." *Industrial Relations* 44, no. 1: 139–63.

Jordan, R. 2005. Interview with the author. November 23.

Kern, J. 2003. Interview with the author. July 20.

Kest, S. 2005. Interview with the author. November 30.

Kuttner, R. 1997. "Boston's 'Living Wage' Law Highlights New Grassroots Efforts to Fight Poverty." *Washington Post*, August 20.

Luce, S. 2004. *Fighting for a Living Wage*. Ithaca, NY: Cornell University Press.

Pollin, R. 2005a. Interview with the author. November 18.

———. 2005b. *Contours of Descent*. 2d ed. London: Verso.

Pollin, R., and S. Luce. 1998. *The Living Wage: Building a Fair Economy*. New York: New Press.

Reich, M., P. Hall, and K. Jacobs. 2003. *Living Wages and Economic Performance*. Berkeley: Institute of Industrial Relations, University of California.

Reynolds, D., and J. Kern. 2002. *Living Wage Campaigns: An Activist's Guide to Building the Movement for Economic Justice*. Washington, DC: ACORN.

Sonn, P. 2005. E-mail correspondence with author. December 3.

Stern, S. 2005. "ACORN's Nutty Regime for Cities." *City Journal*. Spring. Available at *www.city-journal.org/html/13_2_acorns_nutty_regime.html*.

Stone, A. R. 2005. "Campus Living Wage Project: Interviews with Activists." Available at *www.clwproject.org/Files/thecampuslivingwageproject.pdf*.

7

The Battle of Brooklyn
ACORN's Modus Operandi

John Atlas

Bertha Lewis remembers when she first heard about developer Bruce Ratner's plan to "revitalize" a decaying Brooklyn neighborhood. It was at a September 4, 2003, rally for Letitia "Tish" James, a candidate for a city council seat to be determined in November. James was running on the union-backed Working Families Party ticket—a leftist third party created in part by ACORN and co-chaired by Lewis. If she won, it would be the first time since the 1970s that a minor party would elect one of its own members to the New York City Council.

James was a veteran politician with incredible street smarts and a shrewd in-fighter in City Hall. Lewis was one of James's key supporters and a valuable political ally not only because of her personal charm and political savvy but also because she was a veteran political organizer with an important constituency base. Lewis served as executive director of New York ACORN, an organization with 35,000 dues-paying members who could be mobilized to vote as a bloc and, if necessary, to protest, to hold politicians' feet to the fire. Ratner, a wealthy and powerful figure in New York politics, had just won a battle between moguls who dreamed of becoming big-time sports owners. Ratner managed to swipe the New Jersey Nets, a pro basketball team, off the auction block with a bid of $300 million, ending an acrimonious three-month bidding war with Charles Kushner, a New Jersey developer, and his partner, Jon Corzine, then a U.S. senator and later New Jersey governor.

The Plan

Ratner was the chief executive officer and chair of Forest City Ratner Companies (FCRC). He planned to move the Nets to Brooklyn to play in a new 20,000-seat arena, the crown jewel of a $2.5 billion development named Atlantic Yards. Ratner had hired celebrity architect Frank Gehry to design the massive project, which included twelve skyscrapers as high as sixty stories jutting up out of the ground at odd angles, lining Atlantic Avenue, and four more towers bending and circling the sparkling glass-walled arena. Nets and Knicks basketball legend Bernard King and the rapper Jay-Z were supporting the project.

Stretching over some twenty-two acres of land at the congested intersection of Atlantic and Flatbush Avenue, the project would affect at least four tree-lined neighborhoods filled with mom and pop shops, walkable streets, historic two- and three-story brownstones, many occupied by newly arrived professionals who could frequently be seen leaning out of windows to chat. The neighborhoods included owners of million-dollar brownstones as well as long-term poor and working poor residents.

For a politician like Tish James, opposition to such a massive scheme seemed like a no-brainer. A lifelong South Brooklyn resident, James was educated in the city public schools, at Lehman College, and at Columbia University's School of International and Public Affairs. Several of the affected neighborhoods—Prospect Heights, Fort Greene, and Clinton Hill—were in the council district that James was hoping to represent. The district was a mix of African Americans, Caribbeans, Orthodox Jews, Hispanics, gays, and newly arrived professionals.

At the rally, James railed against Ratner's project, citing environmental concerns, traffic gridlock, resident displacement, wasteful government spending, and the government's abuse of its eminent domain powers. James—African American, poised, attractive, and quite capable of working up a rhetorical head of steam—vowed to fight Ratner's development. "It's too large to be in the middle of a low-rise, brownstone community," James roared over the rally's PA system. "We need housing on a human scale where children can play in a yard and neighbors can look out for each other."

Newspaper reports claimed that the project would create some 1.9 million square feet of office space, 300,000 square feet of retail space, six acres of open space, and 4,500 units of housing—more office space than the Empire State Building, and more total commercial square footage than the old World Trade Center. The square footage was equivalent in floor area to three Empire State Buildings. Seventy buildings on six blocks around the site would be condemned and razed. Ratner boasted that Atlantic Yards would be the largest project in Brooklyn's history and the third largest ever in New York City.

Gehry, one of America's most famous architects, designed Ratner's project as a planned residential community smack in the heart of land once eyed by the Brooklyn Dodgers before that team bolted to Los Angeles in 1957. Since the early 1900s, the Dodgers had represented blue-collar America, the children of immigrants. The movies in the 1930s and 1940s were full of Brooklyn characters, with their distinct persona and accent. The Dodgers—"the bums"—were a source of pride, an up-by-the-bootstraps team, in contrast to the pinstriped Yankees. Brooklyn borough president Marty Markowitz, who had solicited Bruce Ratner to buy the Nets and bring them to Brooklyn, would regularly claim that the Nets, like the Brooklyn Dodgers fifty years earlier, would bring the borough together.

New York Times architecture critic Nicolai Ouroussoff thought the project would "radically alter the Brooklyn skyline, reaffirming the borough's emergence as a legitimate cultural rival to Manhattan." Ouroussoff concluded his paean: "What makes the design an original achievement is the cleverness with which he [Gehry] anchors the arena in the surrounding neighborhood. What is unfolding is an urban model of remarkable richness and texture."[1] Another *New York Times* architecture critic, Herbert Muschamp, praised the "arena surrounded by office towers; apartment buildings and shops; excellent public transportation; and, above all, a terrific skyline, with six acres of new parkland at its feet. Almost everything the well-equipped urban paradise must have, in fact." Muschamp called it a "Garden of Eden."[2]

But ACORN's Bertha Lewis was skeptical. To her, Atlantic Yards looked like disguised gentrification, another fancy urban revitalization scheme that would evict the poor to benefit the rich. Since the 1940s, New Yorkers, especially minorities and the poor, have watched politically connected developers and public officials tear down neighborhoods to build cultural centers, office complexes, luxury apartments, public housing, and superhighways. To urban planners such as Tom Angotti, a professor in the Hunter College Department of Urban Affairs and Planning, Atlantic Yards looked too much like the mega-projects that made the name of Robert Moses, New York's former planning czar, a swear word in many neighborhoods.[3] It was exactly the kind of top-down urban planning that the late critic Jane Jacobs, author of *The Death and Life of American Cities* (1961), warned against. The project lacked human scale. It destroyed life at the street level. It would push out the poor.

Ratner understood that if both Tish James and Bertha Lewis opposed the project, he would have a big fight on his hands. Tish James defeated her Democratic and Republican opponents in the November 2003 election with an overwhelming 77 percent of the vote—a huge victory for ACORN and the Working Families Party (WFP). James's landslide victory and the increasing power of the WFP didn't bode well for Ratner's project.

A week after Tish James's November election victory, one of her supporters, Patti Hagan, a leader of the Prospect Heights Action Coalition and former fact checker for the *New Yorker* magazine, approached Bertha Lewis. Hagan told Lewis how much she enjoyed working with ACORN during the election campaign and that she knew ACORN would join the opposition to Ratner's arena plan. Hagan handed Lewis some newspaper articles with photos depicting Hagan and others opposing the Ratner development plan. She told Lewis that a lot more people would be displaced than Ratner claimed. "I did a door-to-door canvass," Hagan said. "I found 463 residents who either rented or owned, plus 400 people in a homeless shelter, and many small businesses, employing some 225 people." After a back and forth discussion, Lewis smiled and nodded and then told Hagan that before she could take a position, she had to do some research and meet with ACORN members. "Our members decide, but I'll definitely get back to you," Lewis said.[4]

Lewis knew that depending on citizen participation and the need to take advantage of any opportunities that could lead to victories for its members often led ACORN down unpredictable paths. This was about to occur.

Seven Months Later

On an overcast day in June 2004, Bertha Lewis attended another rally. Inside Brooklyn's Borough Hall—an Ionic-columned Greek Revival topped with a golden figure of Justice—on a stage packed with New York's most important political, labor, community, and religious leaders, Lewis leaned forward, her arms stretched into a "V," forefingers pointing skyward. To the audience of 1,300 people, she bellowed, "What do we want?" "Jobs! Housing! Hoops!" the crowd mantraed at this rally, where ACORN announced its support for Ratner's Atlantic Yards sports arena and urban development plan.

Outside Borough Hall, protestors—mostly middle-class activists including "old lefties" and ex-hippies—accused Ratner of "Manhattaniz-

ing" Brooklyn and questioned ACORN's backing. Many of these protesters had recently moved to Brooklyn from Manhattan seeking more room
and less congestion. Dismayed at the size of the project, the protesters
represented the views of thousands of Brooklyn residents worried that
the mega-development would overwhelm existing neighborhoods. Why
wasn't ACORN—the leftist, poor people's organization known for public
confrontation campaigns against corporate abuse, gentrification, and political corruption—outside on the picket lines protesting against political
cronyism and developer greed?

The protesters accused ACORN of "selling out" by supporting a deal
that would funnel huge government concessions to a private development
that would increase population, burden traffic, alter the Brooklyn skyline,
and bulldoze many residences through eminent domain condemnations.
Their suspicions were heightened when they discovered that Ratner, like
several other city business figures, had donated money to ACORN, a
nonprofit group that derives most of its income from foundations, private
donors, and membership dues.

What had happened between Lewis's learning of Atlantic Yards in
September and this moment in June?

Soon after the November 2003 election, Lewis began meeting with
Jon Kest, sixteen neighborhood leaders—including Pat Boone, president of New York State ACORN—and Ismane Speliotis, the director of
the New York ACORN Housing Corporation. Speliotis was a nine-year
ACORN veteran with degrees from Barnard College, Columbia University, and Pratt University. Like the opponents of Atlantic Yards, Lewis and
Kest agreed that Atlantic Yards could be a disaster. But they also saw it
as an opportunity to make a big dent in New York's affordable housing
crisis with ACORN getting a lot of credit and boosting its power. But
first ACORN needed to do some research and check with their members.
They reviewed various news articles that were appearing in the downtown
Brooklyn newspapers. Lewis said to Kest, "I'm impressed that the opposition to Atlantic Yards was sucking up to the press."[5]

They consulted with city planners, reviewed the city's housing data,
set up meetings, and talked to ACORN's leaders who lived in Brooklyn.
From years of community organizing, they knew the rental vacancy rate
in Brooklyn was less than 3 percent. New York City's population was projected to jump 16 percent over the next twenty-five years, reaching 9.5
million people by 2030. Brooklyn and the Bronx were projected to sur-
pass their mid-twentieth-century population peaks. The housing crunch

was creating an affordability crisis. More than a quarter of a million families were on waiting lists for Section 8 rent assistance vouchers and public housing.

During November and December, the ACORN staff had to bring the issue to the membership. Participation is ACORN's key weapon against the widespread cynicism and despair that exists in the communities where they organize. Encouraging its members to participate in decision making makes ACORN quite different from most left-wing activist organizations, antipoverty agencies, and community groups that are run by self-appointed leaders, or writers, lawyers, or lobbyists who are hired by professionals, businessmen, and other elites. Most progressive public interest organizations, community development agencies, and antipoverty groups do not have members. If they do, these members are rarely low-income people. The few poor people on the boards of these advocacy groups seldom have a strong constituency base that they can mobilize to change public policy. The staff usually leads. Erecting a democratically run group is just one way that ACORN members participate. Members also pay dues, march, and vote. Before voting on whether to support, oppose, or stay neutral in the Atlantic Yards development, Lewis had to make sure that the members were well versed on the issues. She knew her members wouldn't fight for or against an issue unless they understood it and believed deeply that it was important enough to address.

Critics, such as Mark Winston Griffith, a prominent journalist and community development professional, often accuse New York ACORN of being a "top-down" group manipulated by the staff.[6] The accusation was wrong, but it was not easy for the critics to fully understand how the group works, since there have been few studies that document how ACORN makes decisions. Kest, Lewis, and most of the organizers and leaders claim ACORN is "bottom-up," with all major decisions driven by members. ACORN's campaign in the battle of Brooklyn reveals a complex process in which the staff and grassroots leaders shared decision making. Heidi Swarts's study of ACORN's St. Louis and San Jose chapters characterizes authority as "fluid and frequently negotiated."[7]

This preeminence of participation is so deeply ingrained in most of the staff that it engenders a culture of respect—a byproduct of the organizing culture. This culture enhances the staff's ability to provide effective services, recruit members, mobilize them, and get them to pay dues. ACORN's genius lies in collaboration. Sometimes staff leads; sometimes members lead. The synergy between staff and leaders, feeding off each other's expertise and savvy, brings results.

At training sessions for new organizers, Lewis emphasizes, "In the end, the members call the shots. They vote with their feet, they vote with their level of participation and support for the organization. If you have some deep, hidden issues with poor people, if you are patronizing or really don't like poor people then it will come out. The members will sense it, and this is not the job for you."[8] Bertha Lewis and the other New York staff genuinely like the members and care deeply about their concerns. "The members are the bosses. This is organizing culture!" asserts Lewis. Lewis adds, "If the staff comes up with a plan that is not supported by the members, the members won't volunteer, vote, demonstrate or in any other way support ACORN's action." Atlantic Yards was an example of the staff and elected officers taking the lead, ringing door bells, going to meetings, throwing themselves into the politics of persuasion, with its membership enthusiastically behind.[9]

ACORN's notion of decision making is more like representative government than the direct deliberation of ancient Athens' agora or the New Left's notion of "participatory democracy," embodied in the Students for a Democratic Society (SDS) Port Huron Statement. To SDS it meant something comparable to the old New England town-meeting democracy, where everybody spoke his piece, consensus was the goal, and leadership and hierarchy were resisted. Like Saul Alinsky's organizations, ACORN focuses on solving problems and securing the active participation of its members and neighbors, but it does have a formal decision-making process. ACORN is more in the tradition of Alinsky's approach, which emphasizes strong leadership and centralized decision making by the leaders. ACORN has its bylaws and a hierarchy within the staff and leadership office holders.

Lewis put the ACORN decision-making process into high gear. Lewis, Kest, and other staff began knocking on doors in East New York, Bedford-Stuyvesant, and Brownsville to find out what ordinary residents knew about the project. They held one-on-one conversations with members, helped schedule meetings, and assisted the leaders of the ACORN chapter in drafting agendas. At the meetings, leaders set up role-playing and "what if" discussions: "What's our plan? What if Ratner refuses our plan? What if poor folks who are not members of ACORN begin organizing against us? Who supports Atlantic Yards? Who's against it? If we support it, how much will it cost the organization? If we are against it, can we defeat it?" The most important questions were: "Is this the type of issue that ACORN ought to work on? How will it help ACORN members and the poor? What can we win for our members? How long will it take to win? Will it build ACORN membership? Will it make us stronger?"[10] Lewis had been doing this kind of organizing for more than ten years. She saw this process as a way to train ACORN's leaders and members to become well informed, skilled, and self-confident activists. By now, many of them had the skills to understand ACORN's strategic approach to grassroots campaigns. Although Lewis often played the role of spokesperson, she had also trained a core of twenty leaders who were quite capable of speaking for themselves. Typically black, poor, and working class, without any college credits, they would nevertheless impress their neighbors as well as journalists with their knowledge and sophistication about complex issues.

Lewis and Ratner were not strangers. Lewis had organized a demonstration against Ratner four years earlier over hiring practices in stores like Target and Chuck E. Cheese in the Atlantic Center mall he operated in Brooklyn near the proposed Atlantic Yards site. The protesters wanted the stores to hire more kids from the community and pay living wages. When the police came to throw the rabble-rousers out, ACORN's people kept shouting from the sidewalk. Since then, Lewis had learned how to deal with Ratner. She knew he was tough but reasonable and that he might be willing to negotiate. Ratner knew ACORN could be a serious barrier if it opposed Atlantic Yards, and Lewis knew that partnering with ACORN was not a stretch for Ratner; he understood the benefits.

Ratner was a 1967 cum laude graduate of Harvard University and a 1970 Columbia University Law graduate. His father, Albert, founded Forest City in 1921 in Cleveland and built it into a hugely successful company. With his father's help, Bruce established himself as a critical force in Brooklyn's renaissance by developing some of the most bold, although unattractive, commercial projects during the 1990s years. Ratner brought together the city, the state, and the *New York Times* to plan an $850 million, Renzo Piano–designed newspaper headquarters across from the Port Authority bus terminal. Real estate power brokers are constantly amazed at Ratner's successful government-supported schemes. "He's the master of subsidy. No one does it better," says Fred Siegel, a professor of history at the Cooper Union in New York who focuses on urban issues. "That's not a flat-out criticism of him. It's just that he never builds without someone else taking the risk."[11]

Yet, another side to this real estate tycoon was his civic mindedness. Before becoming a developer, Ratner was director of the Model Cities Program under Mayor John Lindsay and then served in Mayor Ed Koch's administration as New York City's Commissioner of Consumer Affairs from 1978 to 1982. His brother, Michael, headed the Center for Constitutional Rights, the public interest law firm founded by the late radical lawyer, William Kunstler. Bruce's sister, Ellen, created a left-wing radio syndicate and was one of Fox TV's token liberals. At the unveiling of the Atlantic Yards plan, Ratner stated, "Great urban planning incorporates many different uses into a cohesive neighborhood—and truly great urban planning invites the public to participate in the space, whether they work there or live there or they're drawn there to visit."[12]

Ratner, a self-described "old lefty," often distinguished himself from another major Brooklyn developer, Donald Trump's father, Fred. Ratner would say that the Trumps never thought about the broader interests of the population and were concerned only about the bottom line. Ratner, on the other hand, said he would never turn his back to the larger community interests.

In January 2004, while ACORN organizers met with each other and with members, the group's housing expert, Ismane Speliotis, began drafting a plan to present to Ratner. Speliotis's plan would use the Nets arena project to stretch the city housing subsidy programs so more nonwhite people could afford to move to and remain in Brooklyn neighborhoods. Kest and Lewis worked on an organizing strategy to mobilize ACORN members to support, or, if necessary oppose Ratner's plan.

Kest and Lewis wanted to make a deal because they believed that Ratner had the clout to get his project approved and he had the money to influence politicians. The governor, George Pataki, had been his college classmate. Lewis, in discussion with staff and leaders, would argue, "It's better to win something than go into opposition and just yell and scream and ultimately lose. We can't organize our members around issues such as traffic and the environment. What we can kick ass on is housing."[13]

Lewis believed ACORN had a responsibility to steer gentrification to benefit poor and working-class residents. She argued that ACORN's members, like most poor people, didn't want to live in low-income ghettoes. Neighborhoods that only have the very poor—or what sociologists call "high-poverty" areas—have the worst schools and public services, as well as the highest crime rates. The question was whether a neighborhood could be "improved" without its long-term low-income residents being pushed out. The plan ACORN was negotiating with Ratner, if successful, would result in a mix of wealthy, middle-income, and poor people living side-by-side. ACORN was betting that expanding the overall number of market-rate and subsidized housing units in the area would help end the tug-of-war between the poor and the professional class for the existing housing stock. By creating hundreds, perhaps thousands, of new jobs that would provide low-income residents with living wages, Atlantic Yards would ultimately help improve the lives of Brooklyn's poor and working-class residents.

The leaders and the staff agreed that for ACORN to get the support of its members, an unprecedented demand for 50 percent affordable, nonmarket housing would have to be its bottom line. With their demands ready, Lewis then called Ratner to set up a meeting. As usual, Lewis was blunt: "ACORN might support your project if you're willing to build a significant number of truly affordable housing. I mean significant, not the 20 percent stuff. We're thinking half. Poor people, working people, we want half—you can't just do luxury."[14]

Let's Make a Deal

To test the waters, Lewis led about thirty activists in late January 2004 into Ratner's windowless boardroom in a building high over downtown Brooklyn. Sitting across the large oak conference table, one of the Forest City executives asked the group, "Is Bertha going to start something?" As usual, Lewis was charming. Instead of confronting Ratner and his executives, Lewis calmly proposed a partnership that would preserve profits for Ratner and provide major benefits for disadvantaged Brooklynites. Ratner's people also had to contend with Speliotis. Athletic, energetic, cheerful, and attractive, Speliotis would surprise Ratner's negotiators when they realized how cunning and brilliant she was, especially with numbers.

"If we can pull this off," said Lewis, "it would represent a breakthrough, a model for big city development projects. We'll help sell the Atlantic Yards project to government agencies, community groups, and the media."

In exchange, ACORN continued to insist that 50 percent of the proposed 4,500 rental housing units be below market—an unusually large share of subsidized housing for a private development project. Jim Stuckey, the lead manager for Atlantic Yard, said no. He insisted that anything more that 20 percent was not economically viable. "There's no precedent for 50 percent, period," Stuckey emphasized.

At the meeting, Ratner was outwardly relaxed, casually dressed, wearing an open collar and unassuming round glasses. He radiated a rich man's ease and self-assurance. When he heard Lewis's proposal, he smiled, as he often did, with his entire face, the gesture engaging his high brow, warming his eyes and signaling that a deal was likely. After this meeting negotiations continued.

In three months, ACORN would organize over forty-four meetings about Atlantic Yards. These included three with ACORN's thirty-six-member governing board, forty in neighborhood gatherings attended by twenty-five to thirty members, and a borough-wide meeting attended by hundreds of residents. The staff also drafted a series of questions to use in a telephone poll to about 2,000 members, asking their views on what ACORN should do. "You heard about the Nets moving to Brooklyn?" staffers asked. "What would you like to see happen?" Altogether, the process involved more than 3,520 members participating either by phone or at a meeting.

While many of ACORN's members were leery of the Nets arena project, and most were against eminent domain, their overwhelming concern was the lack of affordable housing. At a staff meeting, Bertha Lewis paraphrased members' worries about "housing, housing, housing" and their desire to "stop the rampant gentrification." As a quid pro quo for supporting Atlantic Yards, could ACORN limit gentrification by forcing Ratner to build affordable housing for the poor? The board of trustees gave the green light to ACORN's staff and leaders to negotiate a plan.

On March 15, 2004, the New York ACORN board members gathered at headquarters in Brooklyn. The board included two members from each neighborhood group representing Flatbush, East Flatbush, Bushwick, Brownsville, the Bronx, and Manhattan. It also included four members from neighborhood groups representing Crown Heights, East New York, and Long Island; two members from the ACORN political action committee (PAC); and ten from ACORN'S housing development arm, the ACORN Mutual Housing Association of New York (MHANY). The board unanimously approved an organizing campaign to make a deal with Ratner.

In an effort to carve out a place for low-income families in this mammoth development project, ACORN, along with several allies, began trying to bang out a deal. ACORN wanted a legally enforceable Community Benefits Agreement (CBA) with Ratner and his Forest City partners. Ratner did not need ACORN in order to get his initial governmental approvals for the project. But he believed he needed ACORN's political clout and its endorsement of an affordable-housing program to help promote the project with the public and several city council members, and to make sure key members of the state assembly would include funding for the project in the state budget.

The 2004 November elections added to ACORN's influence, especially among the political pros. The WFP turned out 168,719 votes for U.S. senator Chuck Schumer's reelection on the WFP line. "This party has the organizing capacity to be a triple threat for national Democrats," said Schumer. "They can bring disaffected 'Reagan Democrats' back into the fold, they attract independents, and they provide a place for crossover Republicans. They work very well with Democrats. That's not to say they do everything we want, but they see a common cause."[15]

Painstakingly, Speliotis and ACORN's lawyers, Ratner's lawyers, and the accountants went back and forth to create something that had never been done before. Ratner's people thought 50 percent was outrageous. Speliotis wanted some complexes affordable to families earning as little as $18,400 a year. How many studios? How many one, two, and three bedroom units? The deal was on, then off, then on, and so forth. At times during the negotiations, Ratner's people argued that ACORN'S demands were too costly and would undermine the project's viability. The ACORN negotiators knew that developers typically argue that "the numbers don't work" to fend off demands from community groups or city agencies for more parking spaces, affordable units, open space, public art, and other benefits. "The story could be that a progressive developer gave so much away to ACORN that it sapped the life out of the project," was another Ratner complaint. Meanwhile, the price of the development plan rose to $3.5 billion.

While the negotiations took place, Lewis and ACORN were not putting all their hopes for more affordable housing in Atlantic Yards. She and Kest had been busy negotiating with other groups to build a citywide coalition to support affordable housing. It was beginning to come together. On February 2, 2005, despite the bitter cold, more than 5,000 New Yorkers gathered at City Hall, chanting, "Build it! Fix it! Save it!" They held up signs and banners announcing the name of their union, church, or community-based organization and cheered speakers voicing their demands. Lewis had organized the largest march and rally for affordable housing in decades.

"How can people live in the city without affordable housing?" asked United Federation of Teachers (UFT) president Randy Weingarten, who was also the head of the powerful Municipal Labor Committee. Pointing out how difficult it is for children to learn or teachers to teach if either or both lack adequate housing, Weingarten said, "The mayor talks a lot about making the city a great place to live. But it can't just be a great place to live for millionaires or billionaires."

Lillian Roberts, head of District Council (DC) 37, the city's largest public employee union, called affordable housing "one of the most pressing needs in New York City today." The UFT and DC 37 were just two of the long list of organizations determined to propel affordable housing to the top of the city's political agenda in 2005, an election year.

"For the first time you have the building trades joining with the community because they are the ones who erect the city's housing and they can't even afford to live in it. It's their issue too. It's tremendous," said Lewis.

As the rally ended and the crowd began to disperse, they chanted, "Build it! Fix it! Save it!" Brooklyn's Rev. Herbert Daughtry, who was in discussions with Lewis about Atlantic Yards, shouted, "We will not quit. We will not give up. Go tell Mayor Bloomberg. Go tell Gov. Pataki. Tell every legislator. Every lawmaker. Go tell it everywhere. We will not stop. We will not give up until every New Yorker has a house to live in. When you go to sleep tonight, dream housing. When you get up in the morning, think housing!"

In March of 2005, Ratner, his right-hand man Bruce Bender, a fast-talking charmer, and his press aide Lupè Todd set up a meeting with Kest and Lewis at a Starbucks just across from Councilwoman James's district office to try to finalize negotiations. James was still leading the opposition to Atlantic Yards. Joining them was the prominent New York Daily News columnist Errol Louis. When James walked into the coffee shop, she looked surprised to see Kest and Lewis. ACORN had supported James's election in 2003, but here were their leaders meeting with her arch opponent, Ratner. Why were they meeting here? James wondered if a deal was in the works.

It was. Soon after this meeting, and after a year of negotiations, threats to protest, and compromises, ACORN struck an unprecedented deal with Ratner. Mayor Michael Bloomberg endorsed it. The centerpiece was the 50 percent set-aside for affordable housing in one of the world's most expensive cities. Never before in New York City, or any other city, has a private developer built a large apartment project—an integrated, mixed-income, planned residential community—where half the residents paid market rate rents and lived side by side with the other 50 percent, the subsidized residents. It is rare for low-income community groups to be part of a planning process for a large development. It was exceedingly rare for the developer to agree to sign a legally binding agreement. As Lewis would write in a letter to the magazine *City Limits*,

In an era of increasing housing segregation, Atlantic Yards will be one of the only neighborhoods in Brooklyn where families of all backgrounds will be able to really live and grow together. That's because ACORN insisted, and Forest City Ratner agreed, that the affordable units be spread throughout every rental building at random on every floor. In Atlantic Yards, if the elevator works for the rich folks, it will work for the poor folks. For the first time in a project like this, low-, middle- and upper-income people will live—literally—together. And unless you put your pay stub on your front door, your neighbor will never know whether your unit is market price or below.[16]

At a press conference on May 19, 2005, ACORN, represented by Lewis, along with New York City Mayor Bloomberg and Ratner, announced the agreement. Lewis was known for expressing her activism with a potent, personal, and theatrical flair, from the clothes she wore—lapis lazuli earrings and matching gold-trimmed gown—to her turns of phrase—like the time she contrasted brownstone people (yuppies) with brown people. Lewis had accused Bloomberg's administration of "educational racism" during a fight over school-staffing issues in 2003. This day, Lewis grabbed the mayor's head between her hands and publicly sealed the deal with a kiss.

What Can ACORN Potentially Win?

The agreement with Ratner and his Forest City partners, embodied in a Community Benefits Agreement (CBA), would provide poor and working-class people with more affordable housing, more cultural activities, and more jobs. If the project succeeds, ACORN will have triumphed over community opposition and reaffirmed itself as a serious political force in the city.

The CBA would also provide job opportunities and other services for low-income residents—from hiring to contracting to day care services. In the convoluted jargon of housing subsidy programs, the agreement guaranteed that units would be affordable to families at five different income levels—very low income, low income, moderate income, low middle, and high middle. Twenty percent (900 units) would be reserved for families making less than $31,400 a year. Of that group, 136 units would be reserved for families making less than $25,120 a year. Thirty percent (1,350 units) would be reserved for families with incomes up to $100,480, for a four-person household. "Tiering is a critical component of the program," said Speliotis. "Without it, developers will rent to those families with the highest incomes, those closer to $100,000, not $30,000."[17]

Rent payments would be subsidized by the New York City Housing Development Corporation, a state public-benefit corporation that plans to use a combination of bonds and reserves from investments to finance the subsidies. Speliotis insisted that ACORN be given the responsibility of marketing the units. "Nobody is going to care as much as ACORN that the appropriate people are marketed to, reached and housed," she said.[18] To keep the displacement rate low, the agreement stipulated that displaced property owners would be fairly compensated and that displaced tenants would be given a new, comparable apartment at their existing rent in the new complex. Minority-owned and women-owned construction firms would receive 20 percent and 10 percent (respectively) of the construction contracts, and public housing residents and low-income people from the immediate area would have priority for any jobs.

Ratner also promised space for a health clinic and daycare center, and that the arena would serve as a community resource, housing high school and collegiate sports, games, tournaments, graduations, and community activities. Ratner would later agree to build an additional 600 to 1,000 affordable condo units either on or off the project site—significantly increasing the number of for-sale units available to working families in Brooklyn.

ACORN wasn't the only player in the negotiations. The seven other signatories of the agreement were the Downtown Brooklyn Neighborhood Alliance, the All-Faith Council of Brooklyn, the First Atlantic Terminal Housing Committee, the Downtown Brooklyn Education Consortium, the Public Housing Communities, the New York State Association of Minority Contractors, and Brooklyn United for Innovative Local Development (BUILD). The prominent civil rights activist and pastor of House of the Lord Church, Rev. Herbert Daughtry, led the Downtown Brooklyn Neighborhood Alliance. BUILD would run a program to recruit and train neighborhood residents for jobs in the Atlantic Yards project. At the urging of Assemblyman Roger Green, the Downtown Brooklyn Educational Consortium was added to the mix at the last minute, several months after ACORN began negotiations. Its chair, Freddie Hamilton, was the vice chairwoman of the Brooklyn Democratic Party and the executive director of a nonprofit child-welfare agency. In 1993, after her youngest son was shot and killed by another youth in the community, Hamilton, an African American, channeled her grief into activism. Her new organization would also try to create a charter school devoted to technology. The eight groups were essentially made up of African American members. James Caldwell, the president of BUILD, said it would be a "conspiracy against blacks" if Forest City did not win the right to build Atlantic Yards.[19]

After the press conference, Lewis said she believed that this deal would have a domino effect because it would be used as a model to show other developers that the interests and needs of the local community can be served. Few people with experience in grassroots work thought that ACORN could have won any more concessions. "They did better than I thought they would," said Brad Lander, the director of the Pratt Institute and a leading authority on community development.[20]

The conservative *New York Sun*, in an editorial, blasted the deal as another example of "ACORN's anti-free-market tendencies. . . . New York's housing market certainly needs many things, but an extra 2,250 units of market-distorting, dependence-inducing housing on a prime spot in the heart of Brooklyn isn't on the list."[21] But most of the opponents of the project—the community groups representing existing residents and small businesses—thought that, if anything, ACORN compromised too much. While many of the critics applauded ACORN's housing plan, they thought the project was fundamentally flawed. Tish James, who continued to lead the opposition, felt she was left out of the negotiations, and did not believe this was the best agreement ACORN could have gotten.

Opponents would gather around the most vocal and effective adversary of the Atlantic Yards, Develop Don't Destroy Brooklyn (DDDB), which was led by Daniel Goldstein, a former graphic designer. Goldstein had bought a condo on Pacific Street overlooking the defunct rail yards. When he saw a poster pasted on a lamppost that read THIS NEIGHBORHOOD IS CONDEMNED, he became anxious. Goldstein, in his early thirties, the son of an investment fund manager, was determined to stop the development.

Goldstein suspected that other than ACORN, most of the other signatories of the CBA were what he called "shell organizations."[22] He had a point. According to a report in the Daily News, BUILD had no membership income for 2004 and only $10,000 in revenues. For 2005, however, the group suddenly reported a whopping increase in its budget to $2.5 million, and another $2.5 million for 2006. Most of its budget for 2005 and 2006 was coming from Forest City Ratner. Just two of the eight signatories to the agreement—ACORN and the New York State Association of Minority Contractors—existed as incorporated entities before the negotiations. What Goldstein did not understand was that ACORN's deep grassroots support was sufficient to give Atlantic Yards street credibility and some political juice.

Goldstein called the CBA process a "sweetheart, back-room deal that bypasses the democratic public approval process."[23] To some extent, he was correct on that score as well. Because Forest City Ratner was building on state-owned property, it was exempt from the usual approval process. The Empire State Development Corporation, a state authority, sponsored the project; approval was not dependent upon the state legislature, city council, or local planning boards. State assemblyman Roger Green, an ACORN supporter, acknowledged that the groups signing the Atlantic Yards CBA represented only part of the community. When the project was announced in December 2003, that it had endorsements from the mayor and borough president signaled a planning process that was less than ideal and that could establish a dangerous precedent. As another ACORN ally, the eminent Pratt University planning professor, Ron Shiffman, wrote in opposing the project, "A private developer shouldn't be allowed to drive the disposition of publicly owned or controlled land without a participatory planning process setting the conditions for the disposition of that land."[24]

The opposition also insisted that the project was too massive for this community. A young architect who lived near the proposed building site said, "Office towers, high-rise towers, sports arenas, that's not a community. Brooklyn doesn't want to be Manhattan. If we wanted Manhattan, we'd live there." City councilman Charles Barron, a former Black Panther, joined his colleague Tish James in opposing the project. He complained that rents would be too high and that too many of the below-market units would go to households with high income.

Then there was the big issue of eminent domain and displacement. While Ratner originally announced that only a hundred people would have their homes taken by eminent domain, DDDB conducted a door-to-door survey that found the number closer to 850. Many homeowners said there was no excuse for government to take their property just so a big-time developer who makes large campaign contributions could run roughshod over their property rights. A young architect who had lived in the neighborhood for ten years would be a victim of eminent domain. "This is an abuse of eminent domain. If they can take my home under these pretenses, they can take anyone's," he said.

In the midst of the battle over Atlantic Yards, on July 23, 2005, the U.S. Supreme Court ruled that local governments may force property owners to sell, to make way for private economic development, when city officials decide it would benefit the public, even if the property is not blighted and the new project's success is not guaranteed. The five to four ruling gave state and local governments wide latitude for using eminent domain for urban revitalization. As a result, condo owners and others facing displacement were not likely to prevail if they sued Ratner and the city.

For a while, despite the opposition, it looked like Ratner would get the government approvals and vindicate ACORN's decision to partner with him. But Ratner and ACORN had underestimated Goldstein's tenacity. After three years of assembling in living rooms and church basements, his group began to gain momentum. A long-time institutional ally of ACORN—the Pratt Institute Center for Community and Environmental Development, an urban planning center situated a mile from the proposed arena site—came out in opposition to certain aspects of the project. Mafruza Khan of the Pratt Institute testified at a hearing, stating that, "Given the wide divergence in [subsidy] estimates, from $200 million to over $1 billion, we do want to emphasize that it is impossible for the public to know whether this project is a good deal without knowing how much it will cost to taxpayers. It is being asked to buy something without knowing how much it will cost."[25]

Another long time ACORN ally, the pastor of Lafayette Avenue Presbyterian Church in Fort Greene and social activist David Dyson, joined the opposition. (Dyson's church had provided the space for ACORN's first office in 1982.) Dyson said, "We're trying to prevent the misuse of eminent domain, trying to increase the number of affordable housing units, trying to decrease the number of high-rise luxury office buildings. Those are the kinds of issues that a community group should have, but the Reverend Daughtry—who's also an old friend—and our friends at ACORN are trying to cut a personal deal so that they can be brokers over whatever little piece or crumb of this pie falls from Ratner's table."[26]

Goldstein used a smart public relations ploy and got a bandwagon of local celebrities and authors to join the opposition, including Heath Ledger, Steve Buscemi, Jennifer Egan, Jonathan Safran Foer, Nicole Krauss, Peter Galassi, Jonathan Lethem, and Rosie Perez. They joined DDDB's advisory board. DDDB's legal case was looking better. DDDB's lawyers noted some fine print in the Supreme Court Kelo decision that allowed the city of New London to use eminent domain to turn private property over to a private developer. The Court noted that the private developer could not drive a redevelopment plan that relied on eminent domain. It had to go through city planning and a legislative review. A number of local officials, including Brooklyn Borough president Marty Markowitz, called for the project to be scaled down.

As the hot 2006 summer approached, it still seemed clear that Atlantic Yards would get the approvals it needed, despite the growing opposition. Bertha Lewis continued to speak out on behalf of the project. She also thought ACORN could coast on the power of Ratner's powerful political supporters, freeing her to organize other projects. The environmental study by the project's sponsor, the Empire State Development Corporation (ESDC), would set into motion a public comment period. Then the project would face a final vote by ESDC's board in the fall. Since Charles A. Gargano, the chairman of the development corporation, had publicly supported the project all along, the opposition assumed that the ESDC would produce a satisfactory review and approve the process.

Final approval was needed from the obscure Public Authorities Control Board (PACB), the body that had killed the football stadium deal for the Jets that Mayor Bloomberg had pushed. But since Governor Pataki, who supported Atlantic Yards, appointed the chairman of the board, final approval was likely. The only tactic left for the opposition would be a court battle over Ratner's right to acquire some land by eminent domain.

Just when it looked like Atlantic Yards would move closer to fruition, something unexpected occurred. When, on July 19, the ESDC gave its nod of approval for what had grown from a $2.5 billion to a $4.2 billion project, it released a 1,400-page environmental impact statement. This statement for the first time laid out all the potential effects of the proposed Atlantic Yards project, and to the opponents they weren't pretty. The project would worsen the already tangled web of traffic. It would cast a huge shadow over the surrounding neighborhoods, while street-level signs would bring more neon at night in the concentrated commercial corridors on the project's western tip. By August, pace-setting opinion makers in the *Village Voice*, *New York Magazine*, and the *New Yorker* characterized the project as a mistake, helping to galvanize the opposition.[27]

With public opinion appearing to go his way, Goldstein and his allies had two big opportunities to defeat Ratner's plan. They would have to mobilize their supporters in the upcoming September 2006 primary elections to send a message to pro–Atlantic Yards Brooklyn politicians. Then they would have to mobilize their supporters at the October public hearings required by law. The elections did not go their way; the pro–Atlantic Yards candidates in two congressional districts won, while Goldstein's ally and an outspoken opponent of the project, Charles Barron, lost.

Tensions came to a boiling point at the public hearings. Supporters and opponents from unions, local block associations, community boards, and business groups filled the 880-seat auditorium at the New York City College of Technology in downtown Brooklyn. Both sides took turns applauding, booing, and interrupting one another. Opponents mounted a mordacious refrain of catcalls when borough president Marty Markowitz described the project as "a wonderful addition to Brooklyn."

Race and Class

Those supporting Atlantic Yards put the subtext of race front and center. A fifty-one-year-old Brooklyn resident advanced to the front of the hall. "I'm here to speak for the underprivileged, the people that don't get the opportunity to work, the brothers that just came over out of prison," he said. "Those who opposed the plan," he said, "were not true Brooklynites." As to traffic congestion, he said, "That's nothing." Injecting the issue of race, he said, "Stopping this project would force young black men into a life of crime." Staring at the opponents to Atlantic Yards, he said, "You go back up to Pleasantville." Like many black residents attending the hearing, he saw Atlantic Yards as a beacon of hope.[28]

A few black leaders opposed the project, but most blacks in Brooklyn supported Atlantic Yards. Opposition leaders like Goldstein were clueless when it came to effectively reaching out to the older, more established network of black community activists. In May 2006, Goldstein shot an e-mail message to a *Daily News* columnist, attacking ties between the groups that supported Atlantic Yards and what he termed their "wealthy white masters," referring to Ratner's corporation. The reporter publicized the message, stirring an outcry from Lewis and other black supporters. Goldstein made a half-hearted apology, calling his remarks "unfortunate." But the damage was done.[29]

Opponents like Tish James, who is black, saw a cynical race ruse. She accused Ratner of intentionally stirring up racial divisions, typecasting upscale white residents as the main source of resistance and as numb to the needs of black Brooklynites. James and other critics may have been correct when they said that a better-planned project could provide more affordable housing, with less harmful impact on the area.[30] But, in truth, the opposition was mostly middle-class and affluent whites. James complained that ACORN's success in turning out black participants, who supported the project at community meetings, rallies and hearings, helped fuel perceptions that black support for the project was high. Again, James's problem was that a large majority of blacks did support Atlantic Yards.

In the urban trenches, race and class often intersect. As Brad Lander, the director of the Pratt University Center for Community Development and an advocate for low-income housing, commented, "This is not about race per se. But when you layer on that the people who live near Atlantic Yards are more likely to be whiter and wealthier, and the people who live farther out are more likely to be people of color without good jobs or housing, the race elements have become stronger."[31]

According to census data, the number of whites living near the project site—in neighborhoods like Fort Greene, Boerum Hill, and Prospect Heights—had grown steadily in recent years. Those new arrivals were affluent and highly educated, especially compared with residents of the nearby public housing projects, where most residents were black and concerned about jobs. As white yuppies boosted the area's median incomes, they forced up housing prices. In Fort Greene, for example, which bordered on the project site to the north, average apartment prices rose faster from 2004 to 2005 than in any other Brooklyn neighborhood.

When Forest City sponsored an information session in July 2006 about the project's subsidized housing, the forum was packed with thousands of the area's black working-class and poor residents.

Controlling Gentrification

ACORN firmly stood by its decision to support Atlantic Yards. In New York, the housing crisis for the poor and working class was indeed getting worse. Rents were sharply increasing. More professionals were settling in the outer boroughs. A February 2006 survey released by New York City housing officials confirmed what ACORN already knew. While income in New York fell by 6.3 percent from 2001 to 2004, the median monthly rent increased by 5.4 percent from 2002 to 2005. The number of units with gross monthly rents between $1,000 and $1,499 went up by 17 percent, and those costing $1,500 or more rose by 20.6 percent. Brad Lander said, "Rents are up, low-rent units are almost impossible to find, and people are struggling to pay the housing bills."[32]

For years, ACORN had tried to stem the tide of gentrification, only to find that the combined forces of market pressures, real estate industry political influence, and the acceptance by liberals and the press that rent control and public housing were bad, were difficult to beat. New York still had rent control, but it had been so watered down by political compromises that the number of tenants protected by its regulations declined each year. In addition, owners of New York's famed Mitchell-Lama buildings, which spurred affordable working-class housing by providing low-interest mortgages and significant tax abatements in exchange for caps on rents, were withdrawing from the program so they could increase rents.

A March 2006 ACORN study highlighted the problem. The study examined eighty-seven new development projects in various stages of progress in downtown Brooklyn, containing 5,934 housing units. ACORN's report found that only 201 units, or just 3 percent of the total, were affordable to moderate-income people. Only 266 units, or 4 percent of the total, were affordable to low-income families. In almost all of those projects, city tax dollars were being used to subsidize luxury development in the form of 421a and J-51 tax abatements for purchasers of luxury housing. The result: between 1990 and 2000, the African American population of Community Board 2 (including downtown, Fort Greene, Brooklyn Heights, and Boerum Hill) decreased by 17.2 percent.[33] Francis Byrd, a Democratic district leader from the area who opposed Atlantic Yards, understood ACORN's dilemma: "Certainly, there's a sense among many folks who have seen this happen before that putting up a fight with a developer won't get you anywhere. So whatever little you can get is the best you can hope for."[34]

As of December 2006, the deal was not settled. Supporters and opponents turned their focus to a coming vote by the Public Authorities Control Board (PACB), which would have the final say. This obscure board required all three members—Senate Majority Leader Joseph Bruno, Assembly Speaker Sheldon Silver and Gov. George Pataki's appointee—to approve. A meeting was set for December 20. Pataki, whose term ended December 31, was an enthusiastic supporter of the project. Governor-elect Eliot Spitzer said he favored the project but expressed a desire to look more closely at its financing. According to a KPMG audit commissioned by the Empire State Development Corporation, a copy of which was provided to the *New York Times*, Forest City estimated that the overall rate of return on the $4 billion project, excluding the arena, at about 10 percent over thirty years. Bruno and Silver had gone on record as supporters.

While most people were preparing for their December 2006 holiday vacations or engaged in last-minute Christmas shopping, opponents mounted pressure on Silver to postpone final approval. DDDB delivered thousands of letters from city residents to Pataki, Bruno, and Silver urging them to delay approval until their lawsuit was finalized. On December 19, on the steps of City Hall, several civic organizations, including the Municipal Art Society, the Regional Plan Association, the Citizens Union, and the Natural Resources Defense Council, rallied for a postponement of a final vote based on the lack of financial transparency and the failure to address traffic and other environmental concerns.

On December 20, the previously little-known PACB voted to approve Atlantic Yards. To sweeten the deal, Forest City offered important eleventh-hour concessions. At least 200 of the market-rate condominiums would be subsidized and made affordable to first-time homeowners, and Forest City agreed to spend $3 million to improve parks near the development. Ratner had made an earlier concession to Silver when he cut the amount of Atlantic Yards office space, so as not to compete for tenants that Silver would rather see in his downtown Manhattan district.

Goldstein was not prepared to give up without a fight. "The federal eminent domain lawsuit brought by citizens protecting their constitutional rights is rock-solid, and without those plaintiffs' properties, Atlantic Yards as we know it cannot be built," Goldstein said. But it was a long shot. Lewis, who had been dispatched to Missouri to help stabilize the ACORN St. Louis office, was busy, but not too busy to savor the victory. She knew that ACORN's clout was critical to Atlantic Yard's success. The deal with Ratner helped ACORN organizationally and politically, which would add weight to ACORN's next battle. Lewis called ACORN's PR man, Jonathon Rosen, and asked him to draft a statement for her: "The Atlantic Yards project represents a historic 50/50 commitment to affordable housing and jobs and will help in the ongoing revitalization of Brooklyn while ensuring that long-time residents also benefit. We've worked hard to ensure that there are direct benefits for the community—from ensuring that 50% of all apartments are affordable to low income and middle class families, to unequalled participation of minority and women owned businesses." When called by the press, Lewis said, "It's a holiday gift for Brooklyn families. We are ecstatic. Score one for the people of Brooklyn."

The opposition's criticism had merit but was utopian. A private developer shouldn't be allowed to drive the disposition of public property. But ACORN was not powerful enough to stop Ratner's project, so it chose to force a different type of planning process and then guarantee a different process would bring a better result. In fact, the urban development planning was usually less than ideal, and the poor were typically left out.

While Brooklyn had become the place of choice for many upscale

households, more than 20 percent of its 2.5 million residents lived below the poverty line. In a place where the working poor and even the
middle class were already being driven out by rent gouging and gentrification, arguments from the gentrifying class about its right to preserve its
neighborhood were not very compelling to ACORN. Greg Blankinship,
co-chair of ACORN's Prospect Heights/Crown Heights chapter argued,
"Downtown Brooklyn is growing, and if it's growing, let's get a piece of
the action. Let's get something for the low income community."[35]

This battle over Brooklyn captured the tensions between the legitimate concerns of middle-class professionals who wanted their particular
vision of the city to reign, and the poor who needed the new jobs and
housing and the integrated neighborhood that a big development project
like Ratner's could provide. Lewis believed her coalition spoke for the
majority of the community. She believed that in a conservative era, where
government had substantially withdrawn from supporting the poor, community groups must wrench concessions directly from private corporations. "We've been in that community for twenty-two years. It seems to
me that a lot of organizations have come and gone," Lewis explained.
"Our mission in life and who we are is about protecting that community." Lewis bristled at the self-righteousness of her opponents. "Most of
those people opposed appear to be earlier gentrifyers," Lewis said. "We
just think that folks who have been part of the gentrification of the community don't get to define the community."[36]

Daily News columnist, Errol Louis captured the feeling of many
blacks and certainly ACORN's staff and members: "Standing in the path
of progress are middle-class civic groups whose mostly white leaders profess concern for low-income New Yorkers—and even claim to speak for
them—but shed the illusion of liberal compassion the minute the poor
folk get uppity and start negotiating their own deals for the future of their
families and communities."[37]

Unlike many of the Atlantic Yards opponents, ACORN was not an ad
hoc, one-issue organization. It did not pin all its hopes for the future on
Atlantic Yards, and it had a larger agenda. If the project prevails, which
is likely, this victory, although significant, will be a small step in a long-
distance run to a better life for the poor and working class. In the unlikely
event that the project goes under, ACORN will have gained because it
has garnered lots of publicity, shown elected officials that ACORN can
mobilize a constituency, and revealed to the business community that
ACORN can be pragmatic in order to win victories that benefit the poor.
Most importantly, ACORN has raised the bar regarding the high percent-

age of affordable housing required in private developments. Also, with the money ACORN raised from Ratner, it gained the resources it needed to employ more organizers to fight for more victories. ACORN quickly hired two organizers to recruit new members from a list of thousands of people seeking affordable housing, who attended various events paid for by Ratner. Some of these folks will join ACORN's army of activists and help fight to win the next battle.

ACORN mixed political pragmatism and radical ideas. Unlike ideologues on both ends of the political spectrum, ACORN knew that the perfect is often the enemy of the good. It understood the art of compromise, but only after pushing the limits by mobilizing its grassroots base through confrontation and protest. "Rather than wait until something happens to us," said Lewis, "we go out and help shape the results." If ACORN had joined the opposition, it was doubtful the Atlantic Yards deal would prevail. Instead, ACORN (the activist, poor people's organization) and Ratner (the rich developer) found a way to work together for the common good. "We've been in that community for twenty-two years," Lewis repeated. "It's ACORN's mission to protect it."[38]

Epilogue, 2008

Delays in Atlantic Yards caused by the recent economic downturn, the credit crunch, and legal challenges have emboldened the projects' critics. They claim Ratner has consistently overpromised regarding the project's progress. *New York Times* architecture critic Nicolai Ouroussoff, a strong supporter of the project, warned architect Frank Gehry to walk away if Ratner diminishes the original "bold ensemble of buildings as a self-contained composition." The dazzling skyscraper at the intersection of Flatbush and Atlantic Avenues, called "Miss Brooklyn," awaits an anchor tenant before construction. The fact that the arena will be built well before the affordable housing, and that costs keep increasing, has led to speculation about the exact future of the project. But at this point it is just conjecture.

Bertha Lewis, however, remains unconcerned: "My members are confident this will get done as originally conceived. We have to deal with development and the numbers changing. . . . We don't speculate about this. It is work that is actually going on and anybody who's ever done development would understand." Forest City has demolished buildings and has let out over $42 million worth of construction contracts with nearly

50 percent going to women and minority firms. "We are confident we have the clout to push the developer to make good on his promises of the affordable housing component."[39]

NOTES

"The Battle of Brooklyn" is adapted from a book Atlas is writing about politics and community organizing as seen through the work of ACORN, forthcoming from Vanderbilt University Press.

1. N. Ouroussoff, "Seeking First to Reinvent the Sports Arena, and Then Brooklyn," *New York Times*, July 5, 2005. See also N. Ouroussoff, "Outgrowing Jane Jacobs and Her New York," *New York Times*, April 30, 2006.
2. H. Muschamp, "Courtside Seats to an Urban Garden," *New York Times*, December 11, 2003. For additional information on this struggle over low-income housing in Brooklyn, see J. Atlas, "The Battle in Brooklyn," *Shelterforce*, Spring 2006, as well as the websites of Brooklyn United for Local Development (*www.buildbrooklyn.org*), Develop Don't Destroy Brooklyn (*www.developdontdestroy.com*), and Forest City Ratner (*www.fcrc.com*).
3. T. Angotti, "Atlantic Yards: Through the Looking Glass," *Gotham Gazette*, November 15, 2005, available at *www.gothamgazette.com*.
4. Interview with the author.
5. B. Lewis and J. Kest, interview, October 2006.
6. M. W. Griffith, "Calling the Question of ACORN," DMI Blog: Politics, Policy and the American Dream, December 30, 2005, available at *www.dmiblog.net/archives/2005/12/calling_the_question_of_acorn.html*.
7. H. Swarts, *Organizing Urban America* (Minneapolis, University of Minnesota Press, 2008).
8. B. Lewis, conversation with the author, October 2006.
9. B. Lewis, conversation with the author, October 2006.
10. Conversations with B. Lewis and observations at ACORN meetings.
11. C. Montgomery, "Cleveland Is Home, But Is That Enough? Urban Revival: Forest City's Rise," *Plain Dealer*, December 1, 2005.
12. See *basketball.ballparks.com/NBA/BrooklynNets/index.htm*.
13. Conversation with B. Lewis, October 2006.
14. Conversations with B. Lewis and officials from Atlantic Yards, May 2006.
15. G. Sargent, "First among Thirds," *American Prospect*, April 16, 2006.
16. B. Lewis, "Supporting Atlantic Yards: Simply Not Enough Housing in Brooklyn," *City Limits Weekly* 546 (July 31, 2006).
17. Conversation with Speliotis, September 2006.

18. Ibid.
19. Conversation with Caldwell, September 2006.
20. Conversation with Lander, October 2005.
21. Editorial, "Brooklyn Fairy Tale," *New York Sun*, June 6, 2005.
22. See DDDB's website, *www.developdontdestroy.com*.
23. Ibid.
24. See Ron Shiffman, "Atlantic Yards: Staving Off a Scar for Decades," June 3, 2006, *dddb.net/php/reading/shiffman.php*.
25. Chris Smith, "Mr. Ratner's Neighborhood," *New York Magazine*, August 14, 2006.
26. See "Pastor of the People: David Dyson in conversation with Norman Kelley," April 2005, *www.thebrooklynrail.org/local/april05/dyson.html*.
27. P. Goldberger, "Gehry-Rigged," *New Yorker*, October 16, 2006; C. Carr, "Voices of the Fading Community in the Shadow of the Atlantic Yards," *Village Voice*, July 25, 2006.
28. Author's notes from meeting.
29. See "Divisiveness: Is It about Goldstein—or Ratner?," Atlantic Yards Report, June 6, 2006, *atlanticyardsreport.blogspot.com/2006/06/divisiveness-is-it-about-goldsteinor.html*.
30. See N. Confessore, "Perspectives on the Atlantic Yards Development through the Prism of Race," *New York Times*, November, 12, 2006.
31. N. Confessore, "Perspectives on the Atlantic Yards Development through the Prism of Race," *New York Times*, November, 12, 2006.
32. A. Feuer, "Affordable Apartments a New York Luxury," *New York Times*, February 11, 2006.
33. New York ACORN, "Sweetheart Development: Gentrification and Resegregation in Downtown Brooklyn," March 16, 2006, available at *www.acorn.org/fileadmin/Afforable_Housing/03.16.06_sweetheartdevelopment.doc*.
34. TimesRatnerReport, available at *timesratnerreport.blogspot.com/2005/12/more-on-observers-roger-green-story.html*.
35. J. Murphy, "The Battle of Brooklyn: Grassroots Groups Split on Whether Arena Plan Scores for Borough," *Village Voice*, July 19, 2004.
36. Conversation with B. Lewis, October 2006. See also J. Murphy, "The Battle of Brooklyn," *Village Voice*, July 12, 2005.
37. E. Louis, "A Groundbreaking Coalition," *New York Daily News*, December 22, 2006.
38. Conversation with B. Lewis, October 2006.
39. Conversation with B. Lewis, February 2008.

8

Community Resistance to School Privatization
The Case of New York City

Janelle Scott and Norm Fruchter

As public schools serving poor children of color continue to struggle on standardized assessments, many reformers propose that school choice and the privatization of public school management could be remedies. This approach marks a shift from efforts to improve schools from within the system. Choice advocates and reformers seeking to reduce the role of government in education tend to define the schooling desires of poor parents of color as universally favoring school choice. While urban parents increasingly favor school choice plans like vouchers or charter schools, the popular portrayal of their support tends to be simplistic. For example, descriptions of poor communities of color's support of choice often fail to put such support in social context and exclude consideration of the race and class dynamics that have historically denied equal opportunity to poor urban children. The flat portrayals of community support of school choice also tend to ignore past and contemporary organizing for better educational options by these communities, and the way they have used school choice strategically as part of broader educational and social movements (Anyon 2005; Fruchter 2007; Margonis and Parker 1995; Oakes and Rodgers 2006; Wilson 1987). Moreover, many poor parents of color have opposed such initiatives and organized to resist their implementation. Yet analyses of school choice politics have focused far more on choice advocacy than on choice opposition.

This chapter describes the opposition in 2001 to school choice and privatization, largely led by the New York City chapter of ACORN in collaboration with other groups. Next, we consider ACORN's model for organizing against the initiative and argue that it offers lessons for other grassroots groups seeking to resist the school choice efforts in many urban school districts. Our goal is to provide a descriptive analysis of a movement that has been all but ignored since it achieved its short-term goal. This case study of ACORN's successful opposition to a privatization effort raises questions about the future structure and dynamics of urban education, and the extent to which community groups and parents will be involved in its development as private providers enter the public sphere. Ultimately, we conclude that more attention to these localized opposition movements is needed in order to better contextualize and understand community and parental preferences for school choice.

Our description of the ACORN-led opposition movement against educational privatization does not deny the existence of support for school choice measures in urban communities, where parents and their advocates have long struggled for quality public schools, only to be met with resistance from public officials, often with devastating results. School choice—as a diverse set of policy options—indeed enjoys substantial political support, and some local ACORN chapters have supported charter schools. But parents, community-based organizers, and educational advocates have also at times fiercely contested market-based school choice options. The private management of public schools, vouchers, and some charter school plans are examples of market-based choice plans that have drawn such opposition.

On the surface, market-based choice can conflict with the traditional, progressive orientations of community-based organizations like ACORN. For example, market-based school reforms tend to emphasize the values of choice, competition, and consumer accountability over other democratic values such as equity, access, and quality (Scott and Barber 2002; Stone 2002). But the relationship between market-based school reform and political progressives has always been complicated, and not necessarily in complete conflict. Many market aficionados do not totally reject democratic values; advocates of market-based educational reforms commonly argue that the policies they champion will result in greater educational opportunity (Chubb 1997; Chubb and Moe 1990; Viteritti 2000). And while choice supporters often assert that traditional civil rights leaders and teacher unions are out of touch with the preferences of low-income parents who, they claim, increasingly favor vouchers and other privatization measures (Fuller 2000; Moe 2001), new civil rights organizations have emerged whose policy agendas put the growth of school choice at the center of their advocacy work (Scott, Lubienski, and DeBray-Pelot 2008). Still, while important coalitions have formed between market-based reformers and some low-income communities of color (Apple 2001; Holt

2000), and there is evidence that growing constituencies of color support vouchers (Carl 1996; Wilgoren 2000), many community groups and parents have often opposed these very same reforms (Johnson, Pianna, and Burlingame 2000).

The coalitions formed to defeat the 2000 voucher ballot initiatives in Michigan and California, the resistance to Edison Schools in Philadelphia and San Francisco, the three failed charter school referenda in Washington state between 1996 and 2004, and the advocacy efforts against vouchers in Florida, Ohio, and Wisconsin (Witte 2000) represent key examples of this opposition. But current research literature and popular media coverage often ignore local communities' resistance to market-based choice initiatives. These omissions are exacerbated when resistance is organized and led by communities of color who are neither strongly connected to nor supported by local or national political elites. But if, as some market advocates argue, educational policy should respond to parent and community preferences, we need much closer analyses of the composition, ideologies, and strategies of these moments of resistance to the imposition of local school choice.

This chapter examines New York City's attempt to give the Edison Schools Corporation the management of five public schools that were low-performing and thus designated as Schools Under Registration Review (SURR), which resulted in their being monitored by the then Board of Education and the New York State Department of Education. We discuss the successful campaign to resist that takeover by a coalition of local parent groups, the school system's teachers' union (the United Federation of Teachers, or UFT), and ACORN.

Management Organizations and Urban Education

Educational Management Organizations (EMOs) emerged in the 1990s as private, for-profit companies that promised to weed out the inefficiency of large urban school district bureaucracies. So wasteful were school districts, EMO founders argued, that a private company could manage schools with better academic results, and they could do it by expending fewer resources and could even turn a profit. As school districts experienced decidedly mixed results with EMOs, and as several EMOs failed to become profitable, districts began terminating contracts or allowing them to end (Richards, Shore, and Sawicky 1996). With the arrival of charter school reform in 1992, EMOs could now contract with individual charter school boards, and Edison Schools became the largest, most controversial, and best-known EMO, largely due to the development of charter schools (Miron and Nelson 2002). As the charter school movement matured, and as the for-profit management sector has consolidated, nonprofit charter school management organizations—CMOs—have taken their place. Though CMOs have tended to be less controversial, researchers have not reached consensus on their academic, fiscal, and social impacts[1] (Bulkley 2005; Honig 2004; Molnar and Garcia 2007; Molnar et al. 2007; National Charter School Research Project 2007; Peterson 2007; Scott and DiMartino 2008).

Much of the controversy surrounding MOs has centered on profits, academic effectiveness, community involvement, and the role of teachers unions. To date, the data on student achievement and MOs are inconclusive. For example, in the aggregate, they have not been able to produce significantly higher academic performance on standardized assessments, and in some contexts, the test scores of MO-run schools are worse than those of the local public schools (Miron and Nelson 2002). In many cases, EMO-run schools have proven to be more costly than traditional public schools (Schrag 2001). Where EMOs have been profitable or financially stable, much of the reduced cost is attributable to the lower salaries earned by teachers and support staff in these schools, which typically eschew teachers unions. And there has been significant instability in the MO sector, with for-profit EMOs especially merging or closing their doors altogether. In 2000–2001, in the midst of the controversial New York City campaign, the price of Edison Schools' stock plummeted, and executives began selling their shares. (Edison Schools is no longer publicly traded.) As the nation's largest EMO, Edison drew much attention, and while many of its contracts with districts and schools were successful, there were also multiple incidences of lackluster academic performance, mismanagement, and teacher dissatisfaction. Despite these issues, public officials—especially those in troubled urban systems—enamored with the notion that private management could be superior to public management, have pursued contracts with private management in multiple cities (Herszenhorn 2006).

Although EMOs had a mixed record of accomplishments in charter school management in 2001 (Ackerman 2001; Ascher et al. 2001; Miron and Applegate 2000), the leaders of New York City's then Board of Education (now Department of Education) proposed a major high-profile initiative to give EMOs the management of poorly performing public schools in August 2000. The (then) New York City Board of Education initially issued a *Request for Proposals* for EMOs to convert up to fifty-one low-performing schools to charter status and then manage them. A series of internal negotiations eventually reduced to five the number of schools to be immediately transferred to private management: Public School 161 in Harlem, Public School 66 in the Bronx, Middle School 246, Intermediate School 111, and Middle School 320 in Brooklyn. These schools had been identified as failing under New York State's SURR program, and the New York State Education Department had been pressing the city school system to close and restructure them. As Bertha Lewis, a citywide ACORN leader and the anti-Edison campaign organizer, explained, there was some intention that "the next phase would be fifty and then they would go up to a hundred" (interview, 2001).

Fourteen education companies responded to the city's RFP, and from these bidders, the New York City Board of Education selected the Edison Schools Corporation as the sole provider. Edison's Marshall Mitchell explained that Edison responded to the city's RFP because "it was a huge opportunity for us right in our own backyard to demonstrate that we had an incredibly good product that could turn around the public schools and the community in a positive way" (interview, 2001).

New York's charter school law, which legislators enacted in 1998, somewhat constrained Edison Schools' growth aspirations. The original New York State charter law required the conversion of SURR schools to charter status before an EMO could assume their management since EMOS were not allowed to directly hold the charter. A school would have to first be converted to charter status and then contract with Edison as its manager. A key process for the purposes of ACORN's organizing was also in place. The law mandated a vote on the schools' conversion to charters by the parents of each targeted school and allowed those schools that achieved a 51 percent parent approval vote to officially become charters. In the five schools, parents of almost 5,000 children were eligible to vote, and the Board of Education scheduled the vote for the period of March 19 through 30, 2001.

The New York Board of Education chose Edison as the sole conversion and management agent during the winter of 2000. During the winter holiday break, parents were notified that, as Lewis recalls, "either your school will be shut down or you have the option to change to charter. But if you do change to charter, only the Edison Corporation will be the management company." ACORN and a range of other community groups responded with anger, resistance, and a determination to develop an oppositional campaign.

ACORN's Opposition to the New York City Board of Education's Privatization Proposal

After several months of conflict, controversy, and campaigning, the parents of students in the five schools overwhelmingly rejected the Edison management takeover.[2] The elections drew 2,286 parent voters, and 1,883, more than 82 percent, voted no. Some 2,700 parents who did not vote were counted as negative votes. In all, fewer than 10 percent of the eligible parents voted in favor of the conversion/management proposal. What follows is an analysis of the ideologies and strategies the participants in this conflict pursued and an examination of how the events played out in terms of the community-level politics of privatization. The analysis examines four key questions:

- How was the conversion/management process structured, and why did Edison agree to participate, given the difficulty of succeeding?
- What arguments did the opposing forces advance?
- What organizing strategies did the opposing forces deploy?
- What explains the overwhelming defeat of the conversion/management proposal?

The Conversion/Management Process

Some seven New York City public schools had previously been converted to charter status, following the procedures mandated in the charter law established by the New York state legislature in 1998. The law required an election in which all the school's parents were eligible to vote, and a 51 percent majority of the school's parent body, not simply a majority of those voting, was required to approve the conversion/takeover process. As Jude Hollins, then a staff person in the New York City Board of Education's Office of Charter Schools, explains, "it's not the majority of parents who vote [that's necessary for approval], it's literally the majority of the parents. If you have 1,000 kids enrolled in that school, you need 501 of the parents to say yes" (interview, 2001). Some charter advocates see this provision in the New York State Charter School legislation as overly burdensome and designed to stymie charter efforts, while other public school advocates see it as an important regulation to ensure community buy-in.

This process essentially defined all parents not voting as voting no and thus required a highly intensive mobilization, recruitment, and persuasion effort. In each of the seven schools that previously converted to charter status, the school's leadership led the conversion process, organized the vote, and recruited a majority of yes votes from the school's parent body. Before the Edison conflict, there had never been opposition to any of the conversion efforts; Edison was the first contested conversion/management takeover. Still, many charter organizers prefer to create new schools rather than convert existing ones; organizers perceived of as outsiders have a tougher time than local school leaders convincing local stakeholders to accept their leadership.

Many activists argued that Mayor Giuliani had the privatization plan in progress well before school leaders embraced it. For example, ACORN's Lewis claimed, "the Giuliani administration and other politically connected folks in the city had been plotting to have Edison come in for over a year and a half" (interview, 2005). Rudolph Giuliani, New York City's mayor during this conflict, was a persistent privatization advocate and had forced out Dr. Rudy Crew, the school system's previous chancellor, because of a fierce disagreement about the legitimacy and effectiveness of vouchers. Giuliani was such a staunch advocate of vouchers that in December 2000 his office sponsored a major conference, at which he officiated, on the importance of vouchers for school reform. Many elite advocates and researchers from New York City and from out of state attended the conference. Subsequently, Giuliani pressured Crew's successor, Harold Levy, to institute a major privatization initiative. Levy, a corporate lawyer committed to the need for increased funding for the city's schools, was not enthusiastic about market-based reforms. Among the many hindsight explanations for the Edison defeat were suggestions that Levy had set up the process to fail.

According to former deputy chancellor for instruction Judith Rizzo, Levy's support for the plan was a political compromise, since he was accountable to both the mayor and the citywide Board of Education: "That's very different from being a lackey or a puppet whose strings are being pulled. The fact is, does the Mayor like the notion of privatization? He does; he's been unequivocal about that. On the other hand, there are members on our board who feel differently about it, [and] Harold works for our board. They sign his paycheck. What Harold did was he sort of weighed both . . . and said, 'Let's give it a shot'" (quoted in Franck 2001).

Why did Edison accept a process and a set of conditions almost impossible to fulfill? Asked whether a direct contract from the Board of Education would have been more desirable than the charter conversion process, Edison's Marshall Mitchell replied, "Absolutely. There are a lot of people who feel this was set up to fail." Mitchell argued that the process itself was problematic: "The RFP went out in August and then there was deafening silence until December, just before Christmas, [when] the Board of Education announced that Edison had been named the conversion agent and that we would go out and inform the community, teachers, principals about what all this meant. . . . You had parents and community who had historically been locked out of school decisions now being asked to make fundamental decisions about the lives of their children and the future of the schools" (interview, 2001).

Given Edison's analytic capacity and forecasting acumen, it is difficult to imagine that Edison did not understand the difficulty of producing a majority vote of approval from the targeted schools' parent voters. Clearly, the corporation understood that losing at the polls would significantly damage their standing, as well as delegitimate privatization advocates' claims that poor communities of color overwhelmingly supported charters, vouchers, and other market-based schooling initiatives. (Indeed, Edison's stock fell 19 percent after the election outcomes were announced.) It is possible that Edison expected a level of participation and involvement from the Board of Education that would have increased the legitimacy of their effort. As Mitchell explained: "[Perhaps] if we had demanded that the process be done differently, that the Board of Education would have to be our partner every step of the way, to explain the conversion process and the options that were available, [the outcomes might have differed]. This never happened, and it set the table for the political scavengers" (interview, 2001).

Perhaps exaggerated assumptions about the spillover results of failing schools, including an antagonism toward public schools by poor people of color, led Edison to decide it could organize a majority of parents not only to participate in the election but also to vote yes to the conversion/ takeover. Chris Whittle, Edison's founder, indicated in a *New York Times* op-ed piece that "we were so excited about the opportunity to transform low-performing schools right in our own backyard that we agreed to the plan" (2001). (The reference to Edison's backyard refers to the proposal, eventually abandoned, to build the company's national headquarters facility in Harlem.) Perhaps the Edison strategists believed other privatization advocates' arguments that parents of children in failing schools were desperate for market-based alternatives. Whatever the ultimate reasons, Edison took on a daunting and ultimately impossible task in initiating a campaign to garner a majority vote of approval from parents in the five schools.

The Opposing Arguments

Edison made a series of arguments about its capacity to improve the targeted schools that had, according to the city and the state's data, been failing students for many years. Gaynor McCown, an Edison official at the time, said, "We bring a very rigorous and good design, [which is] research-based [to those failing schools]. We bring structure and accountability, which many schools do not have" (interview, 2001). Edison argued that they had developed considerable expertise in improving poorly performing schools across the country. Moreover, Edison hoped that its "ability to invest huge sums of money" in school management and improvement, as Marshall Mitchell indicated, as well as its commitment to provide cutting-edge technology infrastructure, would convince parents that these significant new resources would dramatically improve student achievement.

Other city officials weighed the proposal and came out publicly against it. Many African American elected officials, including Manhattan borough president Virginia Fields argued that "the Board of Education is abdicating its responsibility to our public school children. We must invest in our public schools. And the Board of Education must direct resources to the classroom—to the programs that work" (Fields 2001). U.S. representative Charles Rangel, city council members William Perkins and Guillermo Linares, other citywide African American leaders such as Al Sharpton and David Dinkins, and many community school board members opposed the conversion to charters and Edison's management takeover. At an anti-Edison rally at P.S. 161 in Harlem, Linares demanded: "Why do they always come to our communities to rape us, privatize our schools, and take away our dignity and our future?" Crown Heights school board member Agnes Green explained, "We didn't like the idea of taking an institution that is there to serve the public and changing it into a for-profit company. If they don't make money, they can just cut bait and leave the fishing pond—and that's too large a gamble" (quoted in Kaplan 2001).

ACORN articulated many of the themes that the citywide campaign to stop the conversion/takeover ultimately employed. ACORN's opposition to Mayor Giuliani was longstanding and intense, and its organizers had previously collaborated with the UFT and other municipal unions to defeat a mayoral initiative to amend the city charter to increase the mayor's fiscal powers. For ACORN, the conversion/takeover represented, as

Lewis said, "just another arrow in his quiver of privatization." So Giuliani became one of ACORN's primary targets in the campaign against Edison.

Giuliani had been one of the main drivers of the initiative to raise the tuition of the City University of New York (CUNY), to remove remedial courses from CUNY's senior colleges, and to limit such remediation to only one year in CUNY's community colleges. Mayor Giuliani and Republican governor George Pataki appointed the special commission that made these recommendations, and Benno Schmidt, the president of the Edison Schools Corporation, chaired it. Therefore, throughout New York City's communities of color, Edison and Giuliani were considered indelibly linked as opponents of equal educational access.

ACORN had been organizing for several years to improve the poorly performing schools in most of the neighborhoods served by the schools targeted for conversion and takeover. As Amy Cohen, a lead ACORN organizer in the Bronx, remembers, "ACORN had been working to concentrate resources in the South Bronx to focus on certain schools that were low performing and attract teachers with more experience to these schools, and create a space for conversations between parents and teachers, . . . so parents had a lot of ideas themselves about how you could make a school better that weren't necessarily the same way that Edison thought that you could make a school better" (interview, 2005).

These issues of community-based school improvement experience and the legitimation of parental voice surfaced throughout the opposition's campaign. As Megan Hester, an ACORN organizer in Brooklyn, recalls, "Parents definitely were indignant about the possibility of somebody not wanting them to be involved or being able to shut them out. . . . It was important to them that there was a way for them to be involved and that they were valued and the parent voices are important" (interview, 2006). Hester went on to explain that parents were offended that a corporation could come in and run things the way it saw fit without any local involvement or connection to the community.

In addition to the concerns about community voice, ACORN also conducted research across the country into the Edison track record in several school districts. ACORN not only documented the limited and sometimes discouraging outcomes of Edison's efforts but actually recruited school board members and parents from some of those districts to come to New York City and participate in the anti-Edison rallies. An ACORN leader remembers: "The Edison Corporation's track record was not any better than anyone else's. . . . We had had folks come in from San

Francisco and other districts that Edison had come into that showed, in fact, that when Edison came in that things deteriorated and went backwards. So we were saying, you know, 'Parents and kids, yes. Edison no. Don't privatize our schools'" (interview, 2005).

The arguments against privatizing the schools—which in this context meant putting a for-profit company in charge of the schools and providing the opportunity for profiting from their management—were primary and pervasive. ACORN constantly raised the issue of taxpayer dollars going to a for-profit organization. As Amy Cohen recalls, "Ultimately privatization was a huge factor in their [parents] decision for not wanting that school to go to Edison, because they felt like, 'Public schools are for everybody, and we don't want a company making money off of our students, off of our children. So we're not up for signing up for something that's gonna potentially make money for a company'" (interview, 2005).

ACORN linked private management of schools to privately operated prisons and defined both situations as fundamental exploitation of disadvantaged students, parents, and neighborhoods. As Bertha Lewis argued in a *Christian Science Monitor* interview, "There's a feeling in the black and brown community that they're profiting in the prison sector. Now they're saying, let's go straight to the schools and make money" (quoted in Coeyman 2001). ACORN also argued that because the five failing schools had been removed from their community school districts and placed in a citywide virtual improvement zone called the Chancellor's District, the schools should be accorded the additional resources and the time necessary to improve.

The Organizing Strategies
The initial issue that galvanized community opposition was the New York City Board of Education's proposal to grant Edison a $99,900 fee (a $100,000 fee would have required public hearings to approve) for each school that voted to approve the conversion and takeover, or a total potential fee of $500,000 to support Edison's public relations and get-out-the-vote efforts. The fee was designated to cover the costs of establishing and maintaining Edison offices in the targeted schools, as well as for parent outreach materials, translation, and hiring the American Arbitration Association to conduct the vote (New York Teacher 2001). Although the fee was payable only after parents approved the conversion to charters, community groups perceived the offer as another instance of Edison capitalizing on its political connections to the Giuliani administration.

ACORN organized a lawsuit against the Board of Education, challenging the fee and objecting to the Board of Education providing Edison the names, telephone numbers, and addresses of parents in the targeted schools while not providing opponents of the conversion and takeover the same information. In the settlement of the suit, ACORN won the right to have three mailings to parents paid for by the Board of Education and the postponement of the election from February to March. Additionally, ACORN forced the Board of Education to add "Inc." to the Edison Schools listing on the ballot.

Once the Board of Education announced the election period, intense campaigning engulfed all five schools. The borough presidents, other elected officials, local community groups, and ACORN organized large protest meetings at each school. A citywide coalition including the NAACP, District Council 37 Municipal Workers Union, Local 1199 Hospital Workers Union, the UFT, and ACORN quickly formed to coordinate strategy and resources across the three boroughs and to organize citywide rallies. ACORN redeployed its organizing staffs to concentrate on the Bronx school and the three Brooklyn schools because they had already been actively organizing on education issues in those neighborhoods. They also developed alliances with strong neighborhood and Parents Association leaders at the Harlem school. A local community group, Community Advocates for Educational Excellence, which had long been organizing for the improvement of Harlem's schools and had previously worked with ACORN, also helped to mobilize the campaign at P.S. 161.

Organizers were usually denied entry into the five schools; they nevertheless quickly developed neighborhood contact lists from the Parent Association officers, school activists, and other parents they had built relationships with through their previous organizing. As Cohen remembers: "Mostly organizers worked with parents who were in and out of the school all the time, who were parent volunteers at the school and who were always picking up their kids" (interview, 2005). Hester, an organizer in Brooklyn, says, "We got the list from the Parents Association of all the parents in the school, and . . . divided it up by neighborhood" (interview, 2006). What followed was extensive door knocking, night after night, until almost all the eligible parent voters in each school were identified, contacted, interviewed, and often reinterviewed. Cohen explained,

ACORN really followed a strategy of organizers and parents talking to other parents and building a network of parents. . . . They used a lot of traditional organizing techniques, of house meetings, of building lists. . . . And they made these signs; a lot of people posted these signs on their houses and the neighborhood was plastered! Like, the businesses around the schools were all full of signs, because the parents would go and say, "Hey, I shop here all the time. Can we put these signs up? We don't want Edison coming into the neighborhood." And the businesses said, "Yeah. Absolutely!" . . . The signs just said, "No on Edison." They had a big red circle with the line through it.

ACORN and its allies held a series of neighborhood and citywide rallies throughout the three months of the campaign, organized by the coalition of unions, advocacy organizations, and elected leaders who had initially coalesced the citywide opposition. Because some of these rallies were quite large and all were very spirited, their media coverage helped to counter the considerable tilt of the citywide print and electronic media toward the Edison management bid. Although the editorial board of the *New York Times* sounded a note of cautious opposition, important segments of the city's political and corporate elites favored the charter conversion and the Edison takeover, arguing that parents whose children had been forced to attend the five failing schools deserved the same choice as more affluent parents.

Edison's strategy also targeted the eligible voter-parents, and Edison's efforts had the advantage of being school based, since the corporation established offices in each of the five targeted schools. Cohen remembers seeing teams of Edison representatives in each school, supplied with brochures and other promotional materials, including a video about the corporation's school improvement efforts. But these representatives seemed, to Cohen, somewhat inexperienced about how to present the advantages of Edison management to parents and community members:

> I remember them as being sort of like young, almost like sales-type people . . . not folks who the parents related to as, this is somebody from my community, who might get what my experience of this is, and understands what it's like to want to have a better school but [also] wants to have a process to improve this school that I'm involved in. . . . They would have these groups of twenty-somethings who were out spreading the word about Edison and, you know, passing out their glossy literature and all this stuff. But they weren't having conversations with people in the neighborhood in the way that the parents were having conversations with each other. (interview, 2005)

In Bertha Lewis's perception, the Edison representatives were "salesmen. They were selling the services of their corporation. . . . They didn't listen to the parents. . . . They tried to tap into the parents' fears by [saying], like, 'Well, if you don't vote for charter, you're done. You know, you have nothing.'" Lewis remembers that Edison did hire a few parent leaders, including a former chair of the citywide United Parents Association (UPA). But in her view, the UPA was clear that the former chair was not speaking for the organization:

> The UPA didn't really go, you know, on board to sign off on this. The parents' councils, and the Presidents Council, which are the presidents of Parents' Associations all over the city said, "You know, we don't adhere to this. We want a free, open, and fair election." . . . Also what was [subsequently] discovered was with these individual people in these schools that were targeted, these were folks who had been promised that if the school went charter, that they would be the new board of directors for the school. So they had a definite conflict of interest. (interview, 2005)

Edison did attempt to send its representatives out into the neighborhoods. Hester remembers meeting parents who had already been solicited by Edison staffers. But she felt that the Edison people were far less experienced and therefore far less effective in trying to influence parents to vote for Edison: "The people on our side, first of all, were probably more experienced with talking to parents than the Edison people. . . . There was more of a rapport, you know, we were people who had done lots of door knocking, our Spanish was good, we were connected, you know, we knew stuff about the neighborhood, about the schools" (interview, 2006).

But beyond the advantages of organizing skills, previous experience, and the neighborhood connections that past organizing had developed, ACORN and the other community groups involved in the campaign defined and presented the issues in ways that resonated with local parents. Lewis argued that the ACORN message was clear and consistent:

> Don't privatize our schools. Vote no. You know, if you vote no, then you could determine what the schools' futures were. That paying a company all of this money could have best been spent on putting those funds into those schools. The Edison Corporation's track record was not any better than anyone else's. . . . With the help of the citywide coalition, and with the help of some of the labor unions, and standing outside and really

organizing the old-fashioned way, we were able to get to the parents. (interview, 2005)

From Cohen and Hester's perspectives as organizers, the campaign's key issues were very persuasive to prospective parent voters. Although Hester remembers meeting parents who were determined to vote for Edison, in her view they were a small minority of the parents she encountered: "There were definitely people who felt like businesses are well run, you know, you can trust corporations, that your government is corrupt, more inefficient [than business]. . . . But there were many more people who were kind of riled about this. 'They're taking advantage of us.' It was kind of like, 'Why are they doing this to our school? Why only the underperforming schools?' Like, 'They're trying to sell us out!'" (interview, 2006.) Cohen stresses Edison's unresponsiveness to the issues that were critical to parents:

> The parents felt really alienated by this company. Even though they [Edison] were there [in the school] and they had these very glossy materials and they had this video, . . . [the parents] didn't feel like anybody was talking to them like real, thinking people and like the parents who matter so much to making a school a good school. And so I think that they felt frustrated and also that they felt like those [Edison] reforms were likely to be like other failed reforms they had experienced. They weren't ready to sign on for just whatever was coming next. They wanted to be involved in making the decision about that. . . . I think ultimately privatization was a huge factor in their decision for not wanting that school to go to Edison because they felt like public schools are for everybody and we don't want a company making money off of our students, off of our children. (interview, 2005)

In retrospect, Cohen and Hester felt that the campaign was far easier and far more overwhelmingly successful than they had expected. Cohen remembers that Edison sent sound trucks throughout her Bronx neighborhood in the final days of the campaign but didn't do any intensive get-out-the-vote effort: "I just couldn't believe that Edison wasn't going to get how to move people to the polls. . . . If we knew how to do it and they had all the resources that they had—how could they not know that?" Hester remembers the campaign as "a really empowering organizing experience." In her view, "it was easier than any door knocking I've ever done before . . . I probably thought it was a lot more difficult when we began, like this was a huge thing to take on because Edison is this, you know, huge nationwide corporation" (interview, 2006). And as Lewis defined ACORN's feelings at the campaign's conclusion: "We're so happy and so proud about it because against a lot of money and a lot of organization, we prevailed, just from door-to-door, old-fashioned grass-roots organizing, networking and parents getting galvanized" (interview, 2005).

Organizing Success

Thus far, we have discussed that the structure of the vote made it difficult for Edison to be successful in converting the schools to charter school status. Yet, without the ACORN campaign and other community organizing and the publicity it brought, it is entirely likely that the company would have prevailed, given the resources the Board of Education promised Edison. Why, then, was "old-fashioned organizing" able to trump the resources and sophistication of what seems to have been a well-funded public relations effort? First, the election was so specifically targeted, and the electorate was so small in number, that ACORN's limited resources could be effectively mobilized to identify and reach all the potential parent voters in the five schools. A more general election involving a much larger number of voters might have dissipated ACORN's resources and privileged the less intensive but more wide-reaching efforts that Edison mounted. In addition, ACORN's organizing strategy is to be aggressive and confrontational and to agitate community members—an approach that virtually guarantees the attention of New York media. ACORN's organizing was quite effective at engaging parents in an issue that they might not have paid attention to otherwise.

Second, Edison seems not to have realized that public relations efforts alone were insufficient to convince and mobilize the majority of parent voters required for a 51 percent approval vote. Edison hired relatively few experienced parent, neighborhood, and community workers, and their staffs tended to stay within the school buildings, where they met relatively few numbers of parent voters. Edison also seems to have relied far too heavily on mailings, sound trucks, and other traditional electoral mechanisms for reaching potential voters. ACORN, in contrast, understood from the campaign's inception that this was not a traditional election and that intensive organizing efforts were required. Gaynor McCown, an Edison official, concurred that the company faltered in its organizing, saying, "We didn't get our message out, and this made a big difference" (interview, 2001).

But intensive organizing efforts alone are sometimes not sufficient to implement a successful campaign. "Parents getting galvanized," in Lewis's phrase, ultimately depends on connecting the issues at the campaign's core to parents' deepest convictions about how their children's education should be conducted. At the critical levels of issue and message, ACORN and its allies succeeded in defining Edison as an unreliable (in terms of past performance), for-profit company that sought to make money off the neighborhood's children. Indeed, at the time of the campaign, Edison was a publicly traded company whose stock prices had plummeted, and investors were suing the company for a range of fiscal issues. ACORN's research revealed that Edison had trouble fulfilling the terms of its contracts in other districts.

ACORN's campaign tapped into parents' fears about privatization and about being taken advantage of by a suspect schooling experiment in for-profit management. Given city governments' decades of disregard for neighborhood needs, along with the universal perception within neighborhoods of color that Giuliani's regime was imperious and racist, it is not surprising that angry parents saw the mayor's attempt to convey the failing schools to Edison as yet another way to rip off poor neighborhoods for private profit. Alternatively, community members could have felt that the schools they had were worth preserving, but more research is needed to capture the range of preferences.

Edison never found a way to counter the arguments that connected with these deep currents of feeling among neighborhood parents. Once Edison's claims of effectiveness based on superior resources and expertise were challenged by the ACORN research into Edison's outcomes at its other sites, Edison's messages became diffuse and less convincing. In the end, it was not "the political scavengers" Marshall Mitchell held responsible for Edison's defeat. Rather, Edison's failure to connect with the core issues of neighborhood parents, who proved far more suspicious of privatization than conservative ideologues had portrayed, turned the election into a debacle for Edison.

There are other plausible interpretations for what happened in the successful campaign against Edison in New York City that also involve the complicated interaction of power, race, and educational opportunity. Some parents, for example, clearly valued the targeted schools despite their students' dismal performance on standardized tests (Coeyman 2001). This phenomenon of local support for failing schools threatened with closure or change has manifested itself across the country during the recent reform waves of school closings and restructurings. Other parents and community members feared the loss of community jobs should a private company take over the public schools, since many neighborhood residents were employed in a variety of educational roles—as teachers, aides, and custodians (Franck 2001).

Additionally, key political leaders such as Manhattan borough president C. Virginia Fields argued that the programs promised by Edison could be implemented under the purview of public management with public oversight. She also accused the city and the state of disadvantaging the struggling schools through years of neglect and then offering them up to the private sector, which was not necessary.

Implications for Community Organizing and School Choice Politics

The current educational policy context is one of increasing school segregation by race and social class, where few legal remedies remain available to those seeking equity of educational access and outcomes through a redistribution of resources (Scott 2005). In this environment, the arguments for more market-based school choice as a necessary response to parental demands for educational opportunity require detailed examination. We conclude that local opposition movements to market-based choice initiatives have been ignored or dismissed by advocates determined to advance educational privatization (Whittle 2005). Yet these opposition movements offer lessons for grassroots political organizing while also revealing the power disparities between elites who advance a privatization agenda and local communities—almost always poor communities of color—that are the targets of privatization initiatives. At the same time, these opposition movements suggest that public officials interested in keeping educational privatization at bay would do well to attend to the long-standing concerns held by community organizers regarding the quality of education for poor children of color. The New York City anti-Edison campaign provides a window into the complex intersection of parental preferences, privatization advocacy, and persistent educational inequality for poor and minority communities. Parenti (1978) expands this point:

> To give no attention to how interests are prefigured by power, how social choice is predetermined by the politico-economic forces controlling society's resources and institutions is to begin in the middle of the story—or toward the end. When we treat interests as *given* and then fo-

cus only on the decision process, our treatment is limited to issues and choices that themselves are products of the broader conditions of power. A study of these broader conditions is ruled out at the start if we treat each "interest" as self-generated rather than shaped in a context of social relationships, and if we treat each policy conflict as a "new issue" stirring in the body politic. (12)

We argue that it is critical not simply to examine the conditions that led to the vote in the short term but also to consider the long-standing social, political, and economic inequality faced by the schooling communities. These conditions shaped ACORN's involvement in the resistance movement and help to explain the suspicion many parents had toward the Giuliani-endorsed measure.

Privatization advocates across the country have defined the resistance to market-based intervention such as the attempted Edison takeover in New York City as not truly representative of community values and preferences (Moe 2001). Examining the tendency to explain away local resistance when it fails to support conservative ideologies about how communities of color respond to privatization initiatives, one researcher (Jacobs 1993) concludes, "When minority leaders do not fall in line with majority group strategies, the former are discredited as not being truly representative of their constituencies. Majority leaders and caretakers then threaten to work around these 'false' leaders, that is, to work with the 'true' community" (189).

In similar fashion, some privatization advocates in New York City, such as the *New York Post* editorial board, argued that the New York City Schools chancellor should have bypassed the conversion and takeover vote altogether and simply contracted directly with private companies to manage the failing schools, effectively excluding the resistance coalition of ACORN, the UFT, and the parents within the schools. Such arguments exemplify the efforts of market-based advocates to maintain the power to implement privatization within elite circles of government. Given the increasing concentration of economic power at the highest levels of American society, this argument for the necessity for elite decision making to impose market-based initiatives in low-income communities of color is likely to intensify.

Thus the Edison initiative may prove to be only an initial foray in New York City's politics of educational choice. City government elites—led by Mayor Giuliani—wanted vouchers and were persuaded to begin their efforts by introducing private management of failing public schools.

Edison was granted the exclusive contract to manage those schools and was provided with Board of Education resources to convince parents to choose the company's management. The severe educational failures of the five schools (and of the next fifty that might have been nominated had the vote for Edison succeeded) created an opportunity to put educational privatization on the policy agenda. Yet, given the political ideology of Mayor Giuliani and his associates, the demonstrated failure of poorly performing schools may have been only a pretext for this first effort to introduce privatization schemes into the city's schools. In future efforts, arguments about civil rights and educational opportunity may become convenient placeholders for other political agendas, and the systemic change benefits of potential reforms such as the fiscal adequacy lawsuit brought by the Campaign for Fiscal Equity (which successfully argued that New York State had shortchanged New York City schools for decades) may well be permanently marginalized.

To complicate this potential for elite imposition of privatization initiatives, researchers and policymakers must move beyond the claims of market advocates and examine the perspectives of community constituencies who struggle with the reality of inequitable education. The need to complicate the debate is not to deny the existence of support for market-based choice within poor communities of color, for this support is real and growing as urban public schools struggle to meet accountability standards under the federal No Child Left Behind Act. Given ACORN's experience organizing against educational privatization in New York City, we question the power dynamics that emphasize this support and define it as more legitimate than the resistance efforts of those same communities, or to simply add opposition as a footnote rather than a central aspect of the politics of urban school reform. Opposition and alternative education strategies are central in the history of educational reform in the United States (Katznelson and Weir 1985). Policy makers committed to meeting the schooling needs of low-income parents of color should carefully examine the claims of privatization advocates and attend to the evidence about the diversity of opinion of urban constituencies confronting privatization initiatives, such as those manifested by the anti-Edison campaign in New York City and other locales.

For community-based advocates, this case shows that organizing can indeed produce desired outcomes. In New York City, ACORN's alliances with key city council leaders, the teachers' union, and other public sector unions, as well as with higher education and civil rights activists, certainly helped the opposition campaign. Also key in the ACORN campaign was a willingness and ability to engage multiple organizing mechanisms that included door-to-door neighborhood canvassing, using legal remedies to gain access to the schools, and successfully engaging the media. Of course, having a privatization proposal that mandated a democratic process helped ACORN and other advocates to have a meaningful voice in the issue, distinguishing the New York City case from other recent state-led efforts in Philadelphia, New Orleans, and Baltimore, where MOs operate a significant proportion of the schools. Without the requirement of a high-stakes vote, the outcome in New York, as well as the organizing strategies, would likely have been quite different. Thus, the New York City case of ACORN's successful campaign against Edison suggests that likeminded organizers should push for the affected community's ability to vote on and organize around privatization proposals in the future. Community-based organizations such as ACORN have been engaged in reforming urban public schools long before elites propose privatized solutions to school failure. Through the engagement process, they are often well positioned to articulate the issues facing their communities, including school finance, facilities, quality teaching and leadership, and quality curriculum.

Epilogue

A question remains: to what extent was the defeat of the privatization proposal in 2001 a good outcome for the targeted schools? Answering this question is complicated and depends upon individual values. Those who favor public management or community voice would tend to regard it as good, while those who favor private management or performance on standardized tests would likely regard the outcome as dysfunctional for the schools. Still, regardless of such complexity, there can be no doubt that the targeted schools continue to struggle academically even as the entire school system has been restructured.

Since the controversy over Edison and the defeat of their privatization initiative, the New York City school system has gone through tremendous structural change. As of 2002, Mayor Bloomberg now directly controls the schools, and Schools Chancellor Joel Klein serves as one of the mayor's commissioners. Locally elected community school boards, the last vestiges of the community control movements of the 1960s and 1970s, have been disbanded, as has the citywide Board of Education. Yet, despite these organizational changes, control of educational policy and decision making has remained constant. The city's elite continues to dominate the citywide educational agenda—the Board of Education is now the Department of Education, overseen by Mayor Bloomberg who appointed Schools Chancellor Joel Klein to his post. Similarly, the Panel for Education Policy advises the mayor and chancellor on issues of school policy, yet the mayor appoints its members. Meanwhile, parents and communities of color continue to struggle for inclusion in the development and implementation of educational policy, as they have done for hundreds of years in New York City (Stafford 2004).

While ACORN and its coalition members successfully fended off the Edison privatization initiative, the schools offered for privatization have hardly flourished as a result. One school was closed by the state due to its low test scores. Another was reconstituted. The other three schools, comprised almost exclusively of low-income Latino or African American students, continue to underperform by ten to twenty percentage points on city and state language arts and math assessments, when compared to all New York City schools. Given the high rates of student poverty in the schools, all are Title I schools, making their students eligible for the school choice options under the federal No Child Left Behind Act, which provides public school choice for students in schools that fail to make annual yearly progress.

Against the backdrop of persistent school underachievement, school choice and privatization measures have morphed and expanded since the earlier effort to turn over SURR schools to Edison Schools Inc. In New York City, with the support of the Bill and Melinda Gates Foundation and other donors, Chancellor Klein has encouraged the growth of small high schools of choice and the expansion of charter schools. New York City parents and community organizers continue their efforts to have their educational concerns heard by public officials. Recent organizing has focused on the reorganization of the city schools, which many parents find confusing. At a recent forum, parents protested outside a community college building where Chancellor Klein was speaking. In these current efforts, parents and community organizers are often employing techniques similar to ACORN's (Hancock 2007).

Grassroots groups such as ACORN that are committed to preserving the public management of urban education face an uphill battle as they work with teachers and parents to improve struggling schools. Under the current federal education policy, No Child Left Behind, states and local education authorities must offer public school choice to students in struggling schools. Local school districts must also provide supplemental educational services (SES) to students in low-achieving schools; this is most often done through private tutoring companies. Title I funds finance the school choice and SES provisions. On a national scale, voucher advocates hope to implement public financing of private school tuition in every state (Debary-Pelot, Lubienski, and Scott 2007). As it stands, there is an inherent but not necessarily irreconcilable tension between community organizers who want more input and public oversight over schools, and reformers committed to private models of educational governance. ACORN's history of expanding democratic participation and access has the potential to ensure that the educational reform agenda of privatization and choice does not neglect the participation of those mostly likely to be affected by these initiatives.

NOTES

1. The research literature's catchall term for EMOs and CMOs is management organizations (MOs). This chapter will use EMOs when discussing for-profits, CMOs when discussing nonprofits, and MOs when referring to the management sector as a whole.
2. This case study employs primary and secondary document analysis, interviews conducted by the authors, and interviews generously shared by Barry Franklin at Utah State University.

REFERENCES

Ackerman, A. 2001. *Edison Charter Academy: Preliminary Report of Findings, Investigation into Complaints.* San Francisco: San Francisco Unified School District.

Anyon, J. 2005. *Radical Possibilities: Public Policy, Urban Education, and a New Social Movement.* New York: Routledge.

Apple, M. W. 2001. *Educating the "Right" Way: Markets, Standards, God, and Inequality.* New York: Routledge Falmer.

Ascher, C., J. Echazarreta, R. Jacobowitz, Y. McBride, T. Troy, and N. Wamba. 2001. *Going Charter: New Models of Support.* New York: Institute for Education and Social Policy, New York University.

Bulkley, K. 2005. "Losing Voice? Educational Management Organizations and Charter Schools' Educational Programs." *Education and Urban Society* 37, no. 2: 204–34.

Carl, J. 1996. "Unusual Allies: Elite and Grass-Roots Origins of Parent Choice in Milwaukee." *Teachers College Record* 98, no. 2: 266–84.

Chubb, J. 1997. "Lessons in School Reform from the Edison Project." In *New*

Schools for a New Century: The Redesign of Urban Education, ed. by J. P. Viteritti and D. Ravitch, 86–122. New Haven: Yale University Press.

Chubb, J., and T. Moe. 1990. *Politics, Markets, and America's Schools.* Washington, DC: Brookings Institution.

Coeyman, M. 2001. "Who Ya Gonna Call?" *Christian Science Monitor*. February 20. Available at *www.csmonitor.com/2001/0220/p13s1.html.*

DeBray-Pelot, E., C. Lubienski, and J. Scott. 2007. "The Institutional Landscape of Interest Groups and School Choice." *Peabody Journal of Education* 82, no. 2: 204–30.

Fields, C. V. 2001. Testimony before City Council Education Committee, March 16. Available at www.cvfieldsmbp.org/press/3-16-01_edcom.htm.

Franck, E. 2001. "Levy Faces a Battle as His Edison Plan Meets Hostile Board." *New York Observer*. March 25. Available at *www.observer.com/node/44167.*

Fruchter, N. 2007. Urban Schools, Public Will: Making Education Work for All Students. New York: Teachers College Press.

Fuller, H. 2000. "The Continuing Struggle of African Americans for the Power to Make Real Educational Choices." Paper presented at the Second Annual Symposium on Educational Options for African Americans. March 2–5.

Hancock, L. 2007. "School's Out." *Nation*. July 9. Available at *www.thenation. com/doc/20070709/hancock.*

Herszenhorn, D. 2006. "City Considers Plan to Let Outsiders Run Schools." *New York Times*. October 5. Available at *www.nytimes.com/2006/10/05/ nyregion/05private.html.*

Holt, M. 2000. *Not Yet "Free At Last": The Unfinished Business of the Civil Rights Movement.* Oakland: Institute for Contemporary Studies.

Honig, M. I. 2004. "The New Middle Management: Intermediary Organizations in Education Policy Implementation." *Educational Evaluation and Policy Analysis* 26, no. 1: 65–87.

Jacobs, G. 1993. "History, Crisis, and Social Panic: Minority Resistance to Privatization of an Urban System." *Urban Review* 25, no. 3: 175–98.

Johnson, T., L. D. Pianna, and P. Burlingame. 2000. *Vouchers: A Trap, Not a Choice.* Oakland: Applied Research Council.

Kaplan, E. 2001. *Lights out for Edison.* Available at *www.psc-cuny.org/lightOut. htm.*

Katznelson, I., and M. Weir. 1985. *Schooling for All: Class, Race, and the Decline of the Democratic Ideal.* New York: Basic Books.

Margonis, F., and L. Parker. 1995. "Choice, Privatization, and Unspoken Strategies of Containment." *Educational Policy* 9, no. 4: 375–403.

Miron, G., and B. Applegate. 2000. *An Evaluation of Student Achievement in Edison Schools Opened in 1995 and 1996.* Kalamazoo: The Evaluation Center, Western Michigan University.

Miron, G., and C. Nelson. 2002. *What's Public about Charter Schools? Lessons*

Learned about Choice and Accountability. Thousand Oaks, CA: Corwin Press.

Moe, T. M. 2001. *Schools, Vouchers, and the American Public.* Washington, DC: Brookings Institution Press.

Molnar, A., and D. Garcia. 2007. "The Expanding Role of Privatization in Education: Implications for Teacher Education and Development." *Teacher Education Quarterly* 34, no. 2: 11–24.

Molnar, A., D. R. Garcia, G. Miron, and S. Berry. 2007. *Profiles of For-Profit Management Organizations: Ninth Annual Report 2006–2007.* Tempe: Commercialism in Education Research Unit, Education Policy Studies Laboratory, Arizona State University.

National Charter School Research Project. 2007. *Quantity Counts: The Growth of Charter School Management Organizations.* Seattle: Center on Reinventing Public Education, University of Washington.

New York Teacher. 2001. "NYC to Finance Edisonís PR Blitz; UFT Asks Parents to Research the Facts on Charter School Revisions.î Available at *www.nysut. org/newyorkteacher/2000-2001/010214charterschools.html.*

Oakes, J., and J. Rodgers. 2006. *Learning Power: Organizing for Education and Justice.* New York: Teachers College Press.

Parenti, M. 1978. Power and the Powerless. New York: St. Martin's Press.

Peterson, P. E. 2007. *School Reform in Philadelphia: A Comparison of Student Achievement at Privately Managed Schools with Student Achievement in Other District Schools.* Cambridge, MA: Harvard University Program on Educational Policy and Governance.

Richards, C., R. Shore, and M. Sawicky. 1996. *Risky Business: Private Management of Public Schools.* Washington, DC: Economic Policy Institute.

Robinson, G. 2001. "The Edison Election." *Gotham Gazette.* March 26. Available at *www.gothamgazette.com/article//20010326/200/253.*

Schrag, P. 2001. "Edison's Red Ink Schoolhouse." *Nation.* June 25, 20–24.

Scott, J. 2005. *School Choice and Diversity: What the Evidence Says.* New York: Teachers College Press.

Scott, J., and M. Barber. 2002. "Charter School Legislation in California, Arizona, and Michigan: An Alternative Framework for Policy Analysis." Occasional Paper No. 40. New York: National Center for the Study of Privatization in Education, Teachers College, Columbia University.

Scott, J., C. Lubienski, and E. DeBray. 2008. "The Ideological and Political Landscape of School Choice Interest Groups in the Post-*Zelman* Era." In *Handbook of Education Politics and Policy,* ed. by B. Cooper, J. Cibulka, and L. Fusarelli, 541–77. Washington, DC: Lawrence Erlbaum and Associates

Scott, J. T., and C. C. DiMartino. 2008. "Hybridized, Franchised, Duplicated, and Replicated: Charter Schools and Management Organizations." *Forum on the Future of Public Education.* Available at *theforum.ed.uiuc.edu/choice.*

Stone, D. 2002. *Policy Paradox: The Art of Political Decision Making.* New York: W. W. Norton.

Viteritti, J. P. 2000. *Choosing Equality: School Choice, the Constitution, and Civil Society.* Washington, DC: Brookings Institution Press.

Whittle, C. 2001. "Edison's Fate, the City's Future." *New York Times.* April 7.

———. 2005. *Crash Course: Imagining a Better Future for Public Education.* New York: Riverhead.

Wilgoren, J. 2000. "Young Blacks Turn to School Vouchers as Civil Rights Issue." *New York Times.* October 9. Available at *www.nytimes.com/2000/10/09/national/09/VOUC.html.*

Wilson, W. 1987. *The Truly Disadvantaged: The Inner City, the Underclass, and Public Policy.* Chicago: University of Chicago Press.

Witte, J. 2000. *The Market Approach to Education.* Princeton: Princeton University Press.

9

"Don't Be a Blockhead"
ACORN, Protest Tactics, and Organizational Scale

Robert Fisher, Fred Brooks, and Daniel Russell

One crucial measure by which to evaluate the potential and limits of community-based work "is the extent to which decentralized organizing can influence the increasingly centralized constellations of economic and political power which delimit the conditions under which people live" (Cloward and Piven 2004). Two possible routes for such influence relate to questions of tactical choice and organizational scale. Of course, not all community efforts should adopt a single type of structure and tactics. Instead, groups must understand the broader challenges faced by urban communities and evaluate the variety of tactics and organizational structures available to address problems and their causes at the local level and beyond. This chapter argues that adding protest to the tactical arsenal of community-based organizations has not only positive internal effects within the community on members and organization building but also external effects on targets that reside outside inner-city communities yet heavily affect life there. Moreover, the study proposes that a national structure of community organizations enables local initiatives to leverage national and global targets that are generally not susceptible to local organizing. It does so in a case study of ACORN's recent national campaign targeting H&R Block for their "predatory" financial service practices.

From its beginning in 1970 as a modest community group in Little Rock, Arkansas, ACORN has grown into an organization that now claims a global reach (Delgado 1986; Johnson 1999; ACORN 2006). It has an annual budget of $37.5 million, not including funds for research and the ACORN housing program, and as of 2006 it planned to continue its recent, dramatic expansion by opening an office in twenty new cities each year for the next five years (Eck 2006). ACORN's basic strategy emphasizes neighborhood-based organizing in low-to-moderate income communities of primarily African American and Latino residents, using a broad array of pragmatic tactics but accentuating direct action. The goal is to force targets—increasingly private sector ones but also public bodies—to address issues concerning its membership and to win victories that build the organization and advance further broader objectives of social, economic, and political justice. Unlike most other community organizations, ACORN's model meshes dues-paying members in local chapters within a national organization. ACORN's multiscale structure—as a federation of local efforts and a national organization—gives it more visibility and clout (Atlas 2005; Atlas and Dreier 2003). In its recent growth phase, a declining percentage of ACORN's funding derives from membership dues, although these remain critical. Membership dues now make up about 10 percent of ACORN's annual income; in the late 1970s it was 45 percent (Eck 2006; Delgado 1986). ACORN helps fund the current organization as well as mobilize members around economic justice issues through corporate campaigns. During 2004, ACORN conducted a national campaign funded by the Marguerite Casey Foundation against the financial service practices of H&R Block, the largest commercial tax preparation corporation in the nation. The campaign, continuing ACORN's work around the democratic control of finance and capital targeted Block's use and promotion of high-interest refund anticipation loans (RALs) to recipients of the earned income tax credit (EITC). It demonstrates the possibilities of community organizing efforts that operate a multispatial organizational structure and mobilize a multitactic campaign built on direct action.

Selected Debates on Social Movements and Community Organizing

The case study engages a variety of issues in the expansive literature on social movements and community organizing. ACORN is a social movement organization (SMO) that explicitly sees itself as a product and continuation of the movements of the 1960s and 1970s. Building on this heritage, one of ACORN's distinctive repertoires is political protest—what it calls "actions." While much of the social movement literature views protest as a form of collective action central to social movements, there is broad discussion about why social movement organizations prefer certain tactics over others (Meyer 2004; Tarrow 1994; Tilly 1978, 2004). Jasper (1997) and others identify a relatively narrow "taste in tactics," in which groups draw upon familiar and limited tactics, despite the broad range of choices open to them, and become highly identified with one or two "core tactics" (Meyer 2004, 169). McCarthy and Zald (1973) see protest tactics as better represented in classical social movement organizations such as the radical and civil rights efforts of the 1930s and 1960s rather than professional social movement organizations such as Common Cause or the National Organization of Women. These organizations also found their impetus and animus in social movement roots, but now, acting more like advocacy interest groups, they pursue more normative strategies. Giugni (Giugni, McAdam, and Tilly 1999) thinks the question of whether disruptive or moderate tactics are more effective is one of the two major debates in the social movement literature. This literature acknowledges the influence of protest tactics on elites (della Porta and Diani 2006), public policy (Giugni, McAdam, and Tilly 1999), the media (Gitlin 2003), and participants (Epstein 1991), as well as the effect of protest on a broader social movement composed of a plurality of actors and initiatives forming "multi-organization fields" with multiple tactics (Diani 1997).

Protest is a core tactic for ACORN, a central aspect of a repertoire that includes a broad array of other tactics, from policy initiatives and negotiation to forming partnerships with former targets and striving for ownership and governance. ACORN is a large, complex organization that uses multiple tactics to achieve varied goals. Nevertheless, it is best known for its direct actions and its ability to turn people out at protests. ACORN uses protest in order to (1) empower its members, (2) build the organization, and (3) win campaigns. In their campaign against H&R Block, ACORN coordinated protests at the local and national levels and added them to the tactics being used by other groups already challenging RALs, thereby complementing a preexisting movement for financial justice.

Moving the debate from the literature on SMOs to that on urban community organizing situates ACORN's use of protest tactics within another academic and practice discourse. In the world of community-based initiatives, direct action tactics are most associated with the work and writings of Saul Alinsky. Alinsky, building on labor and Left organizing models of the 1930s, believed that organization building, strong leadership, and innovative tactics were the recipe for winning victories, developing indigenous leaders, and building a mass people's organization. He proposed to "rub raw the resentments of people in the community" as a way to get them involved in the fight against established powers (Alinsky 1971, 116). Conflict was not the only tactic that Alinsky, his staff, and community residents used. Negotiating, building community, developing relationships in the community, building internal trust and support, and developing indigenous leaders were other elements in their complex political understanding of urban social change. But conflict organizing—groups seeking power and legitimation of claims and claimants by confronting civic and corporate leaders through protest-style actions, often in combination with other tactics—was central to Alinsky's approach.

Alinsky's "radical" community-based social change, begun in 1938 in the Back of the Yards neighborhood in Chicago, received acclaim in the 1960s (Silberman 1964; Katznelson 1981) as well as during the so-called "backyard revolution" of the 1970s and early 1980s (Boyte 1980; Horwitt 1992). In the past decade, despite continued proliferation of new community-based movement forms, Alinsky's model has been criticized from various quarters (Stoecker and Stall 1997; Sen 2003; Williams 1996; Mayer 2003; Cloward and Piven 1999; Marquez 1993). Most pertinent to this study are critiques that see such problem-oriented, conflict organizing as anachronistic (Kretzman and McKnight 1993; Eichler 1995; Beck and Eichler 2000), out of sync with current interest in communitarian perspectives (Sandel 1988; Etzioni 1993, 1995), and marginal when compared to the significant efforts of nonprofit organizations focused on building community, increasing social capital, enhancing local assets, and developing consensus in low-income communities (Putnam 1995; Saegert, Thompson, and Warren 2001).

Most of the social movement literature concludes that contextual factors heavily influence not only overall organizational success or failure but also daily decisions such as tactical choice (Tilly 1978; Tarrow 1994). They shape whether disruptive or moderate tactics are deemed more effective or are even considered. Contextual factors influence the contemporary preference for community building strategies over more oppositional ones (Fisher and Shragge 2000; DeFilippis 2004). Changing opportunity structures produces and allows for different types of political engagement. In the past few decades, economic globalization, urban restructuring, and neoliberal politics have transformed urban neighborhoods and dominated contemporary public policies and discourse, undermining communities and sanctifying "free market" responses to urban and national problems (Kuttner 1996; Heathcott 2005; Pendras 2002). Most community-based organizations adjusted to this new context, often reluctantly, with strategies and tactics that emphasize forming relationships and partnerships with business groups and foundations interested in strengthening the "voluntary sector" and "civil society." In general, they focus on more moderate approaches of building community, developing social capital, identifying and improving local assets, and encouraging consensus, rather than conflict, organizing (Putnam 1995; Kretzman and McKnight 1993; Eichler 1995). In this context, groups such as ACORN, which use multiple approaches but have direct action as their core tactic, seem out of step with current trends. The following case study suggests the contemporary relevance of conflict tactics. Opportunity structures may be more porous, more open to protest tactics, than either community organizing theory or practice reveals. Moreover, a national organizational structure seems to strengthen protest tactics, enabling organizational demands to get quicker attention and response from corporate targets heretofore considered inaccessible.

Method of Study

We used a case study research design (Yin 2003; Feagin, Orum, and Sjoberg 1991) and collected data primarily through interviews and participant observation. We conducted more than thirty individual and collective interviews with ACORN members and staff, corporate executives, and third-party consumer advocates and social scientists studying EITC and RALs during and just after the campaign. We conducted focus groups in Providence, Rhode Island; Philadelphia, Pennsylvania; and Prince George's County, Maryland; each with eight to twelve ACORN members who participated in the RALs campaign. To understand the reaction to this national campaign and its internal impact on constituents, we interviewed ACORN members and staff in various parts of the nation, from Los Angeles and San Diego to Indianapolis, St. Louis, Orlando, and Boston. Because we wanted to interview organizers and members with direct experience, we used purposive sampling techniques to identify key informants. Interviewees must have participated in at least one H&R Block campaign activity. Some interviewees had participated in many other campaigns and actions.

We also used participant-observation techniques, most notably at a Northeast regional action by ACORN in Morristown, New Jersey, where we conducted eleven on-the-ground interviews with ACORN members and staff. In addition, RALs were discussed in focus groups held in San Antonio, Miami, and New Orleans, three target cities where we evaluated ACORN's delivery of free tax preparation services. Data collection during these site visits included participant observation of direct actions as well as press conferences regarding the campaign. Combining participant observation with individual and group interviews allowed for triangulation of data analysis.

To broaden our sources we interviewed H&R Block executives, consumer advocates, and social scientists studying EITC and RALs. Interviews were tape recorded and transcribed verbatim. Content was analyzed using the constant comparative method (Glaser and Strauss 1967). Since the variables were already established prior to the inquiry, themes and concepts were chosen as units of analysis. Themes and categories emerged quickly through open coding of the transcripts (Strauss and Corbin 1990). We interviewed ACORN respondents during and after their campaign, H&R Block representatives afterward, and consumer advocates during and after. Almost all ACORN respondents were positive and enthusiastic about the campaign, partially reflecting their engagement with it. Block executives who would talk with us after negotiations had been concluded were also positive, though not uncritical. Most of their criticism focused more on ACORN's organizational form rather than the campaign or the negotiations. Third-party consumer advocates and social scientists were also generally positive about the ACORN campaign and ACORN's addition to the RALs advocacy, though they were less familiar with the campaign and had the most doubts about H&R Block and its agreement with ACORN. We also mined the literature on these issues in journals and newspapers and closely followed the sizable media coverage of the campaign.

RALs, EITC, and H&R Block

Refund anticipation loans and the earned income tax credit are intertwined for ACORN and H&R Block. EITC is a tax refund program for the working poor; RALs are fast tax refunds. For ACORN the campaign around such refunds was part of a larger initiative to increase the number of people claiming the tax credit and the net amount of EITC funds actually received by taxpayers after filing. More than 50 percent of H&R Block clients in 2003 who were eligible for the EITC received RALs. Therefore, prior to discussing these loans, a few words on the EITC are in order. The tax credit was created in 1975 during the Ford administration in order to offset the Social Security payroll taxes paid by low-income working parents and to encourage parents to work and file federal income taxes. The EITC has been revised and expanded five times over the past thirty years, including under the current Bush administration, whose Economic

Growth and Tax Relief Reconciliation Act of 2001 increased benefits for married families with children (Beverly 2002).

The EITC has received strong bipartisan support over the years because it requires recipients to work and is typically perceived as both antiwelfare and antipoverty (Ventry 2000). At its best the policy intends to reduce income inequality and poverty, help the poor build assets, and promote work by targeting the working poor (Wu, Fox, and Renuart 2002). In 2002 it lifted nearly five million people out of poverty, nearly half of them children, more than any other federal program (Llobrera and Zahradnik 2004; Wu, Fox, and Renuart 2002). In 2003, the IRS estimated approximately 21 million families received EITC tax refunds totaling more than $36 billion.

Commercial tax preparers play a key role in EITC. One of the goals of the IRS is to encourage EITC filers to do so electronically. Filing with commercial preparers increases electronic submissions, partly because filling out the multiple forms for EITC is more difficult than filing a Form 1040 or a Schedule A (Wu, Fox, and Renuart 2002). Maag (2005, 5–6) argues that getting help to prepare taxes heavily influences whether an applicant files for and receives the EITC refund, especially among the poorer and less educated workers eligible for EITC, and therefore the assistance of a paid tax preparer "may be a good thing" for EITC filers.

Other evidence demonstrates that commercial tax preparers drain funds away from EITC recipients. A Brookings study (Berube, Kim, Forman, and Burns 2002) calculates that approximately $1.75 billion of 1999 EITC refunds were diverted to commercial tax preparers, with RALs being a major source of the cost to clients. By definition, refund anticipation loans are "high cost loans secured by and repaid directly from the proceeds of a consumer's tax refund from the Internal Revenue Service" (Wu and Fox 2005, 3). Because the RALs are short-term loans of a week or two (that is, the time until the loan is repaid via the taxpayer's refund), "fees for these loans translate into triple digit annualized interest rates" (Wu and Fox 2005, 3). In 2003 consumers paid "an estimated $1 billion in RAL fees, plus an additional $389 million in 'administrative' or 'application' fees . . . to get quick cash for their refunds—essentially borrowing their own money at extremely high interest rates" (Wu and Fox 2005, 1). As noted above, more than 50 percent of the tax preparer's customers that received RALs that year also received the EITC, whereas only about 17 percent of the entire population gets an EITC (Wu and Fox 2005, 1). More than $500 million was drained out of the EITC program by loan fees in

2003. Customers paid in general about $100 on a $2,050 loan. According to Singletary (2005), "This loan fee is in addition to tax preparation fees averaging $120 and, in some cases, an administrative fee of about $30. A loan under those terms bears an effective APR of about 187 percent (247 percent if administrative fees are charged and included in the APR)."

RALs are a highly profitable product for commercial tax preparers. In 2001 H&R Block, the largest handler, issued 4.5 million RALs—up from fewer than 3 million in the 1999 tax filing season—and made $133.7 million in gross revenue and $68 million in net profits on RALs alone—over a 50 percent rate of return (Berube and Kornblatt 2005; Wu, Fox, and Renuart 2002). Jackson Hewitt, the second largest tax preparation chain in the United States, identified in an annual report for 2004 that 29 percent of the company's revenue derived from RALs and that more than 35 percent of their customers received such a loan. For H&R Block, RALs are a much smaller part of their overall business, although obviously from their profit margin and the fact that in 2003 28.5 percent of Block's customers got a RAL, it is still highly profitable for the company. In 2002 Block handled 4.67 million RALS, and in 2003 it processed 4.65 million. It was only in 2004 that Block experienced an 8 percent decline in RALs for tax year 2003, down to 4.27 million (Wu and Fox 2005; Berube and Kornblatt 2005). Block suggested the decline was due to fewer customers and less aggressive promotion (Wu and Fox 2005). Berube (interview, 2005) thinks the decline results from the disclosure of rapid refunds as loans, not instant cash, a result of initiatives against H&R Block prior to ACORN's campaign. We propose that the decline resulted from the overall impact of a multiorganization activism around RALs during the preceding decade. This effort, part of a broader movement for economic and financial justice, employed a number of tactics to address the problem, publicize the issue, and target H&R Block. ACORN successfully added another ingredient to this campaign—protests staged on a local and national scale—which complemented other tactical approaches.

Prior Advocacy against H&R Block

Social movement efforts are by definition characterized by a plurality of actors who use different tactics and who may not even work in consort but whose collective effort and varieties of engagement, intentional or not, carve out a tactical division of labor and, directly or indirectly, combine for greater impact. Tilly, for example, defines social movements as "not coherent solidaristic groups but . . . clusters of performances by multiple and changing actors" (1999, 256). This definition certainly fits the broader movement for economic and financial justice (Squires 2003b, 2004), as well as the advocacy effort around RALs, which is part of the broader movement. Before ACORN entered the fray, public sector pressure, class-action suits, and consumer advocacy research sought to address the problem with RALs and their relation to the EITC. The class-action suits legitimated the issue and exposed Block's vulnerability. Advocacy research by organizations such as the National Consumer Law Center, the Consumer Federation of America, and the Brookings Institution provided critical information, helped frame initiatives against RALs, and legitimated claimants' grievances. Their aggressive attacks charged Block and other commercial tax preparers with, among other things, exploiting the trust relationship between tax preparer and client and engaging in "corporate profiteering" which undermines "anti-poverty benefits meant to help hardworking Americans" (National Consumer Law Center 2006).

Refund anticipation loans have been under attack since the mid-1970s, when federal agencies first warned Beneficial Life to stop advertising them as an "instant tax refund." In the 1990s, "when RALs really exploded" (Wu 2004), state governments and attorneys general went after Block for failing to discriminate between advertising RALs as a loan and promoting them as a "rapid refund" comparable to "instant cash." More recently Block, along with its bank partner Beneficial/Household, has been the subject of class-action lawsuits organized by consumers, advocates, smaller tax preparation businesses, and even Block shareholders, charging a host of malpractices including racketeering and unfair and deceptive practices (Wu and Fox 2005; Wu, Fox, and Renuart 2002). In 1995 a class-action racketeering lawsuit filed in Chicago against Block accused them of conspiring to trick poor customers into purchasing high-interest tax anticipation loans. At one point during the long trial, there were more than 17 million people in the class. In 1996, consumers filed a class-action suit in Texas against H&R Block for failing to disclose receipt of license fees from lending banks for each RAL it facilitated. The *New York Times* noted that in this and related suits, "the main accusations are that lenders were mistreated when they were not told that Block has a 49.999 percent interest in the loans and receives a fee for each loan Beneficial makes" ("Judge Rejects" 2000).

In 1998 alone Block was the target of at least six lawsuits nationwide in federal and state courts (Kobliner 1998); by 2000 they had been sued no fewer than 22 times ("Judge Rejects" 2000). When faced in the Texas case with a judge's order that would have cost Block $75 million for "intentional, willful, and deliberate" conduct by not disclosing the kickback scheme, Block settled out of court (Hallinan 2002; "Judge Rejects" 2000). But not all suits came from aggrieved consumers. In *JTH Tax v. H&R Block Eastern Tax Services*, filed by John Hewitt, the cofounder of Jackson Hewitt and the founder and current president of Liberty Tax (respectively, the second and third largest tax preparation companies in the United States), a federal judge found in 2001 that H&R Block not only mislead consumers by advertising a RAL product as a "refund" but had engaged in bad faith in so doing. The court noted the "many prior legal actions against H&R Block over similar misleading advertising" (Wu and Fox 2005). It was through this court case that the term *refund anticipation loan* was coined. The case also noted a pattern of Block consenting to a decree in one state and then disregarding it in another, especially concerning its advertising and sales of "rapid refunds."

The court actions, advocacy research, and lobbying against Block wrought significant victories. In 2000, for example, Block began to offer "free cash advances" in California, waiving fees that started at $19.95 and are normally associated with RALs ("Block is Testing," 2000). They expanded this practice to twelve other states by 2004. As recently as 2002 the bad publicity and increasing costs from these advocacy groups and lawsuits caused Block to consider reducing its emphasis on RALs. As a Block executive noted, "Although we probably make more money from this product than anyone else in the category, as a percentage of our overall revenue we're nowhere top quartile. We're certainly the biggest player but this is not as important an activity to us as it is, frankly, to most people who are in our space as tax preparers, because we are a diversified company and do a lot of other things for clients" (interview, 2005). Nevertheless, in 2003 (fiscal year 2002) Block processed 4.6 million RALs, which generated more than $138 million in fees, about 3 percent of its total revenues. Since the mid-1990s, various consumer advocates' attacks have been expensive and unpleasant for Block; as of 2004 the profit that accrued to Block from RALs came with increasing costs for the company. Despite the costs imposed by the anti-RALs campaign, in a broader context of deregulated financial institutions that buttressed the power of companies such as H&R Block and legitimated practices such as RALs, "rapid refund" products remained valuable to commercial tax preparers.

ACORN Enters the Campaign against H&R Block

In the spring of 2003, Wade Rathke, the founder and chief organizer of ACORN, discussed the EITC and the problem of RALs with the Marguerite Casey Foundation. The Casey Foundation indicated interest in funding a broad initiative around the EITC. Quickly, ACORN's Financial Justice Center began to prepare a plan of action and a grant proposal to (1) run free tax preparation sites in three southern cities with low EITC filing rates and (2) develop a national anti-RALs campaign targeting tax preparation companies focusing on EITC recipients. H&R Block would be the first target because it was the biggest and most prestigious. While ACORN prepared to launch the direct action campaign with or without grant funding, the Casey grant, issued in early 2004, provided the resources to run a well-funded campaign simultaneously at the national and local levels. But it offered little start-up time. The prime time for this campaign was the 2004 tax season from January 1 through April 15.

Significantly, ACORN had experience with such campaigns and was already part of a financial justice movement that targeted corporations, for example, defending the Community Reinvestment Act and opposing Household Finance Corporation around predatory lending. In their 1993 campaign against insurance redlining, ACORN targeted Allstate and held actions at sales offices in fourteen different cities. In 1994 Allstate signed an agreement with ACORN for a $10 million partnership with ACORN and NationsBank for below-market mortgages to low-income homebuyers. In addition to their prior experience, ACORN benefited in the campaign against H&R Block from the extensive research on RALs already done by the National Consumer Law Center, the Consumer Federation of America, and the Brookings Institution. ACORN entered an ongoing struggle, equipped with a new tactic of direct action while building on the prior lawsuits, advocacy research, and continuing efforts of loosely connected organizations.

The first ACORN action in the RALs campaign began at the end of 2003 when twenty members held a press conference in front of the IRS building in Los Angeles. Protesters described the dangers of RALs and urged taxpayers to call ACORN to get their taxes done for free. The first nationwide action occurred on January 13, 2004. A day earlier the *Dow Jones Business News* reported, "Tax preparation giant H&R Block will come under fire Tuesday for its popular tax refund anticipation loans, as community groups launch protests planned in more than 30 U.S. cities" (Christie 2004). The protests will include "people wearing boxes on their heads saying, 'DON'T BE A BLOCKHEAD'" (Christie 2004). On January 13, ACORN held actions at forty-three different Block offices across the nation in neighborhoods where ACORN had local chapters. They sought to get the attention of H&R Block and the media. Critical to the effort, ACORN recorded that the day's actions were covered by at least sixty-four media outlets.

On this first day of national protest, the actions at the various local events were scripted by the national campaign. In general, members went to Block offices and demanded to fax a complaint letter regarding RALs to the CEO of H&R Block. Members also chanted and handed out fliers informing Block employees as well as the public, inside and outside the office, about the problems with Block and RALs. One ACORN member described the action:

> When we do go into the office, . . . we go in there holding up signs that . . . you don't have to give them all this money. . . . You can get your tax return done free. And we ask that they fax a letter to the corporate office to let them know that we're against it. . . . Usually, we have the media there so this is being aired and documented. And then when they do tell you [to leave], or they call the police, . . . if they push at us we just back up but we don't kind of push them back or anything like that. . . . Our presence is intimidating enough. . . . We just stick to the issue that we're there to represent and we just inform them and do what we have to do and then we leave. (interview, 2004)

Throughout the nation, protesters accused H&R Block of "stealing from the community," engaging in "price gouging," and being a "rip off" (Steinback 2003). They wore signs in Pittsburgh saying "H&R Block Steals" (Sabatini 2004). In Chicago, they accused Block of "preying on the low-income population" (Shenoy 2004). In Passaic, New Jersey, where a big lighted sign in the window of the H&R Block office on Main Avenue said "Instant Money," nine people stood outside holding hand-written signs in Spanish and English demanding refunds for people they claimed were overcharged. They criticized the "instant money" offer as "deceptive, overpriced, and unfair" (Newman 2004).

ACORN set limits on the tactics used at the actions, pursuing both a tactical preference for direct action (Jasper 1997) and a balance with other political interventions (della Porta and Diani 2006). In order to get to the bargaining table, ACORN chose not to push H&R Block so hard that the company would not view them as a serious organization. As one ACORN organizer noted, "It's a question of what hurts, but doesn't so much that people won't meet and talk about signing an agreement and making some changes" (interview, 2004).

The nationally coordinated local actions continued and expanded on January 31, 2004, when hundreds of ACORN members protested at fifty-five H&R Block offices, demanding that corporate officials meet with ACORN representatives to negotiate an end to predatory RAL practices. According to Murray (2004), ACORN hoped "to shame Block into dealing more forthrightly with their customers." Local efforts were buttressed by the protest being orchestrated again at the national level. Atlas and Dreier (2003, 4) argue, that "ACORN's most impressive attribute" is its federated, membership structure, which enables it "to work simultaneously at the neighborhood, local, state and federal levels, so that its chapter members are always 'in motion' on a variety of issues, and so that its local organizations can link up with their counterparts around the country to change national policy on key issues that can't be solved at the neighborhood or municipal level." Furthermore, the national federated structure enhanced organizational capacity beyond the local chapters. For example, in terms of the media attention generated by the campaign, the ACORN national office not only facilitated local press releases but also helped get the issue covered by national print and television media, including *NBC Dateline*, *ABC Nightline*, *The News Hour With Jim Lehrer*, and the *CBS Evening News*. ACORN's ability to act on a national and local level definitely had an impact on H&R Block. This multispatial approach corresponds with recent scholarship on civic life, especially Skocpol (2003), which emphasizes the benefits of membership-based efforts that operate as active, participatory local chapters of a national organization.

The two national protests were supported with ongoing local activism. According to ACORN's records, in the first two months of 2004, members in fifty-four cities held 402 pickets, protests, and demonstrations at local H&R Block locations—successfully getting the company to the negotiating table (ACORN 2004). Many of the locals were dogged in their efforts around RALs. But they varied in terms of the number of actions, press releases, and distributions of fliers, as well as their interest in the campaign. Combining local units in a national campaign required both organizational discipline and flexibility. Not all locals were pushed as hard to participate in the RALs campaign. Larger ACORN locals—for example, the one in New York City—had other issues absorbing their primary energy. Not all members interviewed were excited about taking up a new issue, preferring to focus on their local issues and not shift attention and resources to the Block campaign. Nevertheless, the national organization was able to exercise discipline, especially with smaller units, through the promise of rewarding local chapters with material benefits won in any agreement with the corporate target. Discipline may seem pejorative among new social movements (Epstein 1991), but it is essential to a national campaign based on coordinated local actions. More important than organizational discipline was that the issue and campaign caught on quickly with members and local staff: "From an organizer's perspective when I was [first] briefed on this campaign I was like, taxes? Oh, that's so unexciting. How do we move people on taxes? [But as it turned out,] it was pretty exciting [and] our members, I mean, they get it . . . They understand when they're ripped off" (ACORN staff interview, 2004). ACORN members we interviewed generally understood as well the value of protest tactics. As one member put her learning process,

> What I like about ACORN is the direct approach, the action. Sometimes I didn't completely understand, like, why don't they just talk to the people. Well, I've learned that—being a member of ACORN—that they have reached out and tried to talk with people that we have some issues with and they just completely ignore us. And so the one thing that we have as citizens, especially just regular working class citizens, we have the power to get with other people and just go out there and have demonstrations and actions. At first I didn't think they'd get anything done, but it worked because people, especially in Indianapolis, they really don't like to be embarrassed like that. (interview, 2004)

Campaign Outcomes

While any evaluation of campaign outcomes is mediated by the brevity and temporal proximity of ACORN's campaign, our study reveals initial results in five outcome areas: local ACORN chapters, ACORN members, ACORN as a national organization, H&R Block, and the broader financial justice campaign against Block's use of predatory RALs. (It is too soon to evaluate impacts in a sixth, though critical area, the proliferation and cost of RALs, especially to EITC recipients.) The nationally coordinated campaign with its national days of action, despite occasionally posing challenges to local chapters, had a synergistic effect. Even organizers in more established locals, where the RALs campaign had to compete with other ongoing issues, spoke to the power of the national campaign and the opportunity afforded by having the national provide directions for more actions. "We can't have enough actions. They're critical to the organization. Actions strengthen people's commitment to the organization" (ACORN staff interview, 2004). Another staff person remarked, "The RALS campaign has made us stronger in a lot of areas in terms of membership, bringing membership together, bringing new members in that we wouldn't have had if it had not been for this" (ACORN staff interview, 2004). The social movement literature concurs. Protest tactics provide important internal functions, among them creating a sense of collective identity and building solidarities critical to action toward a common goal (Rochon 1998).

In terms of member development, our interviews, focus groups, and participant observation revealed results counter to prevailing perspectives on community building. Recent literature on community-based organizations emphasizes the importance of community building approaches to resident empowerment and education, and it critiques protest tactics for failing to build significant identity and solidarity networks among participants (Boyte 2004; Fabricant and Fisher 2002). Conflict strategies, especially ones developed outside the community, are said to do a poor job of participant education and development. The case study reveals more mixed initial results. As a staffer noted, "We had members who, at the beginning of their three months were like, 'What's a RAL?' At the end [of the three months, they] stand up in front of a group of members and talk about RALs way better than I could. That wasn't because we did teach-ins or anything. We did a ton of actions. . . . People love it" (interview, 2004). At their best, ACORN actions seek to move the target, in this case H&R Block, and educate the community. In terms of member education and engagement, we observed that while some participants were personally affected by RALs, most were not. The campaign often took community residents beyond personal concerns to consider larger issues within their communities, the economy, and public policy. RALs were not "just hurting individual families," one member noted, "but our entire economy because this is money that could be filtered back into our communities" (ACORN member focus group, 2004).

Regarding its effect on ACORN as a national organization, almost everyone interviewed spoke positively about the speed of the campaign, the extent of media attention, the engagement of the locals and membership, and the resources it brought to ACORN. Overall, from ACORN's perspective, a well-orchestrated and coordinated national campaign of direct action empowered staff and members, strengthened the organization, and moved a Fortune 500 company to negotiate and support ACORN's work in poor and low-income communities. As ACORN said in its annual report (2004):

> Thousands of ACORN members across the country have been actively engaged in this campaign around increasing EITC and combating RALs, have discussed it in meetings, with their neighbors, and participated in actions. The H&R Block focus in specific has provided a powerful experience of participating in local actions, around problems facing your own neighborhood, but through coordination with similar actions taking place around the country, achieving a level of collective power sufficient to quickly force a major corporation to the table. Block's representative made this point in front of the 2,000-plus ACORN members gathered at the convention when he commented in his speech announcing the partnership that ACORN's activities had accomplished what years of reports and papers had never done in moving the company to make change.

Regarding its impact on H&R Block, while overall it is too soon to tell, some things are certain. Linder (2004) reported 1.2 percent fewer RALs in January 2004 than a year before, resulting from increased attention and changed practices. Roth (2004b) reported a decline in RALs sold by Block from 4.61 million in 2003 to 4.26 million in 2004. More directly, the campaign reaped a nearly instant response from the giant of the commercial tax preparation industry, a powerful multinational corporation. By early February, within a month of the first protest, H&R Block and ACORN were negotiating. As noted earlier, Block was taken off guard by the January 13 action. "When it started, there was a bit of a scramble here. . . . Once the protests started, we were up to speed fairly quickly, but really it wasn't anything we were prepared for. Not something like that. Not protests at our door" (H&R Block executive interview, 2005). Roth (2004a) concurs. "ACORN caught the company's attention when it staged Jan. 13 demonstrations at Block tax offices in 30 cities." That day H&R Block issued a public relations statement in their local newspaper "listing the steps the Kansas City company has taken to benefit low-income taxpayers" (Roth 2004a). A few days later Block's vice president of community outreach and business development made a public announcement noting, "We recognize our low- and moderate-income clients need financial education and financial literacy support" (Davis 2004). In private discussions within the company, H&R Block decided early on to meet with ACORN. They admitted to being vulnerable to bad publicity during the tax season, said they were impressed with the scope of ACORN's actions, and concluded that ACORN was a legitimate representative of low-income community residents. A Block official, sounding as though he had read Skocpol (2003), distinguished between Washington, DC–based national advocacy organizations, which he saw as without real legitimacy, and membership-based organizations such as ACORN:

> Well, I don't think anyone ever engaged us quite the way that ACORN did. . . . We've been engaged in the past by essentially interest groups. ACORN by contrast was a membership-supported organization principally, and last year ACORN had people out there for four hundred office protests, by people who look a lot like our clients. . . . ACORN was the first of its type to engage us, and it was a more credible, more convincing engagement. They know what they are talking about because they've lived it. . . . ACORN, by pounding on the door so to speak, got us to listen a little bit more carefully to our client's perspective. (interview, 2005)

In addition, Block concluded rather quickly, based on a canvass of other companies that had been targeted by ACORN, that it could negotiate with ACORN (H&R Block executive interview, 2005).

ACORN saw a direct relationship between the speed of negotiating with Block and the national action campaign of ACORN. As a staffer put it, "They've been actually much easier to get to the table to negotiate than have been other targets, you know, big banks, or finance companies, like Household Finance" (interview, 2004). Wade Rathke concurred, emphasizing H&R Block's exposure to a well-timed, nationwide, direct action campaign in communities where both ACORN and Block had offices and therefore where Block was a visible and accessible target for ACORN members and community residents. "Their vulnerability to what we were doing was extremely intense, and they knew it and were worried about it and responded very carefully because of that. It was the action profile and the aggressiveness of the campaign that was allowing us to move to negotiations so quickly" (interview, 2005). Our research suggests a variety of factors that moved Block to negotiate: the company's temporal vulnerability; changes in the market for RALs; Block's desire to serve its consumer base more effectively; the work of consumer advocacy groups and legal initiatives, which contributed to Block's vulnerability; ACORN's ability to disrupt Block's business operations on a local and national scale; and ACORN's reputation as reasonable once at the bargaining table.

The results of the negotiations were announced at the ACORN national meeting on June 28 in Los Angeles. "ACORN announced a three-year alliance with Block to help low- to mid-income people better understand tax law," according to Roth (2004a). "Block officials have declined to say how much they will invest in the program. . . . Block will provide expertise and money to develop educational materials about tax credits and other tax saving mechanisms. ACORN will implement the program through its offices in 65 U.S. cities."

The agreement has six main components. First, Block would help ACORN, through monetary contributions of an amount undisclosed at the time of the article, to do work in their communities around EITC outreach. This money would fund a tax literacy and assistance campaign, including information and assistance on EITC and RALs. It would be national in scope; include door-to-door outreach, education, and tax preparation services; and be based in communities where ACORN has local chapters (H&R Block 2005). Second, Block would completely eliminate within the next two years the administrative application fee for RALs, which averages thirty-two dollars nationally. This is the handling fee H&R Block had already eliminated in thirteen states and the District of Columbia. ACORN estimates the value of this savings to be approximately $192 million annually, primarily to poor and low-income people and EITC recipients. They calculate that if prior research estimated $1 billion of EITC funds being lost on RALs, now nearly $200 million, or one-fifth that sum, will stay with EITC recipients. Third, ACORN won a pledge from H&R Block to hire and educate ACORN members to be tax preparers, something that may have seemed less significant to national staff but was highly valued by members returning to their communities with the promise of lowered fees, investment, and new job opportunities. Fourth, H&R Block would provide clearer information to its customers on RALs disclosures and advertising. The language of the disclosure is meant to be as simple as possible so someone does not have to have a great deal of banking knowledge in order to realize that they are about to take out a loan. Fifth, H&R Block agreed to a rebate to ACORN members of twenty-five dollars off tax returns filed during the month of March for the next three years. Sixth, ACORN agreed to cease and desist in their protests against H&R Block. Of course, the impact on the overall issue of RALs and predatory tax preparation practices remains to be seen. Data for tax year 2005 was not available, and the causes of decline in RALs for tax year 2004 are still debated. It is certainly too soon to know the full scope of the agreement, the degree to which H&R Block will uphold its stated intentions regarding RALs and service to low- and moderate-income consumers, and how well a partnership will work out between a social movement organization and a Fortune 500 corporation, with their very different objectives, capacities, and structures.

Third-party consumer advocates, prior participants in the overall effort against predatory RALs, spoke strongly to the contribution ACORN made to the movement against H&R Block. "It definitely made all the difference to have people standing in front of a Block office with signs that say, 'You guys are making predatory loans.' . . . We could write all the reports and issue press releases we want but Block cares about its image and the idea of people standing outside their offices with protest signs, I think was pretty effective" (consumer advocate interview, 2004). Singletary agreed, pointing out that ACORN's addition to the anti-RALs campaign, after years of pressure from other groups, "improved how they [commercial tax preparers] promote, sell, and disclose the terms of refund loans" (2005). Consumer advocates clearly supported ACORN's contribution to the RALs campaign but always situated their evaluation of ACORN's work in the broader movement against predatory RALs. "I think it is all the different tools trying to get to the same thing . . . the research, the reporting, the congressional advocacy, the state level legislative advocacy, the direct action in front of the stores, the direct intervention with the companies trying to move them" (consumer advocate interview, 2005).

ACORN's work must be contextualized in the broader anti-RAL campaign; to view its campaign as the sole agent of change would decontextualize the group's efforts and ignore the complex structure and processes of social movements. Without the prior efforts that disclosed and framed the problem, legitimated and publicized the issue, and attacked and hurt Block, it is highly unlikely there would have been an ACORN campaign on RALs, let alone one that brought Block to the bargaining table so quickly. Some advocates thought less of ACORN's contribution, attributing the 2004 decline in RALs less to ACORN's protest tactics and more to the effect of prior efforts. "I have got to think that one of the reasons that Block is so ready to come to the table with ACORN is that they just see a declining demand for the product. . . . They take a public beating for this [RALs] sometimes and they are doing the calculus, and maybe [it is] seeming less and less worth it to put a lot of their efforts into this product" (consumer advocate interview, 2005). As of this writing, pressure on Block continues with recent lawsuits from the offices of the attorneys general in California and New York, the former regarding RALs, the latter about a new Block product, Express IRAs (Cresswell and Dash 2006).

While in general highly supportive of ACORN's contribution, part of the obvious ambivalence of some consumer advocates results from the secrecy surrounding aspects of the agreement between H&R Block and ACORN. One consumer advocate who praised ACORN's contribution to the movement against predatory RALs noted of the resulting alliance, "I don't know how to evaluate how good the deal was that they got because they did not let it be made public. I don't know whether they got enough of an improvement for consumers. . . . I don't understand why it would be a secret. . . . If they are proud of what they [both] did, I don't know why it is a secret" (interview, 2005). Block has been very protective regarding publishing or posting the whole package of changes agreed to, the ACORN programs that Block will support, and the monetary amount of that support. At a press conference to announce the alliance, a reporter asked if Block was giving ACORN $1 million to fund this initiative. Block's response was "It's a completely inaccurate number" (Alliance Announcement 2005), without any further clarification.

This reluctance to disclose the specifics of the agreement is made even more interesting by an alliance Block created with Operation HOPE Inc. shortly after the one it made with ACORN. "H&R Block Inc. has pledged $1 million plus other support to Operation Hope Inc., whose financial education programs help inner-city residents and low-wealth communities. . . . Block also will encourage employees to volunteer in Operations Hope's youth for literacy program, called Banking on Our Future" (Davis 2004). Admittedly, Operation HOPE Inc. is a community organization of a very different type; it is a formalized, non-membership-based not-for-profit closely allied to the financial industry and with ties to the mainstream public and nonprofit sectors. Nevertheless, it seems contradictory to publicize as a good thing the amount exchanged in one alliance and to keep an agreement with another community-based organization secret, especially a group such as ACORN, which Block publicly applauded for its legitimacy in the community. We assume that ACORN is open to having all the elements of the agreement made public but did not push Block to do so because, among other reasons, Block opposed it and ACORN wanted to move on to their secondary tax preparation targets such as Jackson Hewitt and Liberty Tax. We presume H&R Block opposed making public the monetary transaction in order to avoid being seen as vulnerable to protests such as ACORN's. How well an alliance will succeed based on these shaky beginnings—being forced to the bargaining table, keeping aspects of the alliance agreement secret—remains to be seen.

It is certainly premature to advance definitive conclusions about ACORN's effect on the issue. As time unfolds, IRS data will reveal what trends, if any, have developed since the 2004 protests and alliance agreement. It will be clearer what role ACORN played in the effort to control high-interest RALs. Nevertheless, even with its limits as a modest case study, our research reveals some of the potential of protest tactics as practiced in a national and community-based organization such as ACORN. Evaluations of comparable campaigns come to a similar conclusion. For Taylor and Silver (2003, 169), their study of the Community Reinvestment Act revealed that "activism is not passé; it is essential. Without activism, our society becomes less democratic and less just. This is true in many arenas, but especially in the fight for economic justice and equal access to credit and capital." Squires (2003a) and others concur. Dreier, in his analysis of predatory lending, concludes that "the twenty-first century will certainly see a growing concentration of power in a smaller and smaller number of financial services conglomerates, which will present daunting challenges. . . . Only groups that have a national base such as ACORN . . . will have any reasonable chance to challenge the financial services giants" (2003, 210). Hartman, preferring federal policy initiatives, applauds ACORN's work around the earlier campaign against Household Finance for predatory lending but wonders whether they will be able to find the resources to mount such campaigns nationally and whether "confrontational tactics will produce a backlash" (2004, 210). Perhaps they already have. As a senior vice president from Bank of America put it, "I don't want to hear one more community group tell me something negative and then ask me for $400,000 a week later. That doesn't work anymore" (Hartman 2004, 210).

Hartman and others are correct. Addressing economic exploitation ingrained in the subprime financial markets and contemporary forms of unregulated capitalism will require more than community organizing or the campaign of a single organization, even a national one. ACORN is working in coalitions with other groups advocating for federal and statewide RAL legislation, with some modest early successes in Connecticut and California. Like most of the large community organizing networks, ACORN prefers, when it has enough clout, to work autonomously, but increasingly it works with other groups in ongoing campaigns, such as the RAL protest, or in campaigns where they seek to have greater impact, such as living wage initiatives or electoral efforts.

This case study should encourage theoreticians, researchers, and practitioners to reconsider the choice of protest tactics in community-based organizations as a means of moving vulnerable targets, drawing public attention to neglected issues, building organizations, and mobilizing and sustaining membership. It should also direct attention to the effect of adding protest tactics to existing campaigns; our research reveals direct action was an addition that complemented rather than undermined other tactical repertoires.

This case study should also encourage an increased examination of ACORN by those interested in urban social movements and community-based initiatives. Unlike most current community-based efforts, ACORN has a grander perspective that seeks, as Koehler and Wissen put it in a broader discussion of urban social movements, to "fight the destructive influences which neoliberal globalization exerts on everyday life" and politicize these contradictions through organized "urban social conflict" (2003, 949). ACORN would not use that language, but its staff and members understand the power of multinational corporations under contemporary economic globalization. They know that ACORN must act on a broad scale, at least as a national organization that can hold actions in more than fifty cities as it did with Block. Their strategy to target large corporations, not public agencies or officials, reflects ACORN's understanding of the shift in power and resources under contemporary policies away from the public sector in general and city officials in particular (Weir, Wolman, and Swanstrom 2005). Moreover, ACORN's local as well as national capacity capitalizes on the virtues and helps transcend the limits of small scale, community activism while at the same time addressing some of the key dilemmas inherent in centralized, large scale advocacy organizations (Dreier 2003; Atlas 2005). Moreover, the national structure complements their protest tactics. If ACORN was embedded solely in a single community with a focus solely on that community, not looking beyond local borders for either causes or solutions to local problems, then ongoing protest tactics within the community—what Jane Mansbridge called "adversarial democracy"—would prove counterproductive. But protest tactics, in combination with other approaches, can work well in a national organization focused on both local and national campaigns because its broader practice and focus make it less limited by community values or long-term relationships. If leaders encourage an understanding that community problems are almost always the result of policies and politics from outside the community, and if the organization fights more for the general interests of poor and low-income people than it does for the specific interests of individual community members, then protest tactics, in combination with other tactics, can succeed.

Of course, as noted above, ACORN uses a broad array of tactics: negotiation, partnerships, service delivery, program development and administration, and protest. Protest does not work equally well in every case or place. Not every target, private or public, responds as H&R Block did. Throughout ACORN's history, boisterous, in-your-face, confrontational tactics have consistently alienated officials and business leaders, causing them to react harshly to the organization (Delgado 1986; Swarts 2002). Even within ACORN, especially in its early years, members who do not like the actions drop out of the organization or simply do not participate in the actions. In sites where ACORN has a long-term presence, such as New York City and Chicago, the range of tactics befits a complex social change organization. But even there, conflict and contestation, mobilizing members to protest against local abuses as well as injustices and inequalities originating from outside the community, is central to the organization. Protest is not its only tactic just as protest is not only used in national campaigns. But the mix—direct actions orchestrated at a national level against targets unlikely to be moved by any tactics at the single community level—seems especially appropriate. At the least, this case study suggests that direct action as a tactic, ACORN as an organization, and the model of a national organization of active community-based chapters appear worthy of further study.

NOTE

This article originally appeared in slightly different form as "'Don't Be a Blockhead': ACORN, Protest Tactics, and Refund Anticipation Loans," *Urban Affairs Review* 42, no. 4 (March 2007): 553–82.

REFERENCES

ACORN. 2006. *Annual Report, 2005.* New Orleans: ACORN.
———. 2004. ACORN Actions, 2004. Unpublished reports for staff from local ACORN chapters on H&R Block campaign actions in January.
Alinsky, S. 1971. *Rules for Radicals: A Pragmatic Primer for Realistic Radicals.* New York: Vintage.

Alliance Announcement. 2005. Transcript of ACORN and H&R Block confer-
    ence call.
Atlas, J. 2005. "Out of the Past: What Anti-Poverty Groups Can Learn from the
    American Legion." *Tikkun* 20, no. 4: 41–45.
Atlas, J., and P. Dreier. 2003. "Enraging the Right." *Shelterforce* 129. Available
    at *www.nhi.org/online/issues/129/ACORN.html.*
Beck, E., and M. Eichler. 2000. "Consensus Organizing: A Practice Model for
    Community Building." *Journal of Community Practice* 8, no. 1: 87–102.
Berube, A., A. Kim, B. Forman, and M. Burns. 2002. *The Price of Paying Taxes:
    How Tax Preparation and Refund Loan Fees Erode the Benefits of EITC.*
    Washington, DC: Brookings Institution.
Beverly, S. G. 2002. "What Social Workers Need to Know about the Earned
    Income Tax Credit." *Social Work* 47:259–66.
"Block Is Testing Advances on Tax Refunds." 2000. *New York Times.* January 6.
Boyte, H. 1980. *The Backyard Revolution.* Philadelphia: Temple University Press.
———. 2004. *Everyday Politics: Reconnecting Citizens and Public Life.*
    Philadelphia: University of Pennsylvania Press.
Christie, R. 2004. "Consumer Activists to Protest H&R Block Tax Refund
    Loans." Dow Jones Business News, January 12, 2004. Available at *wsj.com/.*
Cloward, R., and F. F. Piven. 1999. "Disruptive Dissensus." In *Reflections on
    Community Organization,* ed. by J. Rothman, 22–24. Itasca, IL: F. E.
    Peacock.
———. 2004. Introduction to *Roots to Power: A Manual for Grassroots
    Organizing,* 2d ed., by L. Staples. New York: Praeger.
Cresswell, J., and E. Dash. 2006. "Spitzer Sues H&R Block on IRAs." *New York
    Times.* March 16.
Davis, M. 2004. "Block to Support Financial Literacy." *Kansas City Star.* July
    15.
DeFilippis, J. 2004. *Unmaking Goliath: Community Control in the Face of Global
    Capital.* New York: Routledge.
DeFilippis, J., R. Fisher, and E. Shragge. 2006. "Neither Romance or
    Regulation: Reconsidering Community." *International Journal of Urban
    and Regional Research* 30, no. 3: 673–89.
Delgado, G. 1986. *Organizing the Movement: The Roots and Growth of ACORN.*
    Philadelphia: Temple University Press.
Della Porta, D., and M. Diani, eds. 2006. *Social Movements: An Introduction.*
    Oxford: Blackwell.
Diani, M. 1997. "Social Movements and Social Capital." *Mobilization* 2:129–47.
Dreier, P. 2003. "Protest, Progress, and the Politics of Reinvestment." In
    *Organizing Access to Capital: Advocacy and the Democratization of Financial
    Institutions,* ed. by G. Squires, 188–220. Philadelphia: Temple University
    Press.

Eck, E. 2006. "City by City, an Antipoverty Group Plants Seeds of Change." *New York Times*. June 26.

Eichler, M. 1995. "Consensus Organizing." *National Civic Review* 84 (Summer/Fall): 256–62.

Epstein, B. 1991. *Political Protest and Cultural Revolution: Nonviolent Direct Action in the 1970s and 1980s*. Berkeley and Los Angeles: University of California Press.

Etzioni, A. 1993. *The Spirit of Community: Rights, Responsibilities, and the Communitarian Agenda*. New York: Crown.

———, ed. 1995. *New Communitarian Thinking: Persons, Virtues, Institutions, Communities*. Charlottesville: University Press of Virginia.

Fabricant, M., and R. Fisher. 2002. *Settlement Houses under Siege: The Struggle to Sustain Community Organizations in New York City*. New York: Columbia University Press.

Feagin, J., A. Orum, and G. Sjoberg. 1991. *A Case for the Case Study*. Chapel Hill: University of North Carolina Press.

Federal Trade Commission. 2003. "Announced Actions for June 6, 2003." Available at *www.ftc.gov/opa/2003/06/fyi0336.htm*.

Fisher, R. 1994. *Let the People Decide: Neighborhood Organizing in America*. Updated ed. New York: Twayne.

———, and E. Shragge. 2000. "Challenging Community Organizing: Facing the 21st Century." *Journal of Community Practice* 8, no. 3: 1–19.

Forry, B. 2004. "Protesters Target Tax Prep Giant H&R Block in 'Actions.'" *Dorchester Reporter*. February 5. Available at *dotnews.com/h&rblock.html*.

Gitlin, T. 2003. *The Whole World Is Watching: Mass Media in the Making and Unmaking of the New Left*. Berkeley and Los Angeles: University of California Press.

Giugni, M. 2004. *Social Protest and Policy Change*. Lanham, MD: Rowman and Littlefield.

Giugni, M., D. McAdam, and C. Tilly, eds. 1999. *How Movements Matter*. Minneapolis: University of Minnesota Press.

Glaser, B., and A. Strauss. 1967. *The Discovery of Grounded Theory*. Chicago: Aldine.

H&R Block. 2005. "H&R Block and ACORN Partner to Help Working Families Claim and Keep More of What They've Earned This Tax Season." 2005. H&R Block and ACORN News Release. January 13. Available at *www.acorn.org*.

Hallinan, J. 2002. "H&R Block Agrees to Settlement in Texas Lawsuit." November 20, 2002. E-posting.

Hartman, C. 2004. "Predatoriness, and What We Can Do about It." In *Why the Poor Pay More: How to Stop Predatory Lending*, ed. by G. Squires, 203–14. Westport, CT: Praeger.

Heathcott, J. 2005. "Urban Activism in a Downsizing World: Neighborhood

Organizing in Postindustrial Chicago." *City and Community* 4 (September): 277–94.

Horwitt, S. 1992. *Let Them Call Me Rebel: Saul Alinsky, His Life and Legacy.* New York: Vintage.

Hurd, M., and S. Kest. 2003. "Fighting Predatory Lending from the Ground Up: An Issue of Economic Justice." In *Organizing Access to Capital: Advocacy and the Democratization of Financial Institutions,* ed. G. Squires, 119–34. Philadelphia: Temple University Press.

Jasper, J. 1997. *The Art of Moral Protest.* Chicago: University of Chicago Press.

Johnson, K. 1999. "ACORN Branches Out." *City Limits,* February, 2–4.

Joseph, M. 2002. *Against the Romance of Community.* Minneapolis: University of Minnesota Press.

"Judge Rejects $25 Million H&R Block Settlement." 2000. *New York Times.* July 25.

Kahn, S. 1994. *How People Get Power.* Washington, DC: NASW Press.

Katznelson, I. 1981. *City Trenches.* New York: Pantheon.

Kobliner, B. 1998. "Tax Giants Loan Deals Stir Dispute." *New York Times.* April 12.

Koehler, B., and M. Wissen. 2003. "Glocalizing Protest: Urban Conflicts and Urban Social Movements." *International Journal of Urban and Regional Research* 27 (December): 942–51.

Kretzman, J., and J. McKnight. 1993. *Building Communities from the Inside Out.* Skokie, IL: ACTA Publications.

Kristof, K. 2004. "Critics: Tax-Refund Loans Rip Off the Working Poor." *Miami Herald.* February 1. E-posting.

Kuttner, R. 1996. *Everything for Sale: The Virtues and Limits of Markets.* Chicago: University of Chicago Press.

Linder, C. 2004. "Disclosing Refund Anticipation Loans Source Doesn't Quiet Consumer Activists." *American Banker.* March 4.

Llobrera, J., and B. Zahradnik. 2004. *A Hand Up: How State Earned Income Tax Credits Help Working Families Escape Poverty in 2004.* Washington, DC: Center on Budget and Policy Priorities.

Maag, E. 2005. "Paying the Price: Low-Income Parents and the Use of Paid Tax Preparers." February 1. Washington, DC: Urban Institute Report. Available at *www.urban.org.*

Maestri, N. 2004. "H&R Block Sees Office Traffic Falling, Shares Sink." Reuters. April 1.

Mansbridge, J. 1983. *Beyond Adversary Democracy.* Chicago: University of Chicago Press.

Marquez, B. 1993. "Mexican-American Community Development Corporations and the Limits of Directed Capitalism." *Economic Development Quarterly* 7 (August): 287–95.

Mayer, M. 2003. "The Onward Sweep of Social Capital: Causes and

Consequences for Understanding Cities, Communities, and Urban Movements." *International Journal of Urban and Regional Research* 27 (March): 110–32.

Meyer, G. 2001. "H&R Block to Reduce Emphasis on Refund Loans." *Kansas City Star*. September 13.

Meyer, M. 2004. "Organizational Identity, Political Contexts, and SMO Action: Explaining the Tactical Choices Made by Peace Organizations in Israel, Northern Ireland, and South Africa." *Social Movement Studies* 3 (October): 167–87.

McCarthy, J., and M. Zald. 1973. *The Trend of Social Movements*. Morristown, NJ: General Learning.

Murray, B. 2004. "The Cruelest Month." *Nation*. April 26.

National Consumer Law Center and Consumer Federation of America. 2006. "Quick Loans Skim Billions from Taxpayer Refunds." February 2. Press Release. Available at *www.consumerlaw.org*.

Newman, R. 2004. "Consumer Group Protests Alleged H&R Block Price Gouging." Knight Ridder Tribune Business News. January 14.

Pendras, M. 2002. "From Local Consciousness to Global Change: Asserting Power at the Local Level." *International Journal of Urban and Regional Research* 26, no. 4: 823–33.

Phillips, K. R. 2001. "The Earned Income Tax Credit: Knowledge Is Money." *Political Science Quarterly* 116:413–23.

Putnam, R. 1995. "Bowling Alone: America's Declining Social Capital." *Journal of Democracy* 6, no. 1: 65–78.

Rochon, T. 1998. *Culture Moves: Ideas, Activism, and Changing Values*. Princeton: Princeton University Press.

Roth, S. 2004a. "Loans Remain a Lightning Rod for Block Critics." *Business Journal*. March 12. Available at *www.bizjournals.com*.

Roth, S. 2004b. "Block, Critics Find Incentives for Peace: Mutual Benefits." *Kansas City Biz Journal*. July 23. Available at *kansascity.bizjournals.com*.

Sabatini, P. 2004. "High Cost of Quick Tax Refund Loans Blasted." *Pittsburgh Post-Gazette*. January 14.

Saegert, S., J. P. Thompson, and M. Warren, eds. 2001. *Social Capital and Poor Communities*. New York: Russell Sage.

Sandel, M. 1988. "Democrats and Community." *New Republic*. February 22, 20–23.

Scholz, J. K. 1994. "The Earned Income Tax Credit: Participation, Compliance, and Antipoverty Effectiveness." *National Tax Journal* 47 (March): 63–87.

Sen, R. 2003. *Stir It Up*. San Francisco: Jossey-Bass.

Shenoy, R. 2004. "Diminishing Returns." *Chicago Reporter*. February 1. Available at *www.findarticles.com*.

Shragge, E. 2003. *Activism and Social Change: Lessons for Community and Local Organizing*. Toronto: Broadview.

Silberman, C. 1964. *Crisis in Black and White*. New York: Random House.

Singletary, M. 2003. "With Tax Refunds, Haste Makes Waste." *Washington Post*. January 23.

———. 2005. "Tax Refund Loans Show Price of Impatience." *Washington Post*. January 23.

Skocpol, T. 2003. *Diminished Democracy: From Membership to Management in Civil Life*. Norman: University of Oklahoma Press.

Smeeding, T. M., K. R. Phillips, and M. O'Connor. 2000. "The EITC: Expectation, Knowledge, Use, and Economic and Social Mobility." *National Tax Journal* 53 (December): 1187–1210.

Snyder, M. 2005. "Advocate for Affordable Housing Earns Kudos in Lending Law Reform." *Houston Chronicle*. July 4.

Squires, G. 2003a. "No Progress Without Protest." *Shelterforce* 25, no. 2: 12–15.

———, ed. 2003b. *Organizing Access to Capital: Advocacy and the Democratization of Financial Institutions*. Philadelphia: Temple University Press.

———, ed. 2004. *Why the Poor Pay More: How to Stop Predatory Lending*. Westport, CT: Praeger.

Steinback, R. 2004. "Activists Go Straight to Source for Protest of Tax Refund Loans." *Miami Herald*. January 14.

Stoecker, R., and S. Stall. 1997. "Community Organizing or Organizing Community? Gender and the Crafts of Empowerment." COMM-ORG Working Paper. November. Available at *comm-org.wisc.edu/papers96/gender2.html*.

Strauss, A., and J. Corbin. 1990. *Basics of Qualitative Research*. Newbury Park, CA: Sage.

Swarts, H. 2002. "What Makes Community Organizing Succeed? Comparing Church- and Neighborhood-Based Organizations." *Snapshots: Research Highlights from the Nonprofit Sector Research Fund* 21 (January/February). Available at *www.nonprofitresearch.org/usr_doc/Community_Organizing_Snapshots.pdf*.

Tarrow, S. 1994. *Power in Movement: Social Movements, Collective Action, and Politics*. New York: Cambridge University Press.

Taylor, J., and J. Silver. 2003. "The Essential Role of Activism in Community Reinvestment." In *Organizing Access to Capital: Advocacy and the Democratization of Financial Institutions*, ed. by G. Squires, 169–87. Philadelphia: Temple University Press.

Tilly, C. 1978. *From Mobilization to Revolution*. Reading, MA: Addison-Wesley.

———. 1999. "From Interactions to Outcomes in Social Movements." In *How Social Movements Matter*, ed. by M. Giugni, D. McAdam, and C. Tilly, 253–70. Minneapolis: University of Minnesota Press.

———. 2004. *Social Movements*. Boulder, CO: Paradigm Press.

Ventry, D. J., Jr. 2000. "The Collision of Tax and Welfare Politics: The Political History of the Earned Income Tax Credit, 1969–99." *National Tax Journal* 53 (December): 983–1026.

Warren, M. 2001. *Dry Bones Rattling: Community Building to Revitalize Democracy.* Princeton: Princeton University Press.

Weir, M., H. Wolman, and T. Swanstrom. 2005. "The Calculus of Coalitions: Cities, Suburbs and the Metropolitan Agenda." *Urban Affairs Review* 40, no. 6: 730–60.

Williams, J. 1996. "Alinsky Discovered Organizing (Like Columbus Discovered America)." *Third Force* 4 (July–August): 14–17.

Wu, C. C. 2004. Interview with the authors.

Wu, C. C., and J. A. Fox. 2004. "All Drain, No Gain: Refund Anticipation Loans Continue to Sap the Hard Earned Tax Dollars of Low Income Americans." Washington, DC: National Consumer Law Center and the Consumer Federation of America. Available at *www.consumerlaw.org/initiatives/refund_anticipation/content/2004RALReportFinal.pdf.*

Wu, C. C., and J. A. Fox. 2005. "Picking Taxpayers' Pockets, Draining Tax Relief Dollars: Refund Anticipation Loans Still Slicing Into Low-Income Americans' Hard-Earned Tax Refunds." Washington, DC: National Consumer Law Center and the Consumer Federation of America. Available at *www.consumerlaw.org/initiatives/refund_anticipation/content/2005RALreport.pdf.*

Wu, C. C., J. A. Fox, and E. Renuart. 2002. "Tax Preparers Peddle High Priced Tax Refund: Millions Skimmed from the Working Poor and the U.S. Treasury." Washington, DC: National Consumer Law Center and the Consumer Federation of America. Available at *www.consumerlaw.org/initiatives/refund_anticipation/content/RAL_final.pdf.*

Yin, R. K. 2003. *Case Study Research: Design and Methods.* 3d ed. Thousand Oaks, CA: Sage.

10

ACORN Experiments in Minority Voter Mobilization

Donald Green and Melissa R. Michelson

Many observers have noted with dismay the low rates of political participation in U.S. elections. Voter turnout slumps from presidential election years to even-numbered midterm elections. And in off years, during which many local and some state elections are held, turnout levels fall even lower (Morlan 1984). Despite the immediate relevance of local issues to voters' lives, the typical U.S. municipal election draws between one-fifth and one-half of the *registered* electorate. Historically underrepresented minority groups are therefore often underrepresented at the city and state levels, both in terms of descriptive representation and policy preferences. Hajnal and Trounstine (2005) show that low turnout in local elections hurts Latinos because it leads to less representation in city hall. Conversely, Hajnal and Trounstine (2004) find that "increases in voter turnout lead to spending patterns that more closely reflect the preferences of minorities and lower class voters. Greater turnout means more redistributive spending, higher taxes, and less allocational spending."

This chapter reviews several of ACORN's recent efforts to increase Latino and African American turnout in local elections. Researchers have established that nonpartisan, single-contact canvassing, either in person or by telephone, can significantly increase Latino turnout in a variety of election settings (Michelson 2003, 2006; Ramírez 2005). Less is known about how voter mobilization efforts work in African American communities. An effort in the November 2000 elections using direct mail and commercial phone banks increased African American turnout minimally, if at all (Green 2004). Leafleting campaigns in partisan races (Gillespie 2005) and nonpartisan campaigns targeting predominantly African American precincts (Azari and Washington 2006) have also proven ineffective. The various ACORN efforts reviewed here, by contrast, include issue advocacy and efforts to contact voters repeatedly through face-to-face conversations. While one ACORN campaign reviewed here simply focused on increasing turnout in a targeted African American community, in the remaining three elections ACORN made an effort to encourage registered voters who supported certain ballot issues to vote on Election Day. In each case, voters randomly selected into treatment groups were much more likely to vote than those randomized into control groups. Even in low-salience, low-turnout elections, ACORN was able to significantly increase turnout rates in these traditionally low-participation minority groups.

As Harold Gosnell (1927, 108) noted in his path-breaking study of voter mobilization in Chicago during the 1924 and 1925 elections, the quiescence of local elections makes them ideal laboratories for studying methods for increasing voter turnout. Amid limited campaigning and few newsworthy political events, the effects of interventions designed to increase turnout are more readily detected. In addition, low voter turnout rates reduce statistical uncertainty, which is maximal when half of the sample casts ballots. Despite these advantages, local elections tend to attract little attention from students of politics, except insofar as they involve heated racial politics or other circumstances that make them atypical.

In recent years, the study of electoral turnout has increasingly focused on the subject of voter mobilization. Building on the early works of Gosnell (1927) and Eldersveld (1956), the recent scholarship of Rosenstone and Hansen (1993), Verba, Schlozman, and Brady (1995), and Putnam (2000) has emphasized the responsiveness of voters to their social and political environments. A citizen's level of electoral participation and civic engagement more generally is said to respond to blandishments from family members, political parties, and social networks. By implication, a dearth of mobilization activities may account for the low voter turnout rates typical of local elections.

Until recently, the study of voter turnout was dominated by survey research. In the wake of experiments conducted by Gerber and Green (2000a), however, many researchers have turned to field experiments to investigate how to get out the vote. Gerber and Green used nonpartisan door-to-door canvassing, direct mail, and commercial telephone calls to increase turnout in New Haven, Connecticut. They found that door-to-door canvassing increased voter turnout by nine percentage points, direct mail raised turnout by 0.6 percentage points, and commercial telephone calls had no impact at all. They concluded that personal forms of mobilization were more effective, and they encouraged future efforts to focus on personal connections between voters and the electoral process. Subsequent work by other researchers has since expanded that research to include partisan efforts, as well as campaigns aimed at particular demographic groups, including Latinos and African Americans. The main finding—that the most effective methods of voter mobilization are those that involve personal, face-to-face interaction—has held up well after dozens of experimental replications and extensions of the Gerber and Green (2000a) study. As this chapter demonstrates, the personal interaction that typifies ACORN's outreach produces substantial increases in turnout, even in poor neighborhoods where turnout tends to be low.

Method

During the months leading up to the November 6, 2001, election in Bridgeport, Connecticut, and Detroit, Michigan, and the November 2003 election in Maricopa County (Phoenix), Arizona, and Kansas City, Missouri, teams of researchers collaborated with ACORN to examine the effectiveness of door-to-door canvassing, focusing on Latino and African American voters.[1] Names appearing on lists of registered voters were randomly assigned to treatment and control groups. Treatment groups were visited during the days leading up to the election. Control groups were not contacted. After the election, researchers obtained voter turnout records from each county and calculated the turnout rates in each control and treatment group. It should be stressed that, in contrast to most survey-based analyses of voter mobilization, our study does not rely on voters' self-reported turnout or self-reported contact with get-out-the-vote campaigns.

Randomization Procedure
Using official lists of voters gathered immediately after the close of registration, ACORN compiled a database of registered voters' names and addresses. Names of individuals residing at the same address were grouped into households, which were in turn grouped geographically into walk lists. In Bridgeport and Detroit, only voters living in households with fewer than five registered voters are included in the treatment and control groups. One registered voter from each household was selected for study, and these voters were randomly assigned to treatment and control groups. In Phoenix, the experiment included only one and two-voter

households, which were then randomized separately into treatment and control groups. The walk lists given to canvassers contained the names and addresses of people in the treatment group, and they were instructed to approach only these residences. In Kansas City, randomization into treatment and control groups was done at the precinct level.

Canvassing Sites

Although the sites in our study cannot be construed as a random sample of municipal elections occurring nationwide, the external validity of our results is strengthened by the fact that the get-out-the-vote campaigns took place in very different political and demographic settings. An overview of the sites is presented in Table 10.1. Looking solely at the regions within each site that were targeted for canvassing, one sees that the variation across sites is considerable. Data from the 2000 Census indicate that 94 percent of the population in the canvassed regions in Detroit is black, as is 64 percent of the population in the canvassed area of Kansas City. Latinos account for nearly half of the population in the canvassed regions of Bridgeport and 64 percent of the population in the canvassed areas of Phoenix.

SITE 1: BRIDGEPORT, CONNECTICUT

Bridgeport is a racially diverse, low-income urban area that votes overwhelmingly Democratic. The November 6, 2001, election featured a local school board election and city council races. Due to the city's Democratic majority, all but one of these races were uncompetitive, and the remaining election occurred in a district that was outside the area we canvassed. Turnout, as expected, was low.

ACORN conducted a door-to-door campaign in hopes of generating sufficient support among voters for a living-wage ordinance (raising the minimum wage to $11.08 per hour) that had been introduced in the city council earlier in the year. Beginning on October 20 and each weekend thereafter, ACORN volunteers followed walk lists urging every treatment household to vote in the upcoming election. The canvassers included a diverse mix of African Americans and Latinos (some of whom spoke Spanish), who were highly trained before starting their mobilization efforts.

SITE 2: DETROIT, MICHIGAN

With a closely contested mayoral race, the Detroit elections were among the most interesting in 2001. As in Bridgeport, canvassing was conducted

Table 10.1. Characteristics of canvassing sites, focusing only on regions of each site that were actually canvassed

	Bridgeport	*Detroit*	*Phoenix*	*Kansas City*
Total city population	139,529	951,270	1,326,045*	441,545
Population in canvassed areas	19,115	17,412	115,939	46,770
Black	28%	94%	11%	64%
Asian	4%	0%	1%	1%
Latino	47%	1%	64%	10%
Type of election	School Board	Mayoral	Proposition	Proposition
Competitiveness	Low	High	Low	Low
Voter turnout rate among subjects in the control group	9.9%	43.3%	7.3%	29.1%
N of subjects in the control group	911	2,482	545	4,779
N of subjects in the treatment group	895	2,472	5,216	4,933

Source: Demographic profile data is from the 2000 Census.
*This is the population of both the city of Phoenix and the town of Guadalupe (population 5,228). Precincts in both areas were targeted by ACORN for the mobilization effort examined here.

under the auspices of ACORN. However, the crew of canvassers, who were predominantly young, African American, and female, had no previous political experience. After receiving a half-hour training session, the canvassers took to the streets during the weekend prior to Election Day, canvassing all day Saturday, Sunday, and Monday.

SITE 3: PHOENIX, ARIZONA

On November 4, 2003, Maricopa County, Arizona, held an election to determine the future of the county hospital. Proposition 414 asked voters to create a special hospital district, establish a supervising board, institute a property tax, and set a tax rate. It was the only countywide question on the ballot, although in some areas of the county, citizens were asked to vote on other questions. Turnout, as expected, was low.

ACORN, whose heavily Latino membership relied on the hospital's service, focused on mobilizing Latino voters in twenty-nine low- and moderate-income precincts in Phoenix and nearby Guadalupe, where ACORN either had a significant membership or hoped to build one in the near future. Paid canvassers, including a mix of full-time ACORN organizers and inexperienced locals, and a mix of monolingual English, bilingual, and monolingual Spanish speakers, worked from October 13 to 30. From November 1 through 4, canvassers worked to contact a second time those previously identified as supporters or potential supporters of the proposition. Most of these re-contacts occurred through face-to-face interactions, although some people were re-contacted by phone. The use of phones in this part of the campaign muddies the evaluation of the canvassing campaign somewhat, but in light of previous research showing the moderate effects of volunteer phone calls (Green and Gerber 2008), we believe that the strong effects observed in this site were driven primarily by face-to-face interaction.

SITE 4: KANSAS CITY, MISSOURI

A budget crisis forced the Kansas City Transit Authority to place on the November 2003 ballot a proposal requesting a 3/8 percent increase in the city's sales tax. Question 1 asked voters to preserve Saturday and Sunday evening bus service and to add bus lines to the airport and in the inner city. ACORN organized in support of the tax, targeting for mobilization the African American community, which relies heavily on buses for transportation.

Of twenty-eight primarily African American precincts included in the study, half were randomly assigned to a control group. In the fourteen precincts chosen for the treatment group, a pool of seventy-five predominantly African American canvassers walked each precinct twice in the month before the election, with the second contact focusing on those previously identified as supporters of the tax increase proposal.

Canvassing Scripts
Although the characteristics of the sites and canvassers varied, they tended to follow similar procedures when going door-to-door. Each canvasser

was equipped with a clipboard, a map, and a target list of names and addresses. Canvassers were thus responsible for conveying a brief reminder about the upcoming election, in some cases distributing a flier, and recording the disposition of each visit.[2] In Phoenix and Kansas City, some voters were contacted by telephone either when they could not be reached in person or to make a second contact closer to the election.

That the Bridgeport, Phoenix, and Kansas City campaigns focused on local issues of interest to the community being targeted was expected to boost the effectiveness of ACORN's efforts. Schmidt (1989) argues that voters are more likely to vote when a ballot includes initiatives because they are more likely to see tangible results. Similarly, Everson (1981) notes that incentives to participate are clearer for voters when the election includes a ballot proposition. Various studies provide empirical evidence to support these arguments. Schecter (2000, 2003), Smith (2001), Tolbert, Grummel, and Smith (2001), and Tolbert, McNeal, and Smith (2003) all find positive statistical relationships between direct democracy and turnout. Tolbert, McNeal, and Smith find that "exposure to ballot initiatives increases the probability of voting, stimulates campaign contributions to interest groups, and enhances political knowledge" (2003, 23). Using state-level data rather than individual-level data, Schecter (2003) finds that "states with at least one initiative on the ballot in 1996 had higher levels of voter turnout than states without a ballot question."

Raising the minimum wage was expected to be a salient and mobilizing issue for Latinos in Bridgeport. Keeping the local hospital open was likely a key issue for Phoenix-area Latinos (despite the low salience of the election). Maintaining and expanding bus service was important to Kansas City African Americans. In each of these cities, we expected that ACORN's mobilization efforts would have a significant effect on the turnout of targeted voters. However, it should be noted that the issue content of the door-to-door appeals was not varied experimentally; thus, the additional effectiveness of issue-based appeals is a matter of speculation and a subject of future research. To date, this type of experimental manipulation of scripts has been largely confined to alternative nonpartisan canvassing scripts, which do not appear to alter the effectiveness of canvassing (Michelson 2005), or to partisan versus nonpartisan phone scripts (Panagopoulos 2008), neither of which stood out as particularly effective. Whether ACORN's policy advocacy was itself a contributing factor or simply an ancillary part of what otherwise would have been effective, personal outreach remains an open question.

Data and Design Issues

The procedures by which subjects were assigned at random to treatment and control groups varied slightly across sites. Subjects in Detroit were stratified into walk lists before random assignment, while those in Bridgeport were not, but in both sites subjects were assigned the same probability of receiving a treatment. Randomization in Phoenix was done separately in one- and two-voter households, and the probability of being assigned to a treatment group differed for the two types of households. In Kansas City, randomization was done at the precinct level.

After the election, records were obtained from local registrars to calculate voter turnout rates among the treatment and control groups. Turnout records from previous elections were also obtained. This information enables us to check whether random assignment to treatment and control groups was indeed uncorrelated with past voting behavior. It also provides a useful covariate in a multivariate analysis, as past behavior helps reduce the disturbance variance in models predicting voting in the target elections.

Results

Randomization Check
Randomization procedures are designed to create treatment and control groups with equivalent pretreatment vote propensities. In order to check that random assignment performed this function, we calculated voter turnout rates for treatment and control groups in the previous elections. The results indicate that the groups are balanced in terms of background factors such as past voting behavior. As expected, there are no significant differences between the treatment and control groups.

Intent-to-Treat Effects
The intent-to-treat effect refers to the effect of assigning a registered voter to a canvassing list, taking no account of whether the person was actually canvassed. This quantity provides a sense of how effective the overall campaign was in generating additional votes. The intent-to-treat effect can be calculated by examining the turnout rates among those assigned to the treatment and control groups. Table 10.2 presents these turnout rates for treatment and control groups in each city. In every site, the treatment

Table 10.2. Treatment effects, by site

	Intent-to-treat effect (treatment vs. control)		Percentage of treatment group actually contacted	Effects of actual treatment on voting	
Bridgeport (*n* = 1,806)	4.0**	(1.5)	28.1	14.4**	(5.3)
Detroit (*n* = 4,954)	2.4*	(1.4)	30.9	7.8*	(4.5)
Phoenix (1-voter households) (*n* = 3,139)	8.5**	(1.8)	70.9	12.0**	(2.4)
Phoenix (2-voter households) (*n* = 2,622)	14.1**	(3.6)	80.0	17.6**	(6.0)
Kansas City (*n* = 9,712)	4.4*	(2.5)	62.7	7.0*	(3.9)

* $p < .05$, one-tailed test. ** $p < .01$, one-tailed test. Standard errors in parentheses.
Note: Differences between treatment and control groups (column 2) were calculated from OLS regressions of voting in 2001 or 2003 on a dummy variable for experimental treatment assignment, with dummy variables for each walk list as covariates. Actual treatment effects (column 4) were estimated from a 2SLS regression of voting on contact, with the experimental treatment as an excluded instrumental variable. Both stages of the 2SLS regression included covariates for each walk list. The standard errors associated with the Kansas City estimates take clustering (precinct-level assignment) into account.

group turned out at a higher rate than the control group. In Detroit, where over 40 percent of registered voters cast ballots, turnout in the treatment group was 2.4 percentage points higher than in the control group. In Bridgeport, where turnout in the control group was an abysmal 9.9 percent, turnout in the treatment group was 4.0 percentage-points higher. In Phoenix, where overall turnout was only 12 percent, turnout was 8.5 percentage points higher in the treatment group than the control group for one-voter households and 14.1 percentage points higher for the treatment group of two-voter households. In Kansas City, turnout in the control group was 29.1 percent, but was 5.3 percentage points higher in the treatment group.

The Effects of Actual Contact

In order to estimate the mobilizing effect of canvassing among those who are contacted, one must make a statistical adjustment for the fact that many people in the treatment group were never contacted. As shown in

Table 10.2, the limiting factor in these get-out-the-vote (GOTV) campaigns is that they often contact less than half of their walk lists, although contact rates in Phoenix were quite high. When calculating contact rates, all forms of contact are included, even (unusual) instances where people were contacted solely by phone. Excluded from the definition of *contact* are instances where canvassers found no one at home, could not locate the address, discovered that they had the wrong address, or were told to go away before making their GOTV appeal.

The rightmost column of Table 10.2 reports the actual contact effects. The influence of actual contact in Bridgeport, for example, is estimated to be a 14.4 percentage-point jump in the probability of voting, while in Detroit contact increased turnout by 7.8 percentage points. In Phoenix, turnout increased by 12.0 percentage points in one-voter households and 17.6 percentage-points in two-voter households. In Kansas City, contact increased turnout by 8.5 percentage points. The results reaffirm the effectiveness of face-to-face canvassing as a means of mobilizing voters. Across a wide range of electoral settings, ranging from the sleepy local election in Bridgeport to a heated mayoral race in Detroit, and in two low-salience proposition battles in Phoenix and Kansas City, ACORN canvassing had a profound effect on voter participation. Indeed, the ACORN experiments are noteworthy in that they show substantially larger treatment effects than canvassing experiments conducted in conjunction with other organizations (Green and Gerber 2008).

Conclusion

The four ACORN canvassing experiments demonstrate that mobilization campaigns have the potential to substantially increase turnout in local elections. Given low turnout rates in these types of low-salience local elections generally, voter mobilization efforts such as those conducted by ACORN in 2001 and 2003 have the potential to shape election outcomes or at least shape the way in which public officials regard voter turnout rates in minority communities. The success with which these door-to-door campaigns mobilized voters is especially impressive given the austere budgets on which these campaigns operated.

One of the paradoxes of local elections is that individual votes have a greater likelihood of affecting the outcome, yet fewer eligible voters participate. The same logic applies to arguments based on the indirect effects that voters can have on elections by mobilizing their friends and neighbors (Shachar and Nalebuff 1999). With such small numbers of voters casting ballots, mobilization campaigns would seem to be a promising strategy for influencing an election. Yet, the overall level of GOTV activity tends to be low in local elections. In lopsided contests, campaigns have little incentive to do this type of work; in competitive contests, campaigns seem content to focus their energies on persuading voters who regularly vote in local elections. This pattern tends to leave undisturbed the age, socioeconomic, and racial/ethnic disparities between voters and nonvoters that have long been the focus of scholarship on local voter turnout (Hamilton 1971; Oliver 1999). The present study suggests that nonpartisan groups, as well as partisan groups that choose to use nonpartisan appeals, have the potential to alter this pattern through face-to-face contact with potential voters. Even in settings where the election outcome seems to be a foregone conclusion, this type of personal contact has a marked effect on voter participation.

Door-to-door voter mobilization is experiencing a renaissance, as parties, candidates, and organizations turn to old-fashioned, face-to-face precinct walking to mobilize their supporters (Bergan et al. 2005). This study demonstrates that such tactics can be highly effective, even among communities that traditionally have low turnout—low-income Latinos and African Americans. In four local elections, across a variety of electoral contexts and levels of competitiveness, ACORN substantially increased voter turnout.

Scholars and practitioners seeking to understand the process by which canvassing generates votes would be well advised to study ACORN's ongoing efforts. What are the active ingredients? Are they local volunteers who can speak credibly about the importance of the election, scripts emphasizing the relevance of specific issues affecting minority communities, or the combination of the two? The next task is to manipulate these factors experimentally in order to better understand why ACORN's efforts are so successful. Would canvassers from outside the neighborhood be just as effective? Would one achieve the same results using generic nonpartisan scripts that make no mention of issues confronting the community? More generally, could one achieve the same results as ACORN in other demographic or ideological environments, using an analogous formula of local canvassers and issue advocacy?

NOTES

1. Each of these experiments has been discussed in published work. For more details on the Bridgeport and Detroit experiments, see Green, Gerber, and Nickerson 2003. For more details on the Phoenix experiment, see Michelson 2006–2007. For more details on the Kansas City experiment, see Arceneaux 2005.
2. The treatment thus comprises both a personal appeal and distribution of a leaflet. Other experimental evidence seems to show that leaflets alone have minimal effects on turnout (Gerber and Green 2000a). Not reported here are embedded experiments in which the content of the leaflet was varied randomly, sometimes urging subjects to vote and in other cases presenting them with a voter guide culled from a local newspaper. Varying the content of the flyer had small and statistically insignificant effects.

REFERENCES

Arceneaux, K. 2005. "Using Cluster Randomized Field Experiments to Study Voting Behavior." *Annals of the American Academy of Political and Social Science* 601 (September): 169–79.

Azari, J., and E. Washington. 2006. "Results from a 2004 Leafleting Field Experiment in Miami-Dade and Duval Counties, Florida." Unpublished manuscript. Institution for Social and Policy Studies, Yale University.

Bergan, D. E., A. S. Gerber, D. P. Green, and C. Panagopoulos. 2005. "Grassroots Mobilization and Voter Turnout in 2004." *Public Opinion Quarterly* 69:760–77.

Eldersveld, S. J. 1956. "Experimental Propaganda Techniques and Voting Behavior." *American Political Science Review* 50 (March): 154–65.

Everson, D. 1981. "The Effects of Initiatives on Voter Turnout: A Comparative State Analysis." *Western Political Quarterly* 29: 415–25.

Gerber, A. S., and D. P. Green. 2000a. The Effect of a Nonpartisan Get-Out-the-Vote Drive: An Experimental Study of Leafleting." *Journal of Politics* 62, no. 3: 846–57.

———. 2000b. "The Effects of Canvassing, Direct Mail, and Telephone Contact on Voter Turnout: A Field Experiment." *American Political Science Review* 94: 653–63.

Gillespie, A. N. 2005. "Community, Coordination and Context: A Black Politics Perspective on Voter Mobilization." PhD diss., Yale University, New Haven, Connecticut.

Gosnell, H. F. 1927. *Getting-Out-the-Vote: An Experiment in the Stimulation of Voting.* Chicago: University of Chicago Press.

Green, D. P. 2004. "Mobilizing African-Americans Using Direct Mail and

Commercial Phone Banks: A Field Experiment." *Political Research Quarterly* 57, no. 2: 245–55.

Green, D. P., and A. S. Gerber. 2008. *Get Out the Vote: How to Increase Voter Turnout.* 2d ed. Washington, DC: Brookings Institution Press.

Green, D. P., A. S. Gerber, and D. W. Nickerson. 2003. "Getting Out the Vote in Local Elections: Results from Six Door-to-Door Canvassing Experiments." *Journal of Politics* 65, no. 4: 1083–96.

Hajnal, Z., and J. Trounstine. 2004. "Turnout Matters: Voter Turnout and City Spending Priorities." Paper presented at the annual meeting of the Midwest Political Science Association, Chicago, April 15–18.

———. 2005. "Where Turnout Matters: The Consequences of Uneven Turnout in City Politics." *Journal of Politics* 67, no. 2 (May): 515–35.

Hamilton, H. D. 1971. "The Municipal Voter: Voting and Nonvoting in City Elections." *American Political Science Review* 65: 1135–40.

Michelson, M. R. 2003. "Getting Out the Latino Vote: How Door-to-Door Canvassing Influences Voter Turnout in Rural Central California." *Political Behavior* 25, no. 3 (September): 247–63.

———. 2005. "Meeting the Challenge of Latino Voter Mobilization." *Annals of Political and Social Science* 601 (September): 85–101.

———. 2006. "Mobilizing the Latino Youth Vote: Some Experimental Results." *Social Science Quarterly* 87, no. 5 (December): 1188–1206.

———. 2006–2007. "Mobilizing Latino Voters for a Ballot Proposition." *Latino(a) Research Review* 6, no. 1–2 (Summer): 33–49.

Morlan, R. L. 1984. "Municipal vs. National Election Voter Turnout: Europe and the United States." *Political Science Quarterly* 99: 457–70.

Oliver, J. E. 1999. "The Effects of Metropolitan Economic Segregation on Local Civic Participation." *American Journal of Political Science* 43:186–212.

Panagopoulos, C. 2009. "Partisan and Nonpartisan Message Content and Voter Mobilization: Field Experimental Evidence." *Political Research Quarterly* 62:70–76.

Putnam, R. C. 2000. *Bowling Alone: The Collapse and Renewal of American Community.* New York: Simon and Schuster.

Ramakrishnan, S. K., and M. Baldassare. 2003. "Beyond the Ballot Box: Political Participation and Racial Inequality in California." Paper presented at the annual meeting of the Western Political Science Association, Denver, March 27–29.

Ramírez, R. 2005. "Giving Voice to Latino Voters: A Field Experiment on the Effectiveness of a National Nonpartisan Mobilization Effort." *Annals of the American Academy of Political and Social Science* 601 (September): 66–84.

Rivers, D., and Q. H. Vuong. 1988. "Limited Information Estimators and Exogeneity Tests for Simultaneous Probit Models." *Journal of Econometrics* 39:347–66.

Rosenstone, S. J., and J. M. Hansen. 1993. *Mobilization, Participation, and Democracy in America.* New York: Macmillan.

Schecter, D. 2000. "Evaluating the Impact of Direct Democracy on Voter Turnout." Paper presented at the Annual Meeting of the Midwest Political Science Association, Chicago, April 27–30.

———. 2003. "Legislating Morality outside of the Legislature: Direct Democracy and Morality Politics, 1972–2002." Paper presented at the annual meeting of the Western Social Science Association, Las Vegas, April 10–13.

Schmidt, D. 1989. *Citizen Lawmakers.* Philadelphia: Temple University Press.

Shachar, R., and B. Nalebuff. 1999. "Follow the Leader: Theory and Evidence on Political Participation." *American Economic Review* 89:525–47.

Smith, M. 2001. "The Contingent Effects of Ballot Initiatives and Candidate Races on Turnout." *American Journal of Political Science* 45, no. 3: 700–706.

Tolbert, C., R. S. McNeal, and D. A. Smith. 2003. "Enhancing Civic Engagement: The Effects of Direct Democracy on Political Participation and Knowledge." *State Politics and Policy Quarterly* 3, no. 1: 23–41.

Tolbert, C., J. A. Grummel, and D. A. Smith. 2001. "The Effects of Ballot Initiatives on Voter Turnout in the American States." *American Politics Research* 29, no. 6: 625–48.

Verba, S., K. L. Schlozman, and H. E. Brady. 1995. *Voice and Equality: Civic Voluntarism in American Politics.* Cambridge, MA: Harvard University Press.

PART III
Reflections

11

Does ACORN's Work
Contribute to Movement Building?

Gary Delgado

After more than thirty-five years of work in low-income neighborhoods, ACORN's success is hard to deny. With 200,000 member families, and local chapters in thirty-nine states and ninety-eight cities, it is the largest individual membership-based community organization in the United States. ACORN has fought redlining and predatory lending, elected local and state representatives, organized unions, counseled home buyers, achieved passage of 122 living wage ordinances, executed mass actions on a number of federal agencies, and raised hell in thirty-five statehouses. As Bertha Lewis, ACORN's new chief organizer, observes, "Whether you're talking about housing or education or wages, we've been able to deliver. In some ways longevity is our greatest success—we've become an institution" (Lewis 2006).

While size has been key to ACORN's impact, it also has a downside. Smoothly and accountably coordinating offices and staffs in ninety-eight cities, and managing large amounts of money flowing through multiple affiliated organizations, requires bureaucratic systems that are not necessarily consistent with either a movement organization or charismatic, visionary leadership. This problem became particularly apparent in the summer of 2008 when newspapers reported a major embezzlement of organizational funds in 1999 by a senior ACORN staffer who is a member of founder Wade Rathke's family. The discovery had a number of detrimental effects on the organization: staff/board conflict; anger from board members who were not informed of the embezzlement; resignation of key staff, including Rathke; countless "I told you so's" by detractors; a focus on fiscal malfeasance by the press; sanctions and cries of anguish from current and former foundation funders; and a grinding slowdown of organizational activities.

While theft, even in social change organizations, is less rare than many of us would like to think, the lack of an ongoing staff/board system of mutual accountability points to a structural weakness and raises an organizational dilemma. The structural weakness is clear: there was not enough fiscal transparency. The organizational dilemma is less easy to define, but it is reflective of the current disarray in organizational leadership and the question of organizational direction. For almost forty years, ACORN has been led by Wade Rathke, a brilliantly strategic and charismatic, though very controversial, leader. Rathke recruited many senior staff in the 1970s, and they have remained a core of talented organizational actors. Common ideas and history, friendship, trust, and personal loyalty have helped hold ACORN's senior staff together and move the organization forward. At this juncture, many of those connections have been severely tested, and some are permanently broken.

This article was written before the public disclosure of ACORN's internal difficulties. However, given these recently disclosed events and leadership changes, questions of the future direction of the largest community organization in the United States are, I believe, even more important to assess. In this tumultuous period, ACORN will face its greatest test: Will the organization survive and thrive? If it does, what kind of organization will it be?

Although few would argue with ACORN's success on specific issues, the question of the group's overall effect remains. Does ACORN's work help build a progressive movement? Over twenty years ago, in the closing chapter of one of the first studies of ACORN, *Organizing the Movement* (1986), I contended that the work of the growing networks of community organizations, while effective in winning local victories, was actually less than the sum of its parts. At the time, most community organizing networks were comprised of loosely federated and fiercely independent local organizations that seemed to have neither the vision nor the political will to do much more than replicate effective issue campaigns. While winning victories in local communities was important, I argued that the amalgamated efforts of hundreds of small community groups would not necessarily result in large-scale structural change. Instead, actions to change national policies to benefit poor people and people of color would necessarily combine internal organizational efforts to bridge race/gender inequalities with broad-based campaign efforts designed to reframe public debate and win concrete changes in national policies. "The real question," I wrote, "is not whether community organizing networks will survive, but whether they will develop the *internal structures and external strategies* necessary to grow beyond a group of organizations waiting for a movement into a progressive movement for social change" (Delgado 1986). This chapter examines ACORN's work in relation to the elusive concept of "movement building."

Is It Really Possible to Build a Movement?

Movement building has emerged as the trendy term for social change work. From projects to support nonprofit movement building strategies (for example, BuildingMovement.org 2008) to foundation-supported efforts to build movements (Vega-Marquis 2003) to some organizations' forming "movement building departments" (for example, National Gay and Lesbian Task Force), the notion of movement building tops the list of organizational imperatives for many progressive organizations.

While much debate and discussion focuses on the key priorities for movement building work, activists are reaching a consensus on one point: social movements result from conscious and systematic efforts to build them. This consensus did not always exist. ACORN's new chief organizer Bertha Lewis reflects, "As activists in the [19]60s and [19]70s, we fought for the rights of black people and poor people. We weren't trying to create a movement. We were just dealing with the issues in front of us. The movement just happened" (2006). Lewis's sense of history is similar to my own experience in the anti-Vietnam war movement and national welfare rights work. We were part of mass movements, but we viewed those efforts as the happy result of mass sentiment, circumstance, a supportive infrastructure—and luck.

Later, when I began to study social movements, the notion that they were not systematically created was reinforced in my graduate classes at Berkeley. We studied prerequisite political conditions, the kinds of infrastructure that helped support mass movements, and the resources necessary for mobilization and organization, and we debated the "revolutionary potential" of different constituencies. Our common assumption, however, was that while one could build organization and influence public sentiment, social movements could only be hoped for. They simply happened—or, more often, they didn't.

Today the opposite assertion holds sway. Younger activists, especially, assume that it is both necessary and possible to build a large-scale social movement. One key reason for the contention that progressives should make movement building a priority is the issue of scale. Many activists point to the consolidation of global capital, technological advances that make worldwide communications almost instantaneous, and the planetwide detrimental effects of U.S.-initiated military, economic, political, and environmental policies. As Lian Cheun, Director of the Center For Third World Organizing's Movement Activist Apprenticeship Program (MAAP), notes, "the rise of right-wing conservatism in the U.S., coupled with these depressing political developments globally, has created a need in many of us to be part of something larger—something that fights back" (Cheun 2006).

Although many activists agree on the need for movement building, little consensus exists on priorities for movement building activities. For instance, the Peace Development Fund's Listening Project cited the "lack of an overarching set of ideas, themes, and issues that define the movement for the public at large" as the biggest challenge to movement building, concluding that central components for movement building should include "vision, leadership development, addressing multiple issues, active bridging between various sectors, self-transformation, joint strategies, and coordination of resources" (1999). Taj James, director of the Movement Strategy Center, points to "recognizing and addressing structural racism and engaging and mobilizing our traditional base while communicating with the broader public" (2005) as key factors in a movement building strategy. The Marguerite Casey Foundation, a financial supporter of movement building activities, includes "clarity of message, working across generations, and technology sharing and data integration" (Vega-Marquis 2003). Activists Dan Berger and Andy Cornell, authors of *Ten Questions for Movement Building* (2006), refer to a process for developing power "by building coalitions, political infrastructure, and visionary, alternative institutions that prefigure the types of social relationships we desire—while simultaneously confronting the state, right-wing social movements, and other forms of institutional oppression." One without the other, they argue, "is insufficient" (Berger and Cornell 2006).

While these components are not directly at odds with more traditional definitions of social movements, they certainly differ from those that Tilly emphasizes (1997). He lists the elements that differentiate social movements from other forms of politics as "sustained challenge; direction of that challenge to power-holders; action in the name of a wronged population; repeated public demonstrations that the wronged population or its representatives are worthy, unified, numerous, and committed; and actions outside the forms of political participation currently favored by the law" (Tilly 1997). The difference in emphasis between the movement building components suggested by practitioners and Tilly's more traditional view is, at least in part, related to some practitioners' emphasis on internal practices (for example, coalition building, antiracism, leadership development, resource sharing) as opposed to the external manifestations of those practices. Simply put, the activists' emphasis is on the *process* that leads to creating the sustained challenge, while Tilly emphasizes the external *outcome*—the depth, breadth, and disruptive utility of the challenge.

Since the work of social justice organizations, including ACORN, combines internal processes and external outcomes, how do we determine which is more important in assessing ACORN's movement building contributions? Because ACORN's organizational work has clearly tilted toward achieving external outcomes, this brief examination of ACORN's work assesses if and how three interrelated variables—(1) the organization's expanding size and scope of activities; (2) its ability to project progressive vision and values, and (3) the outcomes it achieves—contribute to building a broader social movement. If these are insufficient, what will it take for ACORN to have a greater movement building impact?

Size and Scope

A key task for organizers is building organizational size and scope—developing an organization that has a demonstrative mass membership, strong allies, and the tactical ability to win benefits for its constituency while projecting a cohesive message to the public at large. Although ACORN is best known for its grassroots groups and raucous "in your face" tactics, an important dimension of the organization's success is its ability to replicate those tactics in every major urban center in the country. Pointing to ACORN's chapters in 700 neighborhoods, Manhattan Institute Senior Fellow Sol Stern calls ACORN "the largest radical group in the country." "It is not only big," he continues "it is effective, with some remarkable successes in getting municipalities and state legislatures to enact its radical policy goals into law" (Stern 2003). Critics are appalled by both ACORN's size and breadth. Detractors point to the organization's "presence in more than 100 cities with a national budget of $37 million" (Malanga 2006), "two radio stations, a housing corporation, a law office, and affiliate relationships with a host of trade-union locals" (Stern 2003), and its successful use of "intimidation and other tactics to push for higher minimum wage mandates and to trash Wal-Mart and other non-union companies" ("The ACORN Indictments," 2006). And they are not wrong. As ACORN's national executive director Steve Kest points out,

"When we want to project something nationwide our size insures that a basic level of stuff will happen—and it will happen in a lot of places" (2006). ACORN's ability to "make stuff happen in a lot of places" is due in no small part to the interrelationship of four organizational components: constituent organizing, providing services to constituent members, aggressive activity in the electoral arena, and the organization's newest component, transnational organizing.

The one component that most activists seem to agree is essential to movement building is organizing. In their 2005 *Nation* article challenging progressives, analyst Jean Hardisty and Center for Community Change director Deepak Bhargava wrote that although organizing has always had an uneasy place in progressive circles, "no policy paper or slick message will ever replace the power of organizing" (2005). *Black Commentator* columnist Bruce Dixon agrees, noting that "mass movements don't happen without masses. Organizers and those who judge the work of organizers must learn to count" (2005). Peace Development Fund's Listening Project not only cites the need for grassroots organizing, it contrasts organizing to mobilizing: "Mobilizing may be good for winning reforms, (but) organizing develops critical analysis among people and develops leaders" (Peace Development Fund 1999).

The heart of ACORN's work is neighborhood organizing. By engaging poor people in the issues that directly affect them, ACORN is able to tap human talents and resources that much of the rest of society has written off. When asked why he joined ACORN, one community resident responded, "No one ever came to my door and asked for my opinion before" (ACORN 2005). ACORN's membership base of over 200,000 families provides leadership in local and national campaigns and grounds the organization in the lived experiences of low-income communities. In addition to the organization's neighborhood-based work, strong ties to the Service Employees International Union (SEIU) dating back to the early 1980s has enabled ACORN to work in collaborative campaigns with unions and initiate its own efforts to organize childcare workers and people forced into workfare programs under the 1996 welfare reform act. Clearly, ACORN's membership base is a critical component of the organization's success.

However, although local organizing is what ACORN is most well known for, it is not all the organization does (Table 11.1). After thirty-eight years, its work encompasses a wide breadth of activities. While it is not surprising that the organization's infrastructure includes a policy and research arm, a national campaign staff, and a communications office, activities also include the operation of radio stations in Dallas and Little Rock. ACORN Housing, one of the largest housing counseling operations in the country, serves between 30,000 and 35,000 families a year. Steve Kest says,

> There used to be a lot of debate in organizing circles about whether organizing organizations should deliver services, whether to emphasize clients or constituency. I think the mix we have works well. Mortgage counseling, for example, brings people into our offices where, if they're willing, we can involve them in campaign work. It also gives us real nitty-gritty knowledge on how issues of housing and mortgage discrimination really affect low-income families. So, when we sit down with a target or a legislator to negotiate for changes in policies and practices, because of the volume of the work, we can legitimately talk about trends. Plus, we know what changes to push for, because we know exactly how our members are getting screwed. (Kest 2006)

"Scale matters," Rathke observes. "It was because we had the structure in place in sixty cities that we were able to raise foundation money to test our ability to locate people who were eligible for the earned income tax credit (EITC). Currently, we're working with a group of software experts who are developing a program that will show people all of the benefit programs their families are eligible for once we've entered basic data" (Rathke 2006). Commenting on another advantage of the mix of services and organizing, Bertha Lewis observes, "It provides different points of entry for people to relate to or work with the organization. So, people experience us differently—some people think we're the housing people, or the education people or the union organizing people. The counseling also gives us an opportunity to do ongoing monitoring. It's not enough to expose predatory practices. We have to make sure that the banks do the right thing" (2006).

Politics Up Front

In addition to its service work, ACORN is also directly involved in electoral work. Unlike many community organizations that avoid the electoral arena, ACORN has developed political platforms and endorsed and run political candidates since the early 1970s. In 1976 ACORN launched the 20/80 plan—an effort to expand its organizational base from three to twenty states over the next four years and to use the 1980 presidential campaign to raise issues of concern to low-income people and build

Table 11.1. ACORN and ACORN-related organizational initiatives

Organizational component	Value added
Membership chapters in 39 states and 98 U.S. cities and international organizing projects in Peru, Canada, and Mexico, the Dominican Republic Council, and India	The membership gives the organization a legitimate base in low-income communities of color and enhances its ability to launch campaigns with replicable activities in multiple locations—including transnational work. The membership base also provides a source of organizational income that is not subject to foundation whimsy.
National staff infrastructure	Staff enables ACORN to initiate national strategies, use centrally generated research, and replicate policy advocacy and media messages.
ACORN Housing	ACORN Housing partners with ACORN campaigns directed at HUD and mortgage lenders to assist and counsel members in purchasing housing and to monitor campaign results.
ACORN Financial Justice Centers and Tax Access and Benefit Centers	The Financial Justice and Tax Benefit Centers offer free tax preparation in 62 ACORN offices and partner with allies in an additional 24 locations. Both of these service units also recruit organizational members.
KABF and KNON Radio stations	Both stations are on the air 24/7 and provide access to a broad range of social change activities through a mix of news, cultural programming, and public service announcements.
Project Vote	Project Vote contracts with ACORN to conduct voter registration and education efforts to increase the number of minority and low- and moderate-income citizens participating in the electoral process.
Living Wage Resource Center	This joint project of ACORN and the Labor Studies Program at Wayne State University has tracked living wage initiatives nationally, convened organizers from living wage campaigns across the country to learn from each other, and provided materials and strategies to state and local campaign efforts.

Organizational component	Value added
Organizer's Forum	This forum gives organizers from different networks the opportunity to collectively analyze new issues and technologies, reflect on past work, exchange ideas with organizers working outside of the United States, and strategize and discuss problems and approaches with practitioners outside of their immediate networks.
SEIU Locals 100 and 880	These locals of the Service Employees International Union (SEIU) work hand-in-hand with ACORN chapters organizing lower-wage health care, hospitality, janitorial, and sanitation workers in multiple locations in the South.
Social Policy Magazine	Provides a venue for interchange and analysis among organizers, activists, and public intellectuals.
Working Families Party	Certified as a political party in five states—New York, Connecticut, Delaware, South Carolina and Oregon—the WFP's New York operation, with 21 chapters and the ability to muster over 150,000 votes has had the greatest impact. The party has endorsed and run candidates, successfully advocated for an increase in the minimum wage in New York City, and pushed for and won reform of the state's draconian drug laws and health care for low-wage workers.

Note: Does not include ongoing coalition campaign efforts

the organization's power. The effort succeeded, and ACORN has continued to be involved in electoral politics ever since. ACORN's electoral efforts have expanded to include major voter registration efforts through Project Vote, resulting in the registration of over half a million voters in 2006, and the development of the Working Families Party (WFP)—a direct extension of the organization's ambition to create opportunities for ACORN members to push policies and principles that serve their political interest. Although Working Families has been certified as a political party in five states—New York, Connecticut, Delaware, South Carolina, and

Oregon—it is in New York that the party has had its greatest impact. New York governor-elect Elliot Spitzer called the WFP "a major force in state politics" (Working Families Party 2004), while a conservative columnist writes, "The far-left party won 80,000 votes statewide in the last presidential election and 100,000 in the last U.S. Senate race—the strongest showing of any third party except for the Conservative Party. . . . One-third of Gotham's new city councilors ran with Working Families' endorsement" (Stern 2003). By 2006, the party was able to produce 150,000 votes. With twenty-one chapters across the state, the WFP played an important role in winning a minimum wage increase in New York, reforming the state's draconian drug laws, and fighting for increased health coverage for workers.

Like the organization's service work, the Working Families Party offers ACORN's constituents yet another opportunity to become politically engaged. In some cases, that political engagement has actually led to an expansion of ACORN's organizational role. For instance, as Lewis recounts, "In 1998 we ran a petition campaign to create the Working Families Party in New York, and Gabrial Toks Pearse, a Nigerian Professor at Brooklyn College, sent some of his students over to work with us. He liked the culture of the organization and the commitment to low-income people's issues, so he became an active member. Now he's back in Nigeria and wants to build an ACORN chapter. So, next week I travel to Lagos to meet with an organizing committee and talk about how to start the first chapter" (2006).

The trip to Nigeria is not ACORN's first venture into international organizing. In the last four years, the organization has formed ACORN International, expanding the group's organizing efforts to Peru, Canada, Mexico, the Dominican Republic, and India.

ACORN's trademark ability to replicate campaigns from city to city and to direct actions at the same corporate or governmental target in multiple localities has been a key element of the organization's success. How do the global components of the organization mesh with the work of the domestic chapters? "Frankly, we are operating way past our experience. Although the issues in each country are surprisingly similar, the conditions and culture are very different," says Rathke (2006). "For instance, the notion that you really don't approach people with a preset agenda and that the issues are actually defined by people in the community was initially tough to get across to our new organizers in India. In Peru we learned that a three-month training period in the states for an organizer not familiar with our style and philosophy was simply not sufficient. We needed organizers who really understood the dynamics of both countries. We learned both of these things the hard way—but we learned them" (Rathke 2006).

One example of ACORN's ability to apply its organizing approach cross-nationally is the group's campaign against Sherwin-Williams. In May of 2006 ACORN released *Covering Our Communities in Toxics*, a report prepared by the organization's research staff. The report documented that Sherwin-Williams sold lead paint knowing that it was toxic and contributed to air pollution, and that the company failed to conduct lead dust education classes in violation of agreements with attorneys general in all fifty states ("ACORN Fights," 2006). In an ACORN press release issued six months after the release of the report, ACORN president Maude Hurd said that "the poisonous effects of Sherwin-Williams' years of neglect has spread across two continents" and announced ACORN protests at Sherwin-Williams's headquarters and stores in Toronto and Vancouver, Canada; Tijuana, Mexico; Lima, Peru; and Buenos Aires, Argentina, as well as demonstrations at six U.S. retail, manufacturing, and distribution sites in Little Rock, Arkansas; Jackson, Mississippi; Arlington, Texas; Orlando, Florida; Hartford, Connecticut; and Atlanta, Georgia ("ACORN Fights," 2006). "These companies are global," observed Hurd, "If we want to affect their actions, we've got to build organizations that have the ability to take action across national boundaries. People in those organizations are not outside allies, they're in the same boat we are—they just live in another country" (2006).

Clearly, ACORN's activities cover a wide social and economic span. Examining a cross section of the group's efforts in 2006, we find that ACORN won the elimination of the forty-dollar application fee at Jackson Hewitt, the nation's second largest tax preparer, enabling 16,000 families to file for refunds totaling $19 million. The group also undertook large-scale organizing efforts opposing the privatization of social security and supporting progressive immigration reform. At the state level, ACORN launched initiative campaigns resulting in the passage of minimum wage increases in Ohio, Missouri, Colorado, and Arizona. Local ACORN chapters successfully procured city-funded emergency home repair programs in San Antonio and Philadelphia, prevented foreclosure proceedings for thousands of homeowners displaced by Katrina, and launched campaigns to regulate payday lenders in Toronto and Vancouver. These victories have made significant differences in the lives of poor people. But are they simply isolated victories or have they affected the way fundamental questions are framed and talked about? Have they reframed the public debate?

Projecting Vision and Values

From the colonial rebellion against England to abolitionist, civil rights, and antiwar activism, to the women's and gay rights movements, ideas have played a key role in reframing a commonly held notion of fairness and justice and projecting a vision of a "just future." As writer Jean Hardisty (1999) notes, much of the success of conservative politics can be traced to the Right's ability to use a combination of fear and appeals to commonly held values to develop and popularize a vision and then deliver the public policy to actualize it. Growing out of the anti-ideological community organizing efforts of the 1960s and 1970s, ACORN has resisted both the party-line politics of the Left and the right-drifting Democrats. Has this resistance to a conventional ideological alignment rendered ACORN less effective in projecting vision and values?

As early as 1979, the ACORN People's Platform defined the organization's position in seventeen key issue areas. Neither a top-down nor a staff-generated document, the platform was the result of small group meetings in seventeen states. It called for many corporate reforms, including ending discount rates for commercial consumers of gas and electricity; taxing windfall profits of corporations in the arenas of housing, health, food, and energy; and cleaning up 30,000 hazardous waste sites. It also asked for guaranteed airtime on cable TV for community groups. Ratified at ACORN's national convention, the platform also addressed workers' rights, health access, neighborhood safety, and community development. The process and the product were radical for the time; however, the eclectic platform was less a vision of the future than an internal consolidation of many of the issues that local ACORN groups had worked on. Although the platform unified the organization, it projected neither a framework for those outside the organization nor a clear path for ACORN's future.

It was not until the mid-1990s that ACORN began to use its communicative resources intentionally. The organization's two radio stations regularly host discussions on ACORN's issues, ideas, and political positions, and the quarterly *Social Policy* magazine provides a forum for feature stories and analysis of the work of progressive community and labor groups. "*Social Policy* and the radio stations give us the ability to create and frame discussions—especially among our members and with allies," says Kevin Whelan (2006).

The group has also been successful in projecting issues and frames through mainstream media. A Google search for ACORN-related newspaper articles found 686 links for the period from November 12 through December 13, 2006. Articles ranged from reporting on ACORN's demands for rebuilding housing in New Orleans to coverage on a report on lending discrimination in California, the announcement of an ACORN-endorsed effort to introduce a state-based earned income tax credit in North Carolina, and a story about the possible move of the New Jersey Nets to Brooklyn following ACORN's support for the hotly debated Atlantic Yards development project. ACORN's work, even when it is soundly criticized, is nonetheless news.

However, neither the internally directed work of ACORN's publications and radio station nor the voluminous reporting on day-to-day work necessarily reshapes public debate. "What's worked in the realm of ideas," says Kest, "is to develop a replicable policy that pushes the idea and then to initiate campaigns that force the policy into the public eye. That's exactly what we've done with the Living Wage work" (2006).

The Living Wage Idea

The outcomes of the ACORN living wage campaigns have been little short of astounding. In 1994, a coalition of labor (led by AFSCME) and BUILD, an affiliate of the Alinsky-founded Industrial Areas Foundation, initiated a campaign in Baltimore to require city service contractors to pay a living wage. Using the Baltimore campaign as a model, ACORN successfully replicated living wage campaigns in St. Louis, Boston, Los Angeles, San Jose, Portland, Milwaukee, Detroit, Minneapolis, and Oakland—bringing the national total to 122 ordinances (Living Wage 2007). In addition, in 2005 ACORN organized coalitions in Ohio, Missouri, Arizona, and Colorado that included labor and other progressive groups in efforts to raise the state minimum wage through ballot initiatives in 2006. The initiatives passed handily in all four states.

Passing the initiatives, however, was only one part of the outcome. "We've managed to change the way people think and talk about work and wages," says Steve Kest (2006). Kest is not alone in thinking that minimum wage initiatives and living wage ordinances have transformed the public conversation about work. In a 2006 interview in the *New York Times Magazine*, former labor secretary Robert Reich points out that, "whatever the minimum wage's limitations may be as a policy issue, . . . it demarcates our concept of democracy with regard to work" (Gertner 2006). ACORN's living wage efforts were not immediately successful. Campaign efforts in the late 1990s in Denver and Houston, as well as the state of Missouri, all failed. "We got killed the first time around in Missouri, I think we got a little over 40 percent of the vote," remembers Kest, "but this time at the polls (2006), we got over 75 percent. That's a real change" (2006). To what does ACORN attribute its success? "There are a number of things," says communications director Kevin Whelan. "First, we had to build broad-based support. We knew we couldn't do this by ourselves. Second, attempts to pass living wage ordinances were springing up all over the country, so we had to figure out how to support those efforts even when we weren't directly involved. That's why we worked with the Labor Studies Department at Wayne State University to publish a 'Living Wage Resource Guide' and set up the Living Wage Resource Center. Third, we had to keep at it. We lost many of our initial campaigns. In Houston, for instance, we lost 4 to 1. We used the opportunity to learn what works, and to build our alliances so that the next time out we'd do better. Now we're winning, but it's after over ten years of effort" (2006).

Patience and persistence paid off. As David Neumark, Senior Fellow at the Public Policy Institute of California, observed, "How many other issues are there where progressives have been this successful? I can't think of one" (Gertner 2006, 40). The Living Wage Resource Center carries the full text of 140 living wage ordinances and lists twenty states, twenty-eight colleges and universities, and sixty-three cities or counties where there are ongoing campaigns. Says Steve Kest, "It is no accident that Nancy Pelosi has the minimum wage on the top of her agenda. We've changed the debate on the issue" (2006).

Campaign work is not the only way ACORN attempts to project and consolidate ideas. In 1999, ACORN formed the Organizer's Forum, an effort to enable organizers from a variety of sectors to "reflect, regroup, and then move forward as practitioners in their common work." The forum's board of directors includes organizers from three major organizing networks and union representatives from both sides of the recent split between AFL-CIO unions and the breakaway Change to Win unions. Programmatically, the forum sponsors international dialogues with labor and community organizers doing innovative work. These dialogues take up to twenty U.S.-based organizers abroad for an exchange of ideas and have included discussions with Landless Rural Workers in Brazil (Movimento dos Trabalhadores Rurais Sem Terra), the Congress of South African Trade Unions (COSATU), Dalit Solidarity Peoples in India, and feminist organizers from the Foundation for the Support of Women's Work (FSWW) in Turkey. Program coordinator Barbara Bowen says, "On the one hand, it's been a challenge to really understand the culture and conditions that these groups are working in. On another level entirely, the dialogues have developed a real sense of solidarity and shared mission among the participants. And that's one of the things we're trying to build" (2006).

In addition to the international dialogues, the Organizer's Forum has also sponsored biannual seminars on a variety of issues to advance the work of organizing, including Challenges to Immigrant Organizing, Technology and Organizing, New Constituency-Based Tactics, and Bringing Framing to Organizing. Presenters in these seminars have included community and constituency organizers Marcella Diaz, an organizer with New Mexico's Somos Un Pueblo Unido; Dan Sellers, director of the Ruckus Society; Jennifer Krill with the Rainforest Action Network (RAN); ACORN's own Steve Kest and former Illinois head organizer Madeline Talbott; labor leaders Stephen Lerner and Eliseo Medina (SEIU), and Charles Lester (AFL-CIO). In addition to practitioners, policy advocates and public intellectuals have also made presentations, including Rockridge Institute pundit George Lakoff; pollster Celinda Lake; Donald Green, author of *Get Out the Vote! How to Increase Voter Turnout*; Clarissa Martinez of the National Council of La Raza; Pomona College professor Heather Williams; and scholar-activist Peter Dreier.

Reflecting on her recent return from an Organizer's Forum dialogue in Turkey, Netsy Firestein, Executive Director of the Labor Project for Working Families, says, "I was really struck by the commonalities in issues we're faced with—in both unions and community settings. I think the real value of the dialogue is that it forced me to step outside of my immediate work—it gave me some perspective" (2006). Jeff Fox, former president of the New Democratic Party of British Columbia and Director of Organizing with the B.C. Government and Service Employees' Union, remembers his first experience with the Organizer's Forum. "When I went to the new technology forum in Minneapolis, at first I felt like a fish out of water. I hadn't had much experience dealing with faith-based organizations and the technology stuff was pretty much a mystery to me. But after a day, once I understood what the technology could actually do, I was immediately able to make contributions about the potential strategic uses of the technology in labor organizing. It was both challenging and stimulating" (2006). "The Organizer's Forum," says Rathke, "has given us the opportunity to rip the covers off and really talk about our work. People have been wildly frank. It gives us the opportunity to build trust *before* we discuss possibilities for working together in the future" (2006). Bowen adds, "In initiating the forum, we're taking some responsibility for stewardship. There are very few opportunities for people who are steeped in this work to actually learn from the successes and failures of other organizers. The Forum creates a space where constituency-based organizers can grapple with questions about our work, drawing on experiences outside of our immediate networks" (2006).

In summary, the principal way that ACORN has shaped public discourse is through its issue and campaign work. However, the organization has also developed mechanisms for systematic reflection and refining ideas through *Social Policy* and exchanging ideas and building solidarity among disparate networks in the United States and abroad through the Organizer's Forum. While none of these approaches is perfect, they are self-conscious efforts to address the dearth of progressive ideas and the current collection of isolated issue silos that passes for a progressive landscape.

Outcomes

This chapter has explored two critical elements of movement building: how ACORN has used its size, scope, and national structure to pressure corporate and governmental targets, and its ability to build broad alliances, develop policy alternatives, and reframe public debate. In this section, given that the bottom-line question for organizers at the end of an organizing campaign is—*What did we actually get?*—I'll examine ACORN's major accomplishments.

"The change must move social policy *and* benefit your members," says Bertha Lewis. "That's where you really build power, and it's what attracted me to ACORN. We've been criticized for it—but that's what really makes us a potent force" (2006). ACORN's outcomes over the years have included school reform efforts that stopped school closings in Des Moines, won free transportation to schools in Little Rock, and established alternative schools in Brooklyn, Queens, St. Paul, Oakland, and Jersey City. The group's housing and community reinvestment efforts have led to agreements with banks in St. Louis, New York City, Washington, DC, and other cities, making more than a billion dollars available for loans in low-income neighborhoods. ACORN has lobbied successfully for the passage of a national homesteading bill and pressured the Department of Housing and Urban Development (HUD) to change policies and procedures to make it easier for low and moderate-income people to purchase HUD-owned properties. ACORN also pushed HUD to revamp homesteading programs that turn over vacant houses to low-income residents in Philadelphia, Detroit, Brooklyn, Bridgeport, Chicago, Phoenix, St. Louis, and Little Rock. The group's environmental justice work has forced companies to clean up, move, or cancel plans for toxic chemical plants, dumps, discharges, or waste incinerators in Memphis, Ft. Worth, Philadelphia, Des Moines, New Orleans, Dallas, Minneapolis, Jacksonville, St. Paul, Chicago, and St. Louis. It has also organized parents of lead poisoning victims to pressure local governments for improved screening and treatment in New York, Detroit, Chicago, and Washington, DC, and expanded childhood immunization in New Orleans.

Each of these accomplishments demonstrates the organization's ability to coordinate strategies, develop and actualize policy alternatives, replicate pressure tactics, and negotiate clear-cut victories. But, according to Heidi Swarts, ACORN's low-income membership "has fewer resources than church based organizations, used boisterous tactics that may have alienated officials, and was less successful than church-based groups in achieving policy outcome" (2002).

Swarts's observations are at least partially correct. ACORN's family-based membership base, built almost exclusively through field recruitment, does have fewer resources than organizations built through institutional church memberships. She is also correct in her observation that ACORN's tactics intimidate some public officials and corporate personnel. In fact, Sol Stern of the Manhattan Institute recounts just such an instance, where the mayor of Baltimore was confronted with a protest demonstration at a banker's dinner. Stern's story notes that the mayor "thought it was a pretty cruddy thing to do" but admits that ACORN still got $50,000 a year to provide housing counseling—"despite, or perhaps because of the intimidation" (2003).

Conservatives are not the only critics of ACORN's tactics. New York–based advocate Mark Winston Griffith writes, "It's hard to see their members as . . . more than animated props and set pieces in ACORN's elaborate political theater" (Griffith 2005). "Sure we use disruptive tactics," admits Steve Kest. "We have to use the power of our members to make our case. But it's not just a question of tactics, it's a question of results" (2006). And how are ACORN's results measured? A recent effort by independent consultant Lisa Ranghelli (2006) to measure the outcomes of ACORN's organizing examined the monetary value of ACORN's successful work between 1995 and 2005 in the following arenas:

- the passage of eleven living wage ordinances and minimum wage increases in Illinois, Massachusetts, Florida, New York, and the City of San Francisco;
- legislation limiting predatory lending in Massachusetts, New Mexico, California, New York, and New Jersey, and improvements in federal regulations;

- agreements negotiated with some of the nation's largest subprime lenders, including Household Finance, Wells Fargo Financial, and CitiFinancial, to change abusive practices and provide direct financial assistance to borrowers trapped in harmful loans;
- fee reductions on high-cost tax Refund Anticipation Loans sold by H&R Block, the biggest commercial tax preparation company in the country;
- helping 5,000 low-income households in 2004 claim the Earned Income Tax Credit (EITC) and receive free tax preparation. (Ranghelli 2006)

Ranghelli puts the total monetary value of ACORN victories for the last decade at "$15 billion, or an average of $1.5 billion per year since 1995" (2006) (Table 11.2).

These figures, combined with the steady expansion of ACORN's membership base through unionization and community-based campaigns, the successful passage of significant legislation, numerous local victories, transnational expansion efforts, and ongoing activities to build alliances and increase the analytical capacity of staff and members, suggest that as an organization ACORN has been successful in accruing power and benefits for its low-income base.

But is ACORN a successful movement builder? Interviews with ACORN staff and leaders indicate that many are not sure they wanted to build a movement. "Movement building has not always been our focus," says Kest. "What we've emphasized is developing an organization that enables movements to persevere, contest for power, and deliver results. There's a movement out there among immigrants. ACORN's role is to

Table 11.2. Monetary benefits of ACORN organizing, 1995–2005

Campaign	Monetary benefit
Living and minimum wage increases	$ 2,237,645,466
Predatory lending	$ 6,265,776,423
EITC and tax preparation	$ 8,036,546
Loan counseling and CRA	$ 6,099,012,514
Housing development	$ 33,559,000
Local infrastructure and public services	$ 350,254,300
Budget cutbacks averted/restored	$ 226,230,000
TOTAL	**$15,220,514,249**

help our immigrant leaders provide strategy, structure, and program to that movement so that we can help advance their agenda over the long haul" (2006; 2007). Lewis adds, "Most people concerned primarily with movement think of mobilizing—they don't think of building a permanent institution. In order to multiply your effect you need real organizations. Without institutions there are no protracted movements" (2006). ACORN communications director Kevin Whelan has a different view: "I would resist the notion that movement building and organization building are two different things. You can't have a movement without directly engaging the people most affected by racism and inequality and challenging them to take action. We do that on a daily basis. We also do a tremendous amount of coalition work and are part of coalitions to preserve affordable housing and pass inclusionary zoning laws in places like Los Angeles, Philadelphia, and Minneapolis. All of our living wage work is coalitional. I think the vast amount of what we do is movement building" (2006).

ACORN's Movement Building Contributions

Even though ACORN is involved in coalition work, its primary task is organizing low-income people—predominantly people of color—to act in their own interest. How does ACORN's work contribute to movement building despite internal protestations that the organization's primary task is building power for its members? Below is a list of eight ways.

(1) *Organizing poor people.* It may not sound like a big deal that ACORN still organizes poor people. But in a society where so-called progressives strategize about capturing the imagination of soccer moms and NASCAR dads, a commitment to organizing poor people and doing so directly gives the organization a legitimacy and authenticity that is not replicated in any other national organization. And what kind of movement would we have if poor people were left out?

(2) *A multiracial constituency.* Although the commitment to organize the poor and the interest in organizing a multiracial constituency were part of the original "southern strategy" mandate set out by the national Welfare Rights Organization before ACORN became an independent entity, it is admirable that the organization still adheres to the principle. This is not to suggest that the organization has no racial tensions. It does. The senior staff of ACORN is still predominantly white in a membership organization that is almost 90 percent people of color. However, whereas thirty years ago ACORN studiously avoided addressing issues of race and racial justice,

in the last ten years its work in school reform, predatory lending, housing, and environmental justice have all pointed to racial disparities and worked to address institutional racism. One of the criteria for movement building articulated by Taj James (and cited earlier in this article) is the ability to address racism. ACORN is by no means perfect in this arena, as current staff/board tensions mentioned earlier reflect, but it is one of the few national organizations that has actually launched campaigns with racially explicit demands.

(3) *Challenging the "beauty of localism."* ACORN has successfully consolidated local campaign efforts into national results. Not only was ACORN the first community organization to develop and refine a series of replicable organizing models to engage different populations of low-income people, the organization expanded the notion of how to build power by establishing federated branches in different states and has developed the infrastructure to support multistate and national campaign efforts. The group's ability to aggregate local living wage work into state legislation clearly flies in the face of my prediction twenty years ago that the amalgamated efforts of hundreds of small community groups would not necessarily result in large-scale structural change. As one of the group's conservative critics writes, "ACORN decided instead it would work city by city, starting in the most liberal places, to enact local wage legislation" (Malanga 2006). Another concurs, "Unlike the old New Left, ACORN is patient, willing to achieve its goals by a thousand modest increments" (Stern 2003). There is no doubt that ACORN's strategy to initiate progressive policy reform through local and state campaigns has been extremely successful.

(4) *Willingness to experiment with and build alternative institutions.* Berger and Cornell (2006) argue that a key component of movement building is "building coalitions, political infrastructure, and alternative institutions while simultaneously confronting the state, right-wing social movements, and other forms of institutional oppression." ACORN has rejected the traditional community organizing practice of building a wall between organizers and service providers—the classic "clients or constituents" debate Kest mentioned earlier. Instead, the organization has managed an uneasy balance between providing housing services while fighting redlining, on the one hand, and starting and managing schools while advocating for quality education, on the other. ACORN does not do these things equally well. It is, for instance, much better at fighting for social justice than modeling successful pedagogical approaches in education. However, because it is a federation, it has the ability to learn from its mistakes and to transfer cumulative lessons to membership and staff.

(5) *Consolidating ideas, strategies, and people.* ACORN's development of the Organizer's Forum is becoming a new arena for developing ideas, sharing strategies, and offering organizers opportunities for collective reflection. In

addition to the work of the forum, ACORN's outreach to nonorganizers—public intellectuals, policy analysts, and planners—demonstrates an understanding that moving a large scale agenda will take intellectual capital as well as a membership base.

(6) *Politics on top.* From its earliest days, ACORN has been willing to advance its interests in the electoral sphere. From candidate endorsement, to organizational expansion based on political opportunity, to issuing direct challenges to the Democratic Party, to large scale voter registration drives and development of the Working Families Party, ACORN has viewed the electoral arena as a key space in which to vie for power.

(7) *Internationalization of membership.* ACORN has not only begun organizing partnerships in neighboring countries (as have the IAF and Gamaliel Institute), it has also learned from the experiences of organizers in Canada, India, and Latin America and initiated transnational fights over environmental safety and immigrant rights. ACORN was not the first U.S.-based community organizing network to initiate projects abroad, but because it is one organization with many chapters, it is currently the only U.S.-based network with the ability to launch and coordinate multiple actions to affect targets in many localities globally.

(8) *Tough, hell-raising tactics.* In a society where more and more community organizations are emphasizing "relationship building" as the cornerstone for political discourse, ACORN is still ready to be rude—to demonstrate the power and importance of militant action. Conflict and an oppositional culture are always central to movement building.

Tell No Lies

So, ACORN is a sophisticated animal. It operates on many levels, is potent on a number of fronts, and has outlived many critics and an even larger number of friends. Even though ACORN's major stated task is not movement building, in order to achieve its goal of building power for low-income people, ACORN may have no alternative but to expand its movement building efforts. In the spirit of Amilcar Cabral's urging to "mask no difficulties, tell no lies and claim no easy victories," there are three areas related to movement building that I think the organization should consider.

First, ACORN's internal structure must catch up to its external ambition. Earlier in this chapter I pointed to the differences between ACORN's emphasis on external outcomes or product versus the importance that younger activists place on the relationship between product and process. As ACORN's current internal disarray illustrates, we ignore or deemphasize internal organizational processes at our own peril. In a way, the attacks on ACORN's voter registration efforts before the 2008 election actually gave the organization a reprieve from internal strife. The external threat served to unify staff, board members, and allies. However, when the dust cleared, the internal tensions, caused in large part by a lack of organizational transparency, remained. ACORN cannot use its own political experience and clout to contribute to a broader movement until it develops an infrastructure that clarifies and rationalizes its many organizational components and builds additional developmental infrastructure to increase the skills and talents of grassroots leaders and newly recruited staff.

Second, ACORN should consider developing and activating a more thoughtful approach to less powerful potential allies. Over the years ACORN has had varied ongoing relationships with local groups. It has tended to work well with more powerful allies (for example, unions), mobilize the resources of liberal groups (for example, the Democracy Alliance), and neutralize, absorb, or ignore less powerful allies. Mostly this approach has worked. However, for some groups—legitimate indigenous community-based organizations—this approach has often caused unnecessary and long-lasting enmity. It is an old axiom in community organizing that you make alliances to "borrow power, never to lend it." But ACORN is in a different place than it was thirty-eight years ago. It has grown up. As Lewis points out, ACORN is an institution. As an institution, its organizational leadership role must expand beyond the important task of developing the unheard voices of its primary constituency. It must also figure out how to work productively with smaller, less powerful groups, allowing them to maintain their own identities and to contribute to even more successful outcomes.

Finally, ACORN should consider initiating a process to redefine and rearticulate its politics. Over twenty-five years ago, ACORN developed the People's Platform as a tool to consolidate new affiliates with the collective political experience of the group's existing membership. By articulating the aspirations of the membership, the platform presented an alternative set of social priorities and arrangements. Although ACORN's recent efforts to promote ideas have been important byproducts of its Katrina and living-wage work, both are single-issue efforts. To move large-scale policy reforms on multiple issues, ACORN may need to envision a new People's Platform. Such an endeavor could engage current members and potential allies in a process that could articulate political principles and the policies and programs to realize them. It could also expand the scope of the organization's work into broader social issues. At a minimum, an endeavor to redefine and rearticulate ACORN's politics could help update the organization's implicit vision and, in the process, make it explicit. At best, ACORN could help catalyze a vision critical to movement building.

ACORN has been active on issues of economic inequality, the bailout, and the foreclosure crisis. However, although the organization has taken progressive positions, it has been significantly less articulate on immigration policy, the Iraq and Afghanistan wars, and a host of post-9/11 threats to civil liberties that affect the organization's constituency. To survive and thrive in these turbulent times, ACORN will have to shake itself up, move out of its comfort zone, and demonstrate its commitment to values and principles that are bigger than the bread and butter issues for which it is known. It is that element—the stepping outside of our experiences—that forces people and organizations to really grow and makes others take notice. And who knows? It might just galvanize a movement.

REFERENCES

ABC News/Washington Post Poll. 2006. Available at *www.pollingreport.com/prioriti.htm*. December 7–11.

ACORN. 2005. *Annual Report*. Available at *www.acorn.org*.

"ACORN Fights Sherwin-Williams on International Fronts." 2006. Press release. November 22. Available at *www.commondreams.org/news2006/1122-03.htm*.

"The Acorn Indictments." 2006. *Wall Street Journal*. November 3. Available at *www.opinionjournal.com/editorial/feature.html?id=110009189*.

Berger, D., and A. Cornell. 2006. "Ten Questions for Movement Building." Available at *mrzine.monthlyreview.org/bc240706.html*.

Bhargava, D., and J. Hardisty. 2005. "Wrong about the Right." *Nation*. November 7. Available at *www.publiceye.org/hardisty/wrong_about_right.html*.

Bowen, B. 2006. Personal communication. October.

Building Movement Project. 2006. Website. Available at *www.buildingmovement.org*.

Cheun, L. 2006. Personal communication. November.

Delgado, G. 1986. *Organizing the Movement: The Roots and Growth of ACORN*. Philadelphia: Temple University Press.

Dixon, B. 2005. "It's Time to Build a Mass Movement." *Black Commentator* 144 (June 30). Available at *www.blackcommentator.com/144/144_cover_movement.html*.

Firestein, N. 2006. Personal communication. December.

Fox, J. 2006. Personal communication. December.

Gertner, J. 2006. "What Is a Living Wage?" *New York Times Magazine*. January 15.

Griffith, M. W. 2005. "Calling the Question of ACORN." December 30. Available at *www.dmiblog.net/archives/2005/12/calling_the_question_of_acorn.html*.

Hardisty, J. 1999. *Mobilizing Resentment: Conservative Resurgence from the John Birch Society to the Promise Keepers*. Boston: Beacon Press.

Hurd, M. 2006. Personal communication. December.

James, T. 2005. "So You Wanna Build a Movement." Available at *www.movementstrategy.org/pdfs/BuildAMovement.pdf*.

Kest, S. 2006. Personal communication. November.

———. 2007. Personal communication. December.

Lewis, B. 2006. Personal communication. November.

Living Wage Resource Center. "The Living Wage Movement: Building Power in Our Workplaces and Neighborhoods." Available at *www.livingwagecampaign.org/index.php?id=2071*.

Malanga, S. 2006. "Acorn Squash." *Wall Street Journal*. August 26.

National Gay and Lesbian Task Force (NGLTF). 2005. Press Release. August 5. Available at *www.commondreams.org/news2005/0805–11.htm*.

Peace Development Fund. 1999. The Listening Project. *www.peacefund.org/resources/rclisdes.htm*.

Ranghelli, L. 2006. *The Monetary Impact of ACORN Campaigns: A Ten Year Retrospective, 1995–2004*. November. Available at *www.afj.org/for-nonprofits-foundations/reco/resources/ranghelli.html*.

Rathke, W. 2006. Personal communication. December.

Stern, S. 2003. "ACORN's Nutty Regime for Cities." *Manhattan Institute's City Journal*. Spring 2003. Available at *www.city-journal.org/html/13_2_acorns_nutty_regime.html*.

Swarts, H. 2002. "What Makes Community Organizing Succeed? Comparing Church- and Neighborhood-Based Organizations." *Research Highlights from the Nonprofit Sector Research Fund*. January/February. Available at *www.nonprofitresearch.org/usr_doc/Community_Organizing_Snapshots.pdf*.

Tilly, C. 1997. "Social Movements as Political Struggle." July. A working paper and draft article for the *Encyclopedia of American Social Movements*. Available at *www.ciaonet.org/wps/tic03*.

Vega-Marquis, L. 2003. "Movement Building." Available at *www.caseygrants.org/documents/fromourpresident/resources_from_our_president_april_2003.asp*.

Whelan, K. 2006. Personal communication. December.

Working Families Party. 2004. "Annual Report, 2004." Available at *www.workingfamiliesparty.org/2004Annual.pdf*.

12

Changing Direction
ACORN and the Future
of Community Organizing

Robert Fisher

This book reveals four critical trends in the theory and practice of contemporary community organizing. First, there is the turn to culture and away from political economy as a major focus of organizing. Second, in terms of strategic and tactical emphasis, there is the turn to community building and away from a more oppositional form of community organizing. Third, in terms of scale, there is the turn to a sole emphasis on the local community and away from building power in but also beyond individual communities. Fourth, in terms of movement orientation, there is the turn to community organizing as a form of social change distinct from social movement building. I offer these as dualisms in tension with each other, although obviously their relationship is more complex. They are often a matter of emphasis in organizations that do both. They are presented here as dualisms partly because many in the field treat them as such. ACORN's model of organizing offers a stark contrast, going against the grain of the dominant trends.

Of course, there are many other trends that could be examined and issues that could be raised, as is evident from the multiple topics discussed in this book. For example, as Dreier, building on the work of Theda Skocpol, underscores in Chapter 1, there is a dominant trend toward advocacy on the national and state levels and away from membership-based organizations, and there is the historic trend for community efforts to withdraw from working with labor unions and political parties. ACORN bucks these trends. Rathke in Chapter 2 emphasizes its membership base. Dreier (Chapter 1), Luce (Chapter 6), and Green and Michelson (Chapter 10), respectively, emphasize its ongoing engagement with union organizing as well as electoral politics. ACORN's model is not completely unique in that it overlaps with comparable efforts such as the Industrial Areas Foundation (IAF) and People Improving Organizing through Communities (PICO). Viewing the four trends together as parts of an integrated model, we see that ACORN's practice is different even from these other large networks, usually diverging on more than two of the four trends. And it is usually completely different, offering a counter model on all four trends, when compared to social capital or assets-building approaches, which have proliferated in the past ten to fifteen years.

The Turn to Culture

The turn to culture can be seen in the shift from old social movement to new social movement forms of organizing, where "postmaterialist" values and cultural identity replace material objectives and class identity. The turn can be seen in discourse and efforts around identity politics where cultural identity—such as race, gender, or sexual orientation—trumps class as the primary lens for social change initiatives. It can be seen in arguments about the decline of social capital in the United States, which emphasize individualist culture and consumerist values as the cause for the demise of community connection. It can be seen in a literature of social change which documents contemporary preoccupation with social issues rather than ones of class. It can be seen in the rapid growth of faith-based, congregation-oriented models of community organizing, such as that of IAF and PICO, which tend to offer a "value driven" model of organizing as distinct from ACORN's "secular model" (Hart 2001; Swarts 2008). For example, Stephen Hart, studying the role of culture in grassroots organizing efforts such as the Milwaukee Innercity Congregations Allied for Hope (MICAH), affiliated with the Gamaliel Foundation, discovered that "congregation-based community organizing is a movement that attends seriously to the cultural dimension of politics. In it people wrestle with their basic values and religious traditions, relating them to practical activism addressing concrete local issues. . . . [and thereby illustrating] ways of constructing a culturally robust politics focused on . . . the pursuit of economic equality and democracy" (Hart 2001, 27, 22). Cynthia Gibson (2006, 9) suggests that a "citizen-centered approach" differs from traditional forms of organizing in its "focus primarily on culture change, rather than short-term outcomes, issues, or victories." Harry Boyte, who has been studying and writing about community initiatives for decades, agrees, expressing concern regarding "the silence among organizers about the deeper cultural implications" (1981, 2005, 2007). Gibson, Boyte, and other progressives argue for exposing the dominant culture—with its emphasis on privatization, hyperindividualism, and consumerism—as the critical source of contemporary problems, and contrasting it with the values of community organizing, democratic participation, and collective engagement. The New Right also emphasizes culture and related social issues such as affirmative action, abortion, and gay rights to mobilize working-class white voters in a "culture war," while deemphasizing political-economic policies, such as reducing taxes on the wealthy, that are not as successful in mobilizing the same constituents.

ACORN has not jumped on the cultural bandwagon. For ACORN, culture is not of primary import. Primary is political economy, the interconnection of economic and political power and policy. ACORN's campaigns are almost always focused on issues of political economy, whether living wages, predatory lending, refund anticipation loans, get-out-the-vote campaigns, or school privatization. Reflecting this emphasis, the authors and chapters in this volume focus almost exclusively on issues of political economy. Of course, movement cultures and political economy go hand-in-hand. The Populist movement of the late nineteenth century blended an alternative culture and a model of an alternative political-economic system into a powerful challenge to the emerging urban-industrial capitalist order. In the 1960s an alternative culture played a critical role in the movements of the day, just as it did in the later women's and gay rights movements.

ACORN's organizational culture, probably best viewed as a "counter-culture," plays a critical role in attracting staff and members, connecting them, and generally sustaining the organization. Certainly, the role of culture in ACORN is a subject that needs greater attention. Nevertheless, ACORN keeps its eyes on issues of economic injustice because that is where members and potential constituents have the greatest need and vulnerability. Cultural and social issues seem a distraction at the least, a divisive element at the worst. ACORN's singular focus on political economy directly exposes the class inequities that symbolize the time and targets the economic elites who increasingly dominate the globe. Swarts (2008, xvi) argues that ACORN deemphasizes cultural work because of the homogeneity of its members, mostly low income and predominantly black and Hispanic, whereas congregation-based community organizing (CBCO) emphasizes cultural issues in order to "unify its cross-class, multi-racial membership." Of course, as Delgado argues in Chapter 11, ACORN could benefit from a more integrated approach that fuses both cultural and class issues. Hart (2001) argues that the leading congregation-based community organizations do an excellent job of integrating the two, that is, using a rich discourse and cultural themes to maintain and strengthen a focus on political-economic issues. On the other hand, this volume also illustrates that ACORN's "eye on the prize" of class-based issues of economic injustice would benefit community efforts, such as those emphasizing social connection or identity politics, which often skirt issues of class.

The Turn to Community Building

The second shift has been to a process-oriented form of community building and away from a more politicized and oppositional form of community organizing. Jack Rothman (1968) referred to these two types of community-based work as "locality/community development" and "social action." The first is process oriented, seeking to build consensus in the community, and interested in working with all community members. The latter is process oriented as well, but it is usually more task centered, sees itself in conflict with the causes of community problems, and targets these sources as enemies whether they are within or outside of the community. While community building approaches have a long and substantial history (Fabricant and Fisher 2002), the contemporary turn to community building is linked to the recent ascendancy of theories of social capital. Discussed by DeFilippis, Fisher, and Shragge in Chapter 5, these theories posit that the central problems communities face are ones of social connection and cohesion. According to this approach, the primary emphasis should be on developing and deepening democratic processes across the community (Warren 2001; Saegert, Thompson, and Warren 2001). Organizing becomes primarily about building connection, trust, and relationships with others in order to advance shared goals. The current interest in community building and relationships is as true for the IAF, the heirs of Saul Alinsky's conflict organizing model, as it is for community building groups just getting started.

Often the community building strategy is exactly what a community needs. The positive effects of such efforts on community and individual well-being are well documented (Fabricant and Fisher 2002; Minkler 1997; De Souza Briggs, Mueller, and Sullivan 1997; Saegert, Thompson, and Warren 2001). Simon and Gold propose in Chapter 3, for example, that congregation-based efforts more interested in community building have more success than groups such as ACORN in developing leaders and building relationships in public schools, two critical elements in school-based community efforts. Gibson proposes elsewhere that it's a more democratic and more long-term approach than "mobilizing models of organizing," which are said to act with "little or no input from communities" and view "residents as foot soldiers in carrying out actions for pre-determined agendas" (2006, 13).

ACORN is typically seen in such analyses as the biggest (and probably "baddest") example of the "old-fashioned," conflict-style mobilizing model. Old-fashioned because it is similar, as Dreier and others emphasize in this volume, to a union model of organizing, with its emphasis on dues-paying members and materialist objectives. Old-fashioned in terms of the old social movement versus new social movements divide, with the former's emphasis on issues of political economy, labor organizing, and class. ACORN is fundamentally about confrontational/conflict-oriented community organizing. ACORN would probably protest the pigeonholing. Clearly, as John Atlas demonstrates in Chapter 7 on the issue of affordable housing, ACORN does more than protest. It delivers services, negotiates with power brokers, and even forms partnerships with economic elites. There are many ways to engage members and for people to participate in an issue or struggle. Some may participate in deliberations at public school meetings. For others, it's turning out to protest at an H&R Block office or against the New York City Board of Education. Significantly for groups such as ACORN, community building is part of the internal process of organizing, something essential to building a local base of members. ACORN would object to being labeled as exclusively using a "mobilizing" rather than "organizing" model. They do both. But organizing is always seen as a means to build power, and community is seen as a vehicle, not an end in and of itself.

The community organizing approach of ACORN and other social action networks such as IAF, PICO, Gamaliel, and Direct Action Research and Training (DART) is grounded in a conflict rather than a consensus model. By conflict model I do not mean conflict as simply political theater, that is, protests designed primarily to attract attention in order to build the movement, galvanize participants, and appeal for allies (Piven 2006). Conflict approaches in community organizing, like Rothman's (1968) "social action" model, Fisher's (1994) "political activist" model, or Smock's (2004) "power-based" and "transformative" models, emphasize that the organization and its members stand in opposition to the system and to the causes of economic injustice. This theme, that ACORN is a social action-type organization rooted in conflict strategies and tactics, runs throughout this book. ACORN and direct action are synonymous. Nevertheless, while almost every chapter emphasizes that ACORN is an oppositional organization, they also emphasize that ACORN is a large, complex organization with a diverse and sophisticated strategic and tactical repertoire that ranges from conflict to negotiation, community building, service delivery, advocacy, ownership, and governance.

Romanticizing the Local

While the history of community organizing has always been characterized by a parochial focus on the community, that has probably never been more true than in our current era. As discussed by DeFilippis, Fisher, and Shragge in Chapter 5, much community theory and practice has turned inward to emphasize self-help perspectives, that is, strategies and tactics that focus on communities as the site, cause, and solution to local problems. This concept is essential to highly popular models of community practice such as asset building, capacity building, or consensus organizing (Kretzman and McKnight 1993; Eichler 2007). The fundamental idea is that the resources for building community organizations and for addressing community problems rest within the community. The solution rests with building broad partnerships with others in the community. It assumes, of course, that others in the community have the same interest, and it assumes that those with capital remain in the community. At their core, these approaches promote a strong belief in the assets and power of local communities and organizations. This focus on the community and the distrust of larger structural or spatial forms has deep roots in the history of community organizing (Fisher 1994).

On the other hand, there is an equally long tradition in the history of community organizing which emphasizes that the causes of significant problems do not originate in the community and cannot be solved solely at the community level. People can organize at the community level, but it takes scales of power beyond local limits to bring about significant change. This is one of the reasons for the formation of IAF's statewide and regional networks, PICO's national network, and ACORN's national organization and national strategy as well as its nascent international efforts. Working with others at the community level has innumerable collective and personal benefits (Breines 1989; Davis 1991; Polletta 2002). It gives people experience with public life and democratic process. It engages them in issues that matter to them. It's the essence of community organizing. But it does not have the power to pass Community Reinvestment Act legislation in DC, win living wage initiatives across the nation or force a multinational corporation to negotiate. In contemporary organizing, scale, scope, and size matter. Economic globalization demands it. Capital concentrates into larger and larger corporate entities in order to wield more power. So must the opposition.

ACORN knows the importance of size and scope. Almost from its start, ACORN has measured success in terms of expanding size and scope, be it in annual growth in locals, cities with local chapters, members, or funding. The bigger-is-better model includes ACORN-run radio stations, housing development, union locals, public schools, tax preparation services, and so on. A bigger-is-better model means seeing community as both a site for civic engagement and as a base for mass organizing. It means not only building a national organizational structure but also not constraining community work to narrowly defined, delimited practice. It means expanding community organizing to include continuous work with electoral politics, unions, and labor, work avoided still by most other community efforts. Unlike IAF and PICO, ACORN isn't a network of community groups. It is a powerful national organization.

National community organizations not only wield more power, especially if they are grounded in a local-based membership, but they have the ability to experiment and fail. That's one of the keys to ACORN's success—being able to experiment, fail, wield enough organizational power to revise strategies and tactics, and succeed. For example, initial living wage campaigns in Houston and Missouri met with disaster (Swarts 2008). Bigger-is-better means as well that, as Luce (Chapter 6) and Squires and Chadwick (Chapter 4) put it, ACORN can form coalitions and even support the efforts of other organizations on causes such as living wage initiatives without as much fear of losing turf. In a world in which most community efforts focus solely on their own communities and are therefore fragmented and detached from each other, ACORN and other groups, such as PICO and the IAF, which function at spatial and structural levels beyond the local, are significant exceptions. At the moment there aren't any other membership-based, locally grounded, national organizations like ACORN. Its model of integrating local chapters with a national organization that can mobilize locals into on-the-ground national and even global campaigns is unique. Regarding this third trend, the counter model ACORN offers is clear: community efforts must expand beyond their local limits and struggle for power on broader scales. In terms of better integrating both parts of the trend, ACORN could do a better job—especially where locals are small and poorly resourced—at building community and connection, integrating locals and members in national decisions, and sustaining staff who seek to focus more on community building and member participation.

Disconnecting Community Organizing from Social Movements

A fourth trend of much community organizing is the distancing of community organizations from social movements and the activists involved with them. Community organizing is different from social movement. Community organizers address multiple issues, build a local base, encourage deliberative decision making, develop leaders, invest resources in the community, emphasize commitment to internal process, and view organization building as critical to building power. Discipline and accountability are central to organization building. Social movements, on the other hand, have a short lifespan, tend to be episodic, charismatic, and ideological, and are tied to the salience of a single cause. They are less interested in building leadership, a long-term base, or a powerful grassroots organization. Because community organizing efforts are grounded in a power-oriented base and organization, they tend to see social movements as fleeting, ephemeral, with a lot of "shouting," as Rathke puts it Chapter 2. Social movement seems to most community organizes as a head without a body, as a less effective means of social change because it lacks a dependable base. Swarts emphasizes that organizers and participants in congregation-based models of community organizing, including the IAF, are taught right away "who they are *not*: neither movements with activists or paternalistic agencies with clients" (2008, 51). The hostility of the IAF to movements and activists dates back to its founder, Saul Alinsky, who in the 1930s and 1940s distanced himself from Old Left movements and in the 1960s distanced his work even more so from New Left efforts (Alinsky 1971). More recently, this antagonism derives in large part from IAF's desire to appeal to a broader base, including middle-class moderates. But the phenomenon is certainly not limited to the IAF. It is engrained in the cold war culture of so-called "non-ideological" community organizing to be wary of "activists" with "agendas" from social movements (Gecan 2002).

This trend and the antagonism, however, are shortsighted. Many of the chapters here emphasize the important connection between community organizing and social movements. Fisher, Brooks, and Russell

(Chapter 9) speak to the movement qualities of ACORN's H&R Block campaign. Delgado (Chapter 11) calls for ACORN to engage in more intentional efforts at social movement building. ACORN, like other community organizing efforts, guards its own turf carefully, being wary of the "organizing," "base," and "community" that current social movements profess as part of their work. Most of the ACORN leadership, however, sees their organization as linked to social movements, at least through its past as a product of the civil rights and welfare rights movements of the 1960s. ACORN is also linked with social movements through most of its staff, who are shaped, directly or indirectly, by movement experience or analysis. It is hard to imagine ACORN continuing to expand and survive without these movement roots. The organization's culture understands that social movements have always been central to the growth and development of community efforts. The civil rights movement brought Alinsky's model and community work back to life in the 1960s, just as the movement stimulated the founding of the National Welfare Rights Organization and then ACORN. There has always been a dialectical interaction between mass social movements and local community groups, each affecting the other. Social movements have always been critical to any large-scale, fundamental change in the United States, and in most movements the participation of local organizations plays a central role. Regarding the fourth trend, at its best ACORN acts more like a hybrid between a community organizing effort and a social movement organization.

Of course, the tensions inherent in these four trends challenge ACORN as well. Critics think ACORN does a poor job of community building. They think it "mobilizes" instead of "organizes" and therefore does not sink deep roots in many communities where it has local chapters. They point out its high staff turnover as undermining the continuity essential to community building. Critics argue furthermore that ACORN is largely a staff-led, rather than member-based, organization, and point to its recent disclosure of financial improprieties nine years after they occurred as a classic example. They recognize ACORN's strength and success, but argue that it lies not in ACORN's membership but in the skills and savvy of its staff. Others more to the Left propose that ACORN is too willing to take on any and all opportunities, that it is fueled by an unbridled pragmatism focused on growth, which fragments the organization and dilutes its politics. Some think its politics should be more radical, offering a radical critique to accompany its often radical tactics. If ACORN were more sincere about movement building, it should have aggressively opposed the Iraq war and lent more support to the mobilization around immigrant rights. Still others argue that in places where it has large organizations and a deep history, such as New York City, ACORN has been incorporated into the local power structure. And these criticisms do not even include those from the Right, which, as was evident in the recent presidential election, see ACORN as an evil left-wing organization that threatens the very fabric of our nation. (See, for example, Employment Policies Institute 2008.)

The People Shall Rule demonstrates that in terms of the varied approaches and potential effect of community organizing, ACORN advances an alternative model. Using ACORN's recent growth as well as its impact on critical issues such as living wage, predatory lending, and voter registration as indicators, this model is playing an increasingly significant role in the field of community organizing and the broader struggle for economic justice. In terms of the four trends, it offers a counter trend more focused on political economy, oppositional organizing, building national and even international structures and power, and creating synergy by connecting with social movement opportunities. Those are some of its major strengths. The four elements of the counter trend should be considered by all those interested in social change, especially those organizations and activists that now exclude them. But there should also be "methodological integration," which proposes that the most effective organizing occurs when both aspects of the dualisms are incorporated into the organizing model. Accordingly, ACORN's power and potential may be lessened if it is not willing to address both sides of the dualisms inherent in the four trends, particularly if it continues to deemphasize the value of culture in organizing, the role of community building, and more social movement building. We hope that the lessons learned in this book and those emphasized in this concluding chapter will offer direction to current and future community organizations, organizers, and members, as well as to those who study their efforts.

REFERENCES

Alinsky, S. 1971. *Rules for Radicals*. New York: Random House.
Boyte, H. 1981. *Backyard Revolution*. Philadelphia: Temple University Press.
———. 2005. *Everyday Politics: Reconnecting Citizens and Public Life*.
    Philadelphia: University of Pennsylvania.
———. 2007. Introduction to *We Make Change: Community Organizers Talk about What They Do—and Why*, ed. by K. L. Szakos and J. Szakos. Nashville: Vanderbilt University Press, xvii–xxi.

Breines, W. 1989. *Community and Organization in the New Left, 1962–1968.* New Brunswick: Rutgers University Press.

Davis, J. E. 1991. *Contested Ground.* Ithaca: Cornell University Press.

De Souza Briggs, X., E. Mueller, and M. Sullivan. 1997. *From Neighborhood to Community: Evidence on the Social Effects of Community Development.* New York: New School for Social Research.

Eichler, M. 2007. *Consensus Organizing: Building Communities of Mutual Self Interest.* Newbury, CA: Sage.

Employment Policies Institute. 2008. *Rotten ACORN: America's Bad Seed.* Available at *www.EPIonline.org.*

Fabricant, M., and R. Fisher. 2002. *Settlement Houses under Siege: The Struggle to Sustain Community Organizations in New York City.* New York: Columbia University Press.

Field. J. 2003. *Social Capital.* London: Routledge.

Fisher, R. 1994. *Let the People Decide: Neighborhood Organizing in America.* Updated ed. New York: Twayne.

Gecan, M. 2002. *Going Public.* Boston: Beacon Press.

Gibson, C. 2006. *Citizens at the Center: A New Approach to Civic Engagement.* Washington, DC: Case Foundation Report.

Hart, S. 2001. *Cultural Dilemmas of Progressive Politics: Styles of Engagement among Grassroots Activists.* Chicago: University of Chicago Press.

Kretzmann, J., and J. McKnight. 1993. *Building Communities from the Inside Out: A Path toward Finding and Mobilizing a Community's Assets.* Chicago: Acta.

Minkler, M., ed. 2004. *Community Organizing and Community Building for Health.* New Brunswick, NJ: Rutgers University Press.

Piven, F. F. 2006. *Challenging Authority: How Ordinary People Change America.* Lanham, MD: Rowman and Littlefield.

Polletta, F. 2002. *Freedom in an Endless Meeting: Democracy in American Social Movements.* Chicago: University of Chicago Press.

Rothman, J. 1968. "Three Models of Community Organization and Macro Practice Perspectives: Their Mixing and Phasing." In *Strategies on Community Organization*, ed. by F. Cox, J. L. Erlich, J. Rothman, and J. E. Tropman, 3–26. 4th ed. Itasca, IL: Peacock.

Saegert, S., J. Thompson, and M. Warren, eds. 2001. *Social Capital and Poor Communities.* New York: Russell Sage.

Smock, K. 2004. *Democracy in Action: Community Organization and Urban Change.* New York: Columbia University Press.

Swarts, H. 2008. *Organizing Urban America: Secular and Faith-based Progressive Movements.* Minneapolis: University of Minnesota Press.

Warren, M. 2001. *Dry Bones Rattling.* Princeton: Princeton University Press.

Contributors

John Atlas is President and Founder of the National Housing Institute, which publishes *Shelterforce*. He has been the executive director of the award-winning Passaic County Legal Aid Society, a radio talk-show host, and an organizer. His work has appeared in numerous publications, and he is the co-author of *Saving Affordable Housing* (published by NHI and the Ford Foundation). He is writing a book about politics and poverty seen through the work of ACORN.

Fred Brooks is an Associate Professor in the School of Social Work at Georgia State University in Atlanta. His research focuses on community and labor organizing and affordable housing. His recent scholarly publications include articles on union organizing of child-care teachers, racial diversity in community organizations, and the living wage movement.

Jan Chadwick is a doctoral candidate in public policy at George Washington University. She has taught public policy as an associate faculty member at Eastern University and served for twelve years as the assistant director of the Fair Housing Council of Suburban Philadelphia.

James DeFilippis is an Associate Professor in the Edward J. Bloustein School of Planning and Public Policy, Rutgers, the State University of New Jersey. He is the author of *Unmaking Goliath: Community Control in the Face of Global Capital* (Routledge, 2004), which was named the best book on urban politics in 2004 by the American Political Science Association.

Gary Delgado is a Senior Research Fellow at the Applied Research Center. His analytical work includes over forty articles and studies on social change practice. His background includes stints as one of ACORN's initial organizers, lead organizer with the National Welfare Rights Organization, and cofounder of the Center for Third World Organizing. He has been recognized as a Hellraiser by *Mother Jones* magazine and profiled as one of sixty-one visionaries by *Utne Reader*.

Peter Dreier is the Dr. E. P. Clapp Distinguished Professor of Politics, and Director of the Urban and Environmental Policy Program at Occidental College in Los Angeles. He served for nine years as senior policy advisor to Boston mayor Ray Flynn. He is coauthor of *The Next Los Angeles: The Struggle for a Livable City* (University of California Press, 2005); *Place Matters: Metropolitics for the 21st Century* (University Press of Kansas, 2001); and *Regions That Work: How Cities and Suburbs Can Grow Together* (University of Minnesota Press, 2000), and writes frequently for the *Los Angeles Times, American Prospect*, and the *Nation*.

Robert Fisher is Professor of Community Organizing at the University of Connecticut School of Social Work. He has published five books, including *Let the People Decide* (Twayne, 1994) and more recently the coauthored *Settlement Houses Under Siege: The Struggle to Sustain Community Organizations in New York City* (Columbia University Press, 2002). He has received two Fulbright faculty fellowships and the Moses Distinguished Professorship at Hunter College.

Norm Fruchter has recently retired as the Director of the Community Involvement Program of the Annenberg Institute for School Reform at Brown University. Fruchter previously directed the Institute for Education and Social Policy at New York University. His latest book is *Urban Schools, Public Will* (Teachers College Press, 2007).

Eva Gold is a founder of and Principal at Research for Action. She has served as primary investigator for numerous local and national studies concerning the relationships among parents, communities, and schools. Gold and Elaine Simon have published widely on youth and community organizing for school reform. Gold also teaches in the Urban Studies Program and the Graduate School of Education at the University of Pennsylvania.

Donald Green is the A. Whitney Griswold Professor of Political Science at Yale University, where he has taught since 1989. He has written extensively on the topic of voter mobilization. He is the author of *Get Out the Vote: How to Increase Voter Turnout* (Brookings Institution Press, 2008), coauthored with Alan Gerber.

Stephanie Luce is an Associate Professor and Research Director at the Labor Center, University of Massachusetts–Amherst. Before earning her PhD in sociology, she worked as an economist with the U.S. Department of Labor. She is the author of *Fighting for a Living Wage* (Cornell University Press, 2004).

Melissa R. Michelson is Associate Professor of Political Science at California State University, East Bay. She is principal investigator for the evaluation of the James Irvine Foundation's California Votes Initiative. Her research includes work on immigrant political incorporation and voter mobilization of youth and ethnic/racial minorities.

Wade Rathke is the founder of ACORN and served as its chief organizer for thirty-eight years. Currently, he is chief organizer of ACORN International, working in Canada, Peru, Mexico, Dominican Republic, Argentina, India, and other countries, as well as directing Local 100, Service Employees International Union, the Organizers' Forum, and many other projects in community and labor organizing. He is author of two books, *Citizen Wealth: The Campaign to Save Working Families* (Berrett-Koehler, 2009) and *The Battle for the Lower Ninth: ACORN and the Rebuilding of New Orleans* (Verso, 2009).

Daniel Russell, Professor of Social Science at Springfield College, Massachusetts, analyzed ACORN's organizing strategies in *Political Organizing in Grassroots Politics* (University Press of America, 1990). He also coauthored two recent articles on ACORN with Fred Brooks and Robert Fisher and is working on a history of ACORN's leadership.

Janelle Scott is an Assistant Professor in the Graduate School of Education and the African American Studies Department at the University of California at Berkeley. Her research examines the racial politics of public education, with a focus on school choice. Recent publications include an analysis of venture philanthropy and charter school advocacy. She is a 2008–2009 National Academy of Education–Spencer Foundation Postdoctoral Fellow, and the editor of *School Choice and Diversity: What the Evidence Says* (Teachers College Press, 2005).

Eric Shragge taught at McGill University School of Social Work for twenty-five years. He went to Concordia University's School of Community and Public Affairs in 2000 to direct a new Graduate Diploma Program in Community Economic Development. His most recent book is *Activism and Social*

Change Lessons for Local and Community Organizing (Broadview, 2003). He is a cofounder of and is active in the Immigrant Workers Centre, Montreal.

Elaine Simon, Senior Research Associate at Research for Action, is an urban anthropologist who has conducted ethnographic research and evaluation in the fields of education, employment and training, and community development. She is Co-Director of Urban Studies and adjunct Associate Professor in the Graduate School of Education at the University of Pennsylvania. She has published a number of articles on education organizing and school improvement with Eva Gold and others.

Gregory D. Squires is a Professor of Sociology and Public Policy and Public Administration at George Washington University. His recent books include *Privileged Places: Race, Residence, and the Structure of Opportunity* (Lynne Rienner, 2006), coauthored with Charis E. Kubrin, and *There Is No Such Thing as a Natural Disaster: Race, Class, and Hurricane Katrina* (Routledge, 2006), coedited with Chester Hartman.

Index